READER'S DIGEST

**all-season guide
to gardening**

autumn

READER'S DIGEST
all-season guide to gardening
autumn

PUBLISHED BY
THE READER'S DIGEST ASSOCIATION LIMITED
LONDON • NEW YORK • SYDNEY • MONTREAL

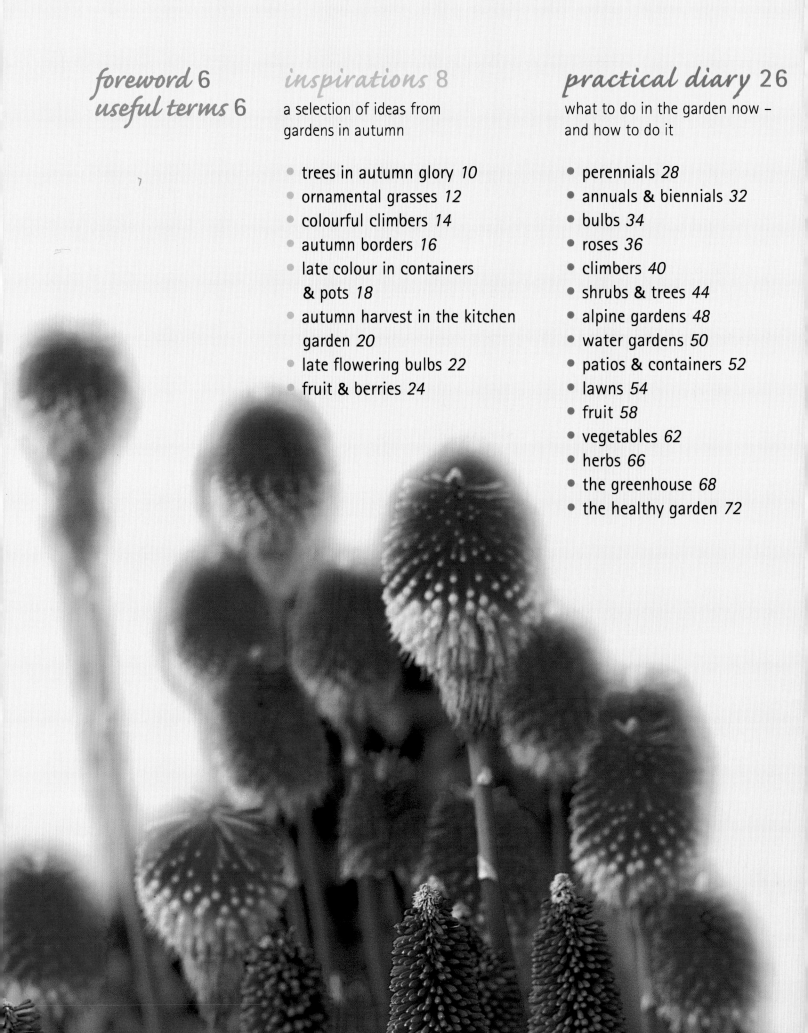

contents

foreword

The *All-Season Guide to Gardening* provides a complete practical and inspirational guide to making the most of your garden season-by-season, with year-round detailed information to help you plan, plant and enjoy the garden of your dreams. Each of the volumes is presented in four key sections:

inspirations offers a source of design and planting ideas taken from contemporary and traditional gardens photographed during the season. The plants featured have been identified to enable you to re-create or adapt the ideas to your own garden scheme.

practical diary is a guide to the most important tasks to be done in the garden at this time of year. The information is divided into subject areas – such as Perennials, Climbers,

or Patios & Containers – that reflect particular gardening interests. The headings appear in the same order in every volume in the series, so you can easily find the information you need. Under each heading is a list of the season's main tasks. The most important jobs are then explained in more detail, with step-by-step photographs and expert tips. The Healthy Garden, at the end of the section, is a full checklist of priority seasonal tasks for the whole garden. Since many jobs require follow-up attention in a later season, a 'Looking

useful terms

alpine Although this strictly refers to a mountain plant that grows naturally in free-draining soil at high altitude, the term is used by gardeners to mean any plant suitable for growing in a rock garden.

annual A plant that grows, flowers, sets seed and dies in one growing season.

anther The part of the flower that produces pollen.

aquatic plant In its widest sense, this can mean any water plant, but usually refers to plants such as water lilies that grow in deeper water, rooted in the bottom of the pond or in special baskets.

bareroot This refers to plants, usually trees and shrubs, that have been dug up and supplied to the customer without any soil on their roots. Roses are often supplied in this way.

bedding (plant) A plant used outdoors for temporary or seasonal display, often as part of a planned 'bedding scheme'.

biennial A plant that completes its life cycle in two growing seasons.

biological control The treatment or prevention of pests, diseases or weeds by natural, rather than chemical, methods, usually involving a naturally occurring parasite or predator.

cloche A glass or plastic cover used to shelter plants from cold or windy weather. Cloches are available as separate units or in tunnel form, often called 'continuous cloches'.

coldframe A low, unheated structure with a transparent top, in which plants can be grown in protected conditions.

cordon A plant restricted by pruning and training to a single, unbranching stem. Examples include apples, tomatoes and sweet peas grown on canes.

corm The swollen stem base of plants like crocuses and gladioli, where food is stored during winter. A new corm forms each year on top of the shrivelled remains of last year's.

cultivar A distinct, named plant variety that has originated in cultivation, rather than in the wild. Cultivars are often simply (but incorrectly) called 'varieties'.

deadhead To cut off the spent flowers.

die-back The result of attack by a fungal disease, which causes shoots or branches to die back from their tips.

direct sow To sow seeds in the ground where the plants are to grow, rather than starting them indoors or in a temporary seedbed for later transplanting.

drill A furrow or channel made in the soil at the correct depth for sowing seeds.

ericaceous Any plant belonging to the erica or heather family, for example pieris and rhododendrons. Also refers to the acid conditions these plants like and the special lime-free compost in which they are potted.

espalier A tree such as an apple or cotoneaster that is pruned and trained as a single upright trunk, with side branches

extending horizontally to form symmetrical layers or 'tiers'.

foliar feed Liquid fertiliser sprayed or watered on the leaves of plants, usually applied for rapid results or when plants are not actively absorbing nutrients through their roots (after injury or in cold weather, for example).

glyphosate A chemical weedkiller that is absorbed through leaves and moves through the plant so that all parts, including roots, are killed (see systemic).

habitat The natural home of a plant growing in the wild. Not to be confused with habit, which is the typical form or shape of a plant.

harden off To gradually acclimatise a plant previously grown indoors to unprotected conditions outside in the garden.

hardwood cutting A piece of this year's shoot taken for propagation from a shrub, tree or climber during the autumn, when their stems are hard and ripe.

heel A small strip of bark torn from the main stem when a sideshoot is pulled off to make a (heel) cutting.

heel in To bury the roots of a plant in a temporary hole or trench when it is not to be planted immediately.

humus The dark, water-retentive component of soil that results from the decay of organic material.

in situ Literally, in position, or where plants are to grow permanently.

internodal cutting A cutting that is trimmed midway between two leaf-joints, rather than immediately below the leaves.

layering A method of propagation in which a shoot is rooted while still attached to the

ahead' feature indicates when you will find details of follow-up action in another volume.

plant selector is a directory of the plants which are at their best at this time of year, as selected by our gardening experts. Within each subject grouping the plants are arranged by colour, and within each colour sequence they are generally listed alphabetically by botanical name. Each plant is shown in a photograph, with information supplied including the plant's common name, size, site and soil preferences, best uses, general care and suggestions for good companions. Each plant is also given a 'hardiness' rating:
● 'Hardy' plants can be grown outdoors in all parts of the British Isles.
● Plants rated 'not fully hardy' can be grown outdoors in milder parts of the British Isles but elsewhere will need some protection in winter.

● 'Half-hardy' plants can withstand temperatures down to 0°C (32°F). They are often grown outdoors in summer displays, but propagated and kept under glass between autumn and late spring.
● 'Tender' plants require protection under glass for all or part of the year.
At the end of the section, there are lists of the plants best suited to different garden conditions and soil types.

garden projects offers ideas and instructions for garden improvements, ranging from building a patio, pergola or raised bed to designing and planting up a new border or pond. Major DIY projects are illustrated with step-by-step photographs and all the projects are within the capabilities of a fit, practical person. Although some projects are specific to a season, many of them can also be undertaken at other times of the year.

---

parent plant. Rooting a branch where it touches the ground is called simple layering, while serpentine layering involves rooting a long flexible stem in several places; long stems can be tip layered by burying their growing tips.

loam A type of soil that contains a balanced mixture of sand, clay and organic material.

marginal plant A waterside plant that is grown at the edge of the pond, either in shallow water or on the bank.

mulch Any material used to cover and protect the soil surface. Organic mulches include straw, manure and lawn mowings, while polythene sheet and stones are examples of inorganic mulches.

naturalise To deliberately plant, or allow plants to grow and spread, as in the wild.

node The place on a plant's stem where a leaf forms.

nursery bed A piece of ground specially reserved for raising young plants.

organic This literally refers to any material derived from decomposed animal or plant remains. It is also used to describe a gardening approach that uses little or no obviously chemical substances such as fertilisers and pesticides.

perlite A granular, absorbent soil or compost additive made from expanded volcanic rock.

perennial (correctly herbaceous perennial) A durable non-woody plant whose soft, leafy growth dies down in winter, but grows again the following year.

pinch out To remove a growing tip, using finger and thumb.

pot on To move a potted plant into a larger container.

pot (up) To transfer a plant from a seedtray or open ground into a pot.

prick out To transplant seedlings from where they have been sown to a container or piece of ground where they will have more space to grow.

rhizome An underground root (strictly, a stem) that behaves like a bulb by storing food from one season to the next. Also used to describe the buried creeping shoots by which some plants, especially grasses, spread underground.

rootballed This describes plants packaged for delivery by wrapping their mass of roots and soil or compost in a net bag.

rootstock (or stock) The rooted portion of a grafted tree. This usually influences the habit and ultimate size of the selected variety joined onto it (the scion).

seedbed A piece of ground for raising seeds, specially prepared by removing all weeds, stones and large lumps of soil.

semi-ripe cutting A section of this year's stem cut off for propagation, usually during summer while the tip is still soft but the base has become firm and woody.

softwood cutting A cutting prepared from a portion of a young new shoot that has not started to harden.

spit A measurement of depth equal to the length of a spade-blade (about 25cm/10in).

standard A trained form of woody plant with a single upright stem that is clear of all leaves and shoots. Full standard trees have trunks about 1.8m (6ft) high, half-standards 1.2m (4ft). Standard roses are about 1m (3ft) high, while half-standards have 75cm (2ft 6in) stems.

subsoil The lower layer of ground below the topsoil (see below). Often paler and relatively infertile, this is usually coarser in texture and hard to cultivate.

sucker A shoot growing from below ground and away from the main stem of a plant, sometimes from its rootstock.

systemic A type of pesticide, fungicide or weedkiller sprayed onto leaves and absorbed into all plant parts in its sap.

tender perennial A plant that can live for several years but cannot tolerate frost or very cold conditions.

thin out To reduce the number of plants, buds or fruit so that those remaining have enough room to develop fully.

tip cuttings Softwood cuttings (see above) formed from the outer ends of young shoots.

top-dressing An application of fertiliser, organic material or potting compost spread on the surface. Also refers to replacing the top layer of compost in a large container with a fresh supply.

topgrowth The upper, visible part of a plant above ground level.

topsoil The upper layer of soil, usually darker and more fertile than the layers below (see subsoil), and where plants develop most of their feeding roots.

tuber A fat, underground root (in dahlias, for example) or stem (begonias), constructed differently from a bulb or corm but used in the same way for storing food from one season to the next.

variety Botanically, a distinctly different variation of a plant that has developed in the wild, but commonly used to mean the same as cultivar (see left).

There is something wonderful about the dishevelment of gardens in autumn. Plants can be allowed to billow and riot in the borders, as their final flowers turn to seed heads and fruits. Meanwhile, deciduous trees and shrubs take on bonfire colours before dropping their leaves. Some plants reach their peak in autumn, their fresh flowers catching the lowering rays of late sun. Apple and pear trees groan under the weight of their crop, and it's time to store kitchen garden produce before the first frosts. Try to spend as much time outdoors as possible, enjoying this precious season.

inspirations

trees in autumn glory

At the onset of autumn, the green pigments of deciduous leaves start to fade, allowing the reds, yellows and oranges to come to the fore. These warm colours are illuminated by the low angle of the sun and provide a succession of interest throughout the season.

Many ornamental maples offer attractive bark as well as good foliage and shape. The moosewood (*Acer pensylvanicum*) is a medium-sized maple whose yellow-orange autumn leaves fall to reveal the splendour of the trunk's pale 'snake bark' stripes (left).

The fan-like leaves of maidenhair trees (*Ginkgo biloba*) turn clear yellow before falling in pools on the ground. Ginkgo (right) is the survivor of an ancient group of plants that were widespread 160 million years ago. Nonetheless, it tolerates urban pollution and is a good choice for a large town garden.

Cercis canadensis '**Forest Pansy**' brightens up a corner of a garden from spring through to autumn (below). The heart-shaped, red-purple leaves take on a rich, glowing quality just before they drop. Plant cercis young and leave well alone, as they resent disturbance.

Among the earliest of plants to colour during autumn are the sumachs. *Rhus trichocarpa* (left) is a small tree with huge pinnate leaves whose leaflets, coppery when young, turn a deep orange-red before falling.

One of the great pleasures of autumn is walking through newly fallen leaves such as those from the Japanese maple *Acer japonicum* 'Vitifolium' (below). In woodland paths and borders, delay sweeping until the crimson carpet turns crisp and brown.

For colour and liveliness, plant the delightful Tibetan cherry (*Prunus serrula*) as a standard or multi-stemmed tree (left). Site where autumn and winter sun will catch the thin layers of peeling bark, then stand back to enjoy dainty spring blossom, willowy foliage turning yellow in autumn, and the polished mahogany-coloured bark.

Acer palmatum

ornamental grasses

The movement and texture of grasses brings a welcome softness to the autumn garden. Most flower in late summer and early autumn, and pass the rest of the season with pale, glistening seed heads. Grasses associate effortlessly with other plants.

Ornamental grasses require little more upkeep than a gentle shearing over before new growth appears in spring. They are ideal choices for a small, low-maintenance garden where the traditional lawn has been replaced by a wide path (above). Here a shingle mulch suppresses weeds and conserves moisture.

The criss-crossing stems of purple moor grass (*Molinia caerulea* subsp. *caerulea* 'Heidebraut') make fine lattice-work behind *Berberis* x *media* 'Red Jewel' (above). This elegant grass appreciates moist, neutral to acid soil.

Different heights of ornamental grasses are used to great effect here, with a stand of tall reed grass (*Calamagrostis brachytricha*) behind *Imperata cylindrica* 'Rubra' (right). This red-leaved beauty may need a protective winter mulch in cold regions.

The soft, feathery flower sprays of *Stipa tenuissima* (above) make it one of the most beautiful ornamental grasses, forming billowing, wispy mounds. It suits most soils and makes a fine complement to other plants, including the mauve-flowered heather *Calluna vulgaris* 'Spring Torch'.

The tall, straw-coloured plumes of *Miscanthus* and teasel heads (below) are caught by the slanting rays of late autumn sunshine. If you leave such elegant dead stems in place during winter, not only do they benefit wildlife, but they will create enchanting scenes like this.

Grasses lend themselves brilliantly to low-maintenance, prairie-style perennial plantings and have a unifying effect (above). Planted randomly among yellow coreopsis, sedums and soft-leaved *Stachys byzantina* is the grass *Stipa tenuissima*, turning parchment coloured with age.

One of the best tufted-hair grasses is *Deschampsia cespitosa* 'Tautrager' (right). Most grasses perform well in a sunny position and in well-drained soil. This one can cope with dry or damp soil and sun or partial shade, but it dislikes chalky or alkaline soils.

colourful climbers

There can be no excuse for dull walls and fences in early autumn, when the leaves of virginia creepers, boston ivies and ornamental vines take on their incredible autumn hues. These climbers need careful management, but repay effort with colourful growth.

Tendrils armed with adhesive suckers enable the magnificent boston ivy (*Parthenocissus tricuspidata*) to cling to walls and tree trunks. In autumn, the three-lobed leaves change to yellow, orange and fiery red. Mature plants against houses (left) need an annual trim to prevent the invasion of gutters and windows.

The dramatic autumn foliage of *Vitis vinifera* 'Purpurea' looks most effective against a coloured wall (below left). Horizontal support wires are hardly visible when strained tight, but must not be allowed to sag. The grapes are sour to eat, but can be used for wine making.

The prince of ornamental vines is *Vitis coignetiae* (below). Its thick stems may need tying in and the massive leaves, suffused with warm colours in autumn, need a substantial pergola or large area of wall to set them off.

An arm of boston ivy (*Parthenocissus tricuspidata*) has crept along some balustrading to great effect (above), brightening the bamboo and ornamental grasses.

Clematis tangutica 'Lambton Park'

Allowed to smother the entire boundary wall of a garden, virginia creeper (*Parthenocissus quinquefolia*) grips with disc-like suckers to make a superb backdrop to a mix of evergreens and variegated dogwoods (left). Trim back this meandering climber thoroughly just after the leaves fall.

autumn borders

Autumn is a season of contrasts, starting with an explosion of colours and growth when late flowering plants reach their peak. Then the first frosts melt the flowers away, leaving behind skeletal outlines mixed with blond grasses and russet leaves.

A mass of hardy border chrysanthemums and michaelmas daisies looks spectacular when their rayed flowers mingle in jewel-like shades (left). Plant in groups and provide discreet supports, and they will all flower in turn.

The ice plant (*Sedum spectabile*), one of the stars of the autumn border, ages beautifully and is superb for edging. Here it combines with asters and grasses, framed by a smoke bush and irish yew (above).

White-flowered sea lavender (*Limonium*) proves an ideal foreground for the blue flowers of *Caryopteris* x *clandonensis* 'Arthur Simmonds' (right). Pruned every spring, this reliable shrub will not overshadow the neighbouring grass, *Miscanthus sinensis* var. *purpurascens*. These are ideal plants for a dry, sandy soil.

Relaxed, informal shrub borders are a delight as autumn brings changing colours to the foliage of maples and azaleas (above). The blurred tones of yellow, orange and red are enhanced by dew and mist.

This abundance of autumnal flowers, foliage and grasses appears effortless (right). But to achieve this, borders need selectively cutting back and extra support throughout summer. The graceful stems of the grass *Deschampsia cespitosa*, metallic *Eryngium giganteum* and the pink blooms of *Monarda* 'Cherokee' can then fade gradually as the season progresses.

Aster amellus

Prunus sargentii (below) and paper-bark maple (*Acer griseum*) add both height and autumn colour to subtle, low-maintenance plantings of ornamental grasses with spurges (*Euphorbia*), hardy geraniums and rodgersias. Grasses like this *Calamagrostis brachytricha* can be lifted and divided in spring, just before they flower.

late colour in containers & pots

Containers are ideal for emphasising the seasons by bringing key plants together. Choose species evocative of autumn and display them individually in pots, or combine them in larger containers.

The graceful *Nerine flexuosa* 'Alba' thrives in a pot (left), flowering better when bulbs are crowded together. Plant in spring with the bulb tips just above the compost, and bring indoors for winter.

Cheerful flowers in containers brighten up areas where there are no beds. Autumn-flowering michaelmas daisies (right) are plunged in their pots into a galvanised receptacle with drainage holes.

Container-grown plants are a movable feast and can take centre stage when in bloom. *Nerine bowdenii* (below) flowers well when pot-bound.

Spare roots of perennials can be potted and grown on to cheer up a part of the garden. *Sedum* 'Herbstfreude' (above) needs a sunny position for its pink flowers to be enjoyed by butterflies.

The dark foliage of *Dahlia* 'Bishop of Llandaff' (above) is attractive all season, but doubly so when joined by red flowers. Plant up tubers into large containers, then water and feed copiously throughout the growing season. Deadhead regularly to keep the flowers coming.

Small containers need more upkeep and will need checking every few days for water requirements. These cyclamen and echeveria (above) are lovely for autumn, but must have protection from winter frost and excess wet.

Nerine bowdenii

Repetition works well and these pink dahlias grown in pots bring an autumn patio to life (below). When the display is over, whisk them away and allow the plants to be frost-blackened before removing and storing the tubers in a cool, dry, frost-free shed over winter.

The pink fruit of *Gaultheria mucronata*, together with the yellow of ornamental chilli peppers, make a jazzy combination (below). The hardy gaultheria can stay put for several seasons in an ericaceous compost, but the pepper is a seasonal filler for summer and autumn only.

A collection of generously sized pots in warm tones are planted permanently with foliage perennials, including phormium and purple-leaved heuchera (bottom). Red cyclamen and *Dianthus* 'Diamond Scarlet' provide seasonal colour and can be swapped, later, for spring and summer flowering plants.

INSPIRATIONS

autumn harvest in the kitchen garden

Onions and shallots are dried and stored, marrows hung in nets for winter use, and pears picked and stored until ready for eating. Old bean and pumpkin growth can be added to the compost heap, leaving behind tidy rows of winter brassicas and leeks.

This potager in autumn is resplendent with nineteenth-century apple varieties 'Pitmaston Pine Apple' and 'Brownlees Russet' (above). Soon the summer crops will have to be cleared, but the strong lines of paths, trellis and box edging provide winter structure.

A rustic division in the kitchen garden provides support for a venerable, lichen-clad 'Doyenne du Comice' pear (right). Beyond, fine crops of winter brassicas and leeks prove that no season need be without its fresh produce.

Apple 'Fiesta'

There is both sadness and beauty in the autumn kitchen garden as plants like sweet peas and cardoons die away. Pumpkins (left) ripen in the sun until their skins are tough, when they can be dried off and stored, safe from frost.

For those who garden on well-drained soils and sunny slopes, the prospect of growing outdoor grapes for wine, juice or even eating becomes a reality (above). Even without the fruit, grape vines are attractive plants and most cultivars offer strong autumn leaf tints.

The key to a truly productive garden is succession (below). Curly kale and other spring-sown winter brassicas will enliven the kitchen garden well into autumn. Strong netting will protect their leaves from hungry pigeons.

Maximum use is made of the space in this intricate kitchen garden (right), where vertical posts are clothed with old apple varieties, summer-pruned as upright cordons. The soil below is carpeted by alpine strawberries.

late flowering bulbs

A little forward planning reaps great rewards when bulbs, corms and tubers push forth their autumn flowers, providing fresh colour when it is most needed. In colder areas, dahlias need lifting for winter, but most bulbs naturalise well, coming up year after year.

The fresh white flowers of *Colchicum speciosum* 'Album' push through a carpet of autumn leaves (far left) and naturalise quickly from a late summer planting. The foliage emerges later, in spring.

Just as everything else in the garden seems to be dying away, the pointed buds of *Nerine bowdenii* open to elegant, glistening blooms (left).

Bringing autumn colour, *Cyclamen hederifolium* spreads beneath a tree (below). The tubers benefit from winter moisture, enjoy dappled shade and are dormant in summer when soil is liable to dry out. This is one of the few plants able to grow well under pine trees.

Dahlias have become popular additions to mixed borders. Especially valued are those like 'Ellen Huston' (above) whose foliage colours complement the flowers. Plant tubers in spring and healthy young plants in late spring when the dangers of frost have passed.

Crocosmias fire up the border in late summer and autumn (right). Plant the corms in spring, which is also a good time to divide and replant existing clumps. In autumn cover them with a dry mulch of leaves or straw to keep them safe from frost.

A sumptuous dahlia enjoys its rightful place in a cutting garden of perennials (above). Dahlias will brighten up vases from late summer to the first frosts.

Plant the tubers of a classy dahlia like 'Hillcrest Royal' in spring and be sure of flowers lasting until the first serious frosts of autumn. Help matters along by providing good, well-nourished soil, adequate support and plentiful water during droughts. Here the purple blooms are complemented by blue *Salvia uliginosa* (right).

Dahlia 'Bishop of Llandaff'

fruit & berries

Fruiting and seeding is the culmination of a plant's efforts during the growing season. Attractive fruits and pods are all designed to scatter and disperse seed in the most efficient way possible, but gardeners prize them for their colour and shape.

Glossy, mop-like seed heads tinged with pink are as much a feature of *Clematis tangutica* 'Lambton Park' (left) as the nodding, yellow flowers that appear from midsummer to autumn.

The purple fruit of beauty berry (*Callicarpa bodinieri* var.*giraldii* 'Profusion') lingers on the branches long after the leaves have fallen (right). Birds usually leave them alone and they shine well into winter.

Chinese lanterns (*Physalis alkekengii* var. *franchetii*) soon spread into a clump, dying back for winter. The stems of bright orange papery calyces dry well for indoor arrangements (below left).

Just when some gardens are fading, this one explodes into colour. Masses of orange pyracantha berries (below) clash spectacularly with sugar-pink *Nerine bowdenii*.

From blossom to fruit, crab apples have a long season of interest. The fruit of *Malus* x *robusta* 'Red Sentinel' lasts well into winter. The gently fading hydrangea flowers and agapanthus seedpods complete a pretty autumnal picture (below).

The characteristic flask-shaped hips of *Rosa moyesii* (left) set abundantly from deep red or pink single flowers when the shrub is planted in rich, moist soil.

Wild places are ideal for imaginative planting. Sow honesty (*Lunaria annua*) in spring for purple or white flowers the next year, followed by translucent seedpods (right). These coincide with the showy fruits of *Arum italicum*.

Mellow autumn weather brings with it the opportunity for garden work put on hold during the hot, dry summer months. Your soil should be moist, though not waterlogged, and still warm, creating ideal conditions for root growth. Don't be in a hurry to clear away the dying stems of herbs and perennials as some are attractive in their own right and, collectively, create delightful outlines when frosted during winter. There is little more satisfying than the glow of working outdoors in the brisk chill of autumn, raking up the leaves and generally setting the garden straight before the onset of winter.

practical diary

perennials

As the growing season comes to a close there is plenty of weeding and tidying to be done, but leave a few seed heads standing for their winter beauty. This is also a good time to lift and divide large clumps, as new plants will establish well in early autumn.

now is the season to . . .

■ **move tender perennials** under cover before the first frosts.

■ **cut back to ground level** perennials that have died down, although there are benefits in delaying this job until spring (see below). Remove supports and destroy all diseased growth.

■ **mulch plants** on the borderline of hardiness (see opposite).

■ **divide clumps of established perennials,** giving priority to those that flower in spring.

■ **treat perennial weeds** with systemic weedkiller.

■ **inspect container-grown plants** for vine weevils (see below).

■ **look for self-sown seedlings** as you weed. Pot these up or transplant to a nursery bed for planting out next year.

■ **order new perennials** from mail-order suppliers, who will despatch them in a dormant state.

■ **plant out new perennials** in September if possible (see page 30), including polyanthus divided in early summer.

■ **pot up rooted cuttings** and layers started in late summer.

■ **move under cover** any young plants growing in pots outside.

■ **prick out seedlings** sown in late summer into modular trays or small pots once they are large enough to handle, usually when the first pair of true leaves has formed.

■ **water plants** in containers occasionally and also new plants in the border if dry spells occur.

■ **collect seed** when ripe for sowing now or storing (see Late Summer).

and if you have time . . .

■ **mulch borders** if weather permits (see opposite).

■ **move container plants** to a sheltered spot before winter.

■ **plant** some winter-flowering perennials.

■ **buy and pot up** plug plants and keep under glass until spring (see page 30).

cutting back perennials

Once the growth of perennials, ferns and ornamental grasses has died back to the ground it can be cut back if you want your garden to look really tidy. However, there are benefits in delaying the traditional autumn tidy-up until late winter or early spring. From an aesthetic point of view, the dead leaves and seed heads of many plants look beautiful when rimed with frost or bejewelled with pearls of moisture on a misty morning. The dead growth also gives the plant extra

Cut down to the ground the stems of dead and dying perennials that are spoiling the border, but leave those with decorative seed heads.

protection from the cold, and provides shelter for hibernating insects like ladybirds and lacewings, which are natural predators of garden pests such as aphids.

Perennials that must be cut back now, however, are lush-leaved plants like hostas, as their leaves quickly turn to mush, and any plants with diseased foliage. This must be removed and destroyed, not left *in situ* where the disease spores could overwinter, and not put on the compost heap.

Tender perennials rarely tolerate frost and need to be moved under cover in autumn. Lift and pot up any plants

vine weevils

Vine weevil grubs can cause considerable damage to container-grown perennials, as they continue to eat through the roots during autumn and winter. Inspect compost for the creamy white, brown-headed grubs. If any are found treat with the chemical imidocloprid or repot in compost that contains this chemical – or consider using biological control. Primulas and polyanthus are favourite plants, and it is worth growing a few for an early warning of this voracious pest.

Seen here with the golden heads of grasses, *Verbena bonariensis* flowers through to autumn, but will need to be protected with a thick dry mulch over winter.

growing in the border and move them into a well-lit, frost-free place such as a greenhouse, porch or conservatory. Plants in an unheated structure will often survive if the compost is kept on the dry side. However, if you have already rooted some cuttings to overwinter indoors, you could leave the parent plant outside to take its chances.

weeding and mulching

Carry out these jobs at any time from autumn to spring, when the ground is workable. A good guide is that if soil sticks to your boots, it is too wet to work without risk of damaging its structure. The advantage of mulching now is that a blanket of material over the soil helps to keep in warmth, but before you mulch clear the weeds.

- **pull up annual weeds** and dig up the roots of perennial ones.
- **treat perennial weeds** with the systemic weedkiller glyphosate if it is not possible to dig out all the roots. Apply early in autumn so the plant draws the chemical down to its roots as it becomes dormant for the winter.

- **lay a mulch** 5–8cm (2–3in) deep of composted bark, cocoa shells, garden compost or well-rotted manure. The drawback with the latter two materials is that they may contain weed seeds. Cocoa shells have the added advantage that they may also help to repel slugs and snails.

- **plants of borderline hardiness**, such as the african blue lily (*Agapanthus*), penstemons and *Verbena bonariensis*, benefit from a thick, dry covering now in cold and exposed areas. Suitable materials include leaves, bracken or straw, and they should be laid about 8cm (3in) thick. Put a few woody prunings over it or peg some chicken wire over the top to prevent the mulch from being blown away.

MULCHING TIP When applying mulch, first cover the plant with an upturned container or bucket to keep its leaves clean.

perennials/2
planting and propagating

Autumn is the ideal time to plant new hardy perennials as well as to propagate existing ones by division and collect seeds for sowing next spring.

planting

The soil holds plenty of warmth from the summer and is usually moist from autumn rain, creating the perfect environment for plants to develop their roots. This means that new plants can establish a good root system in time for an explosion of growth in spring.

Prepare the ground thoroughly in advance of planting by deep digging and working in lots of organic matter such as garden compost or well-rotted manure. Be sure to remove all weeds, particularly every bit of perennial root. Add planting fertiliser to each planting hole to boost root development and make sure you set the plants at the same depth as they were growing previously.

Red hot pokers are some of the best highlight plants for the autumn border. They form large clumps that can be divided once the plants have died down and are dormant.

propagation

Mail-order suppliers offer a limited range of perennials as 'plug' or starter plants and this is an economical way of quickly building up stocks. When the plugs arrive plant them in 8cm (3in) pots and grow them on in a greenhouse or on a cool, well-lit windowsill.

In addition to buying plug plants, seedlings and cuttings also need attention and it is time to divide established plants.

● **pot up cuttings** taken in late summer into 8cm (3in) pots once they have rooted. Stand them on a warm, well-lit windowsill or in a heated greenhouse.

● **detach rooted layers** of border carnations pegged down in late summer and pot them up or move to a nursery bed for planting out next spring.

● **collect seed** of late flowering perennials and grasses as soon as it is ripe and sow in pots or trays of moist seed compost (see Late Summer). Stand the containers in a coldframe or in a sheltered spot covered with a cloche to keep off heavy rain.

● **prick out seedlings** of perennials sown in late summer into modular trays or small pots.

● **thin young plants** growing outside in nursery rows to leave them 10cm (4in) apart.

dividing perennials

When your perennials are several years old and have formed established clumps they can be lifted while they are dormant in autumn or winter and divided into several pieces (see opposite). Be sure to replant the divisions at the same depth as they were growing previously. As long as each piece has a reasonable amount of roots and some buds, they will quickly form a new small clump.

perennials to plant now

These excellent gap fillers for the border include those that bloom from late autumn to early spring and some evergreens: • bugle (*Ajuga reptans* varieties) • elephant's ears (*Bergenia*) • *Carex oshimensis* 'Evergold' • euphorbias • stinking hellebore (*Helleborus foetidus*) • Christmas rose (*Helleborus niger*) • Lenten rose (*Helleborus orientalis*) • gladwyn iris (*Iris foetidissima*) • *Liriope muscari* • 'black' lilyturf (*Ophiopogon planiscapus* 'Nigrescens') • *Saxifraga fortunei* • kaffir lily (*Schizostylis coccinea*)

Liriope muscari

● **wash off the soil** if you have trouble seeing the positions of the roots and shoot buds.

● **discard the centre** if the clump has become unproductive and woody, and replant only the young outer portions.

● **hellebores and peonies** dislike being divided and take several years to settle down and start flowering again, so these are best left undisturbed.

● **spring and summer-flowering** perennials are best divided in autumn so they have plenty of time to settle down before flowering.

● **late summer and autumn-flowering** perennials may be divided now or in early spring. In cold areas, delay dividing fleshy-rooted perennials like hostas until spring.

looking ahead . . .

☑ EARLY SPRING Remove dry mulches from plants of borderline hardiness.

☑ LATE SPRING Plant out young perennials raised from seed, cuttings, layers and plug plants.

there is still time to . . .

● **take cuttings** of tender perennials (see Late Summer), though a heated propagator is usually necessary now for rooting to take place.

dividing sedums

1 Fleshy-rooted plants, like many hostas and *Sedum spectabile*, are best cut into sections using a sharp spade. First, cut back the top growth.

2 Lift the clump using a garden fork. Shake off the excess soil.

3 Use a sharp spade or an old bread knife to cut the root into sections, and replant the divisions.

dividing geraniums

1 Use a garden fork to lift the clump and shake off excess soil.

2 The easiest way of splitting fibrous-rooted plants like geraniums, as well as michaelmas daisies and japanese anemones, is to insert two garden forks back-to-back and lever them apart. Do this several times.

3 Replant the small divisions into soil that has been refreshed with some well-rotted compost or manure and a handful of planting fertiliser. Plant them at the same depth as they were growing previously.

annuals & biennials

Autumn is a gamble. In a mild year continued deadheading can extend the flowering almost into winter, whereas a sudden frost may finish the display prematurely. Many summer bedding plants can be kept over winter, while there is still work to be done to ensure a good show next spring.

Rudbeckia hirta 'Rustic Dwarf' is usually grown as an annual, although it is in fact a short-lived perennial. Its colourful rayed flowers have distinctive cone-shaped centres.

now is the season to . . .

■ **continue deadheading plants** regularly to prolong flowering for as long as the weather remains favourable.

■ **thin late summer sowings** of annuals so that plants stand 8–10cm (3–4in) apart. If you lift thinnings carefully with a fork they can be transplanted elsewhere or potted up for greenhouse display.

■ **remove faded and frosted plants** to the compost heap, weed and rake up fallen leaves so the ground is clear for replanting.

■ **lift pelargoniums, argyranthemums** and other tender bedding perennials before the first frosts, and pot up or take cuttings ready for overwintering indoors (see below).

■ **buy wallflowers** and plant immediately (see opposite).

■ **plant out spring bedding** in display beds and other prepared areas (see opposite).

■ **protect seedlings** of hardy annuals with cloches or fleece in the event of severe frost.

■ **sow sweet peas** indoors for best results next spring (see page 69).

and if you have time . . .

■ **pot up some of the best** summer bedding plants to keep over winter for spring cuttings (see below).

■ **cut remaining flowers** if hard frost threatens, and use for indoor decoration.

keeping bedding plants over winter

Some summer bedding plants are perennial and can be kept from one year to the next.

● Before they are killed by the frosts, carefully lift some of the best and pot them up in 9–10cm (3½–4in) pots of soil-based compost.

● Trim the top growth to about 5–8cm (2–3in) high, and keep just moist in a frost-free greenhouse over winter.

● Increase heat and watering in March to induce new growth suitable for soft-tip cuttings. The main plants will often make large specimens for planting out again next summer.

bedding plants
to keep over winter
● ageratum ● argyranthemum
● *Begonia semperflorens*
● bidens ● busy lizzie
● diascia ● helichrysum
● pelargonium ● petunias
(Surfinia and Milliflora types)

buying and planting wallflowers

Wallflowers are popular spring bedding that many gardeners prefer to buy as bare-rooted plants in autumn, rather than devote space to raising them from seed. Choose compact, branching plants with plenty of rich green foliage. Avoid buying thin, drawn specimens, which seldom bush out after planting, or plants with yellow leaves that indicate starvation or stress from being out of the ground too long.

Before planting, apply a little lime to the planting site unless your soil is naturally alkaline, as wallflowers are cabbage relatives and are similarly prone to club-root disease. Plant wallflowers immediately or heel in (bury) the roots in a spare piece of ground until you are ready (see right).

planting spring bedding

Traditional spring bedding displays combine edging plants around a central 'carpet' of wallflowers or forget-me-nots and bulbs such as tulips. Start planting once summer flowers have been cleared and try to finish before November.

perennials as annual bedding

Although often treated as biennials, spring bedding plants such as polyanthus, primroses and double daisies (*Bellis*) are in fact perennials that can be multiplied and re-used year after year. Whether you started by raising your own from seed in May or June, or you bought the plants, in early summer you can dig up plants that have flowered and split them into smaller portions. Planted out in a nursery bed, ideally in moist shade, the segments will develop into full-size plants by autumn. You can now transplant them as part of the usual bedding routine.

Wallflowers are treated differently: tear off sideshoots from the best plants in late spring and use these as cuttings. Dip the bases in rooting hormone and root them under glass.

planting wallflowers

2 **Plant several together** to make more of an impact than single spaced plants.

1 **Keep the bare-rooted plants** in a bucket of water before planting them.

there is still time to . . .

● **sow hardy annuals** under glass to produce early flowers for next year.
● **gather and dry seeds** of favourite plants and unusual varieties to store for sowing next spring (see Late Summer).
● **take cuttings** from tender perennials, for rooting indoors.

looking ahead . . .

☑ EARLY SPRING Thin autumn-sown annuals to their final spacing.
☑ Prepare sites for hardy annuals, and start sowing *in situ*.
☑ Induce new growth in bedding plants to provide cuttings.
☑ LATE SPRING Sow seed of spring-flowering biennials.

planting spring bedding

1 **Clear all weeds** and prick over the surface with a fork to aerate the soil. Rake the soil level and clear of debris, then leave it for a few days to settle.

2 **Plant the edging first,** spacing plants 15cm (6in) apart. Then plant the other bedding. Space plants closely, 20–23cm (8–9in) apart, because little growth is made before flowering.

3 **Complete the display** by planting bulbs equidistant between the bedding plants.

bulbs

This is the time to plant spring-flowering bulbs in beds or borders, naturalise them in lawns or line them out in generous rows for cutting. As summer varieties die down, bring them indoors to dry, at about the same time as forced spring bulbs show their first fat buds.

now is the season to . . .

■ **continue planting spring-flowering bulbs.** Leave tulips and hyacinths until last (see below); finish planting by November.

■ **plant large-flowered anemones** for flowers from January onwards (see below).

■ **protect autumn-flowering bulbs,** such as amaryllis and nerines, from frost and heavy rain, particularly those growing in pots, by covering them with cloches, fleece or dry mulch.

■ **lift begonias, dahlias and gladioli** before or after frosts (see opposite).

■ **prepare new beds for gladioli** (see opposite).

■ **check that bulbs potted for forcing** for flowers in late winter or early spring are still sound and moist. Bring indoors any that are forward, with buds above soil level, but keep cool.

■ **lift, divide and replant** overcrowded clumps of alliums, summer snowflakes (*Leucojum*) and crocosmias. Collect seeds and bulbils for potting under glass.

and if you have time . . .

■ **propagate hyacinths** by scoring or scooping (see opposite).

■ **propagate lilies** by scaling for forcing indoors (see opposite).

planting anemones

Plant two or three batches of large-flowered *Anemone coronaria* St Bridgid and De Caen Group between September and early November for a succession of colourful flowers to cut in spring.

● **soak the tubers** in water overnight, and then plant ('claws' uppermost) in rich soil, 5–8cm (2–3in) deep and 10cm (4in) apart in rows or blocks.

● **for early blooms,** cover outdoor rows with cloches or plant some tubers in a coldframe or cool greenhouse.

planting tulips and hyacinths

Once you have planted daffodils and other bulbs that prefer an early start, you can turn your attention to hyacinths and tulips. For outdoor use, smaller 'bedding' hyacinths are preferable to the large bulbs sold for forcing. They can be left permanently in borders, although flower size may decline. For best results in spring bedding use fresh bulbs each year and space them about 20cm (8in) apart each way (see page 33). Use old bulbs for propagation (see opposite).

The ideal time to plant tulips is late October or early November to prevent premature leaf growth and the risk of disease. Give them an open sunny position and plant them deep; 20cm (8in) is sufficient for most soils, but 30cm (12in) is better on light ground. Deep-planted bulbs can be left for three years or more, instead of being lifted annually, which is advisable if shallow planted. Space bulbs 10–20cm (4–8in) apart according to size, or plant more closely in layers in containers (see page 53).

Illuminated by autumn sunshine are the spectacular flowers of *Dahlia* 'Bridge View Aloha', with *Verbena bonariensis* weaving through them. The striped foliage of *Canna* 'Phasion' makes a good backdrop.

scoring hyacinths

1 **Clean off any soil,** roots and loose scales. Then make two or three deep cuts across the base, almost a third of the way into the bulb. Pot up the bulb sections with their tips at surface level.

2 **Grow in a greenhouse** or coldframe over winter until the bulblets have formed.

propagating lily scales

1 **Pull the small scales** off lily bulbs after cleaning off the soil.

2 **Plant them** in a seed tray with their base just pushed down into the compost.

propagating from bulbs

Although hyacinths will naturally produce tiny bulblets, they are often extremely slow to multiply. You can speed up propagation by scoring the baseplate on any sound hyacinth (see above). In spring small leaves will appear around the main bulb. Allow growth to die down in summer and remove the bulb from the pot. Up to a dozen bulblets will have formed, and these can be removed for growing on to flowering size.

Scooping is even more productive than scoring. Use a sharp knife to gouge or scoop out a cone of tissue from the baseplate, cutting about a quarter of the way into the bulb. Discard the cone of tissue, then dust the cut surface of the bulb with fungicide, pot up and grow on as for scoring.

lifting summer bulbs

Many summer-flowering bulbs need to be brought indoors just before the frosts or as soon as the first frost has blackened the foliage. This can be early October in some years, or well into November in a mild season.

● **dry bulbs** for two to three weeks, then carefully rub off all soil, roots and papery scales before packing them in dry compost in trays, boxes or bags. Store them in a dry, cool, but frost-free place.

preparing gladioli beds

If you want to grow large-flowered gladioli for cutting, now is the time to prepare a new bed for next season's display. Select a well-drained position in full sun, and thoroughly dig over the site to at least one spade blade deep. If heavy ground lies wet, choose another spot, or create a raised bed with extra topsoil from elsewhere in the garden. Work in plenty of well-rotted manure or garden compost, and leave the ground to settle over winter.

there is still time to . . .

● **pot up arum lilies** for early flowering under glass (see Late Summer).

● **plant daffodils**, muscari, early crocuses, erythroniums, ornithogalums and dwarf irises outdoors (see Late Summer).

---

lifting bulbs

BEFORE FROST ● begonias

AFTER FIRST FROST ● acidantheras ● crocosmias ● dahlias ● gladioli ● ixias ● sparaxis

Clean begonias, gladioli and dahlias after lifting, and box them up in compost for the winter under glass.

---

looking ahead . . .

☑ WINTER Bring in forced bulbs as buds develop.

☑ Check bulbs in store.

☑ EARLY SPRING Feed indoor bulbs after flowering.

☑ Start planting gladioli.

roses

In a mild year, roses carry on flowering well into autumn, so continue with deadheading and disease control. The main task this season, though, is to plant new roses so that they have time to establish before winter.

now is the season to . . .

■ **plant or heel in new bare-rooted roses** as soon as they arrive (see page 38).

■ **water new roses** in a dry season, especially those planted against walls.

■ **continue watering roses** in outdoor containers, but reduce the frequency as temperatures fall.

■ **tie in new growth** on climbers and ramblers, check their supports for stability, and shorten longer stems to reduce wind damage.

■ **prepare sites** ready for planting new roses (see page 38).

■ **continue spraying leaves** against black-spot disease.

■ **tidy beds for winter** when roses have lost their leaves. Gather and remove or burn fallen leaves, clear away all weeds and lightly fork or hoe in surface mulches.

■ **protect newly planted roses** in cold gardens (see right).

■ **cut opening buds** for the house if frost threatens, deadhead faded flowers and remove developing hips to conserve the plant's energy, unless keeping for decorative reasons or for future propagation.

■ **pot up new roses** for forcing under glass (see opposite).

■ **layer climbers**, ramblers and shrub roses (see opposite).

■ **gather ripe hips** if you wish to raise new roses from seed (see Winter).

and if you have time . . .

■ **continue deadheading** in a mild autumn, but remove only the flower, not a long-stemmed section as in summer.

preparing roses for winter

Tall ramblers and climbers are liable to injury from strong winds unless you take the following simple precautions.

● **finish pruning ramblers** by early October (see Late Summer) and make sure all new stems are tied in firmly.

● **for climbing roses,** cut back very long stems by up to half their length in November and tie in temporarily. Leave the main pruning until late February (see Winter).

● **check all supports** and repair if necessary (see page 43). Replace any ties that have broken or frayed.

● **make sure labels are securely tied** and legible before winter. This will avoid future frustration, as pruning methods vary according to variety.

● **protect newly planted roses** against frost. Most roses are fully hardy and will survive the winter, but in very cold gardens, where prolonged hard frost is usual, it is worth mounding

Tie in the stems of climbing roses until late winter when they will be pruned.

Heap a layer of straw or dry leaves around a new rose and hold this covering in place until early spring. Remove it before any new growth appears.

In autumn, the single pink flowers of *Rosa glauca* start to be replaced by hips, while the unusual blue-green foliage continues to bring colour and interest to beds and borders.

potting up **roses**

For perfect blooms under glass from early spring onwards, pot up a hybrid tea or compact floribunda rose in October. Put plenty of drainage material in the bottom of a large pot, 40–45cm (16–18in) deep, and plant very firmly in soil-based compost. Prune stems back to 15cm (6in) and water well. Stand the pots on a hard surface in a sheltered position outside until December, when you should move them into a greenhouse.

layering roses

The usual autumn method of propagating shrub, floribunda, rambler and climbing roses is by hardwood cuttings, but you can also layer any rose with flexible stems (see below). If you do this now, the layers will have rooted by next autumn.

First choose a strong, flexible branch that can be bent easily to meet the ground. Lightly fork over the soil at this position and work in a few handfuls of potting compost. Peg the branch down at least 30cm (12in) back from its tip.

straw, bracken or dry leaves over a young plant. Hold this covering in place with fleece or sacking, and leave undisturbed until February or early March, before new growth appears.

layering roses

1 Cut into and along the underside of the chosen branch to produce a 10cm (4in) 'tongue' of stem.

2 Wedge the cut open with a thin twig and then place the cut section into loosened soil.

3 Hold the cut section of stem down with bent wire, a stone or a forked stick, and cover with a mound of soil.

4 Tie the tip of the stem to an upright cane, then water the area. The following autumn, when the layer has rooted, sever it from the parent plant and move to its new home.

roses/2

planting roses

Prepare the soil at least a month before planting by digging thoroughly, adding plenty of organic matter and allowing it to settle (see Late Summer). It is not too late to do this now, although you might have to tread the soil firm before preparing to plant.

preparing for planting

Just before you expect your bare-rooted roses to arrive, fork over the surface to break up any lumps and remove any weeds. Spread a dressing of rose fertiliser over the whole area, and fork or hoe this in. Finally, rake the site level and mark the position of the roses with short canes.

adapting light soils

Sandy and silty ground can dry out quickly in summer and this will affect the flowering and good health of roses unless you take steps to make the soil more moisture-retentive.

● **dig in ample supplies** of well-rotted manure, garden compost or leaf-mould to increase humus levels and also stimulate beneficial bacteria that aid root growth.

● **mulch established plants** lavishly with an 8cm (3in) layer of well-rotted manure every spring and feed plants in spring and midsummer, because light soils also lose nutrients quickly.

roses for light soils

Most rugosa, gallica, alba and hybrid musk roses tolerate light soils, including:
● 'Alba Maxima' ● 'Blanc Double de Couvert'
● 'Fimbriata' ● 'Madame Legras de St Germain'
● 'Maiden's Blush' ● 'Mrs Anthony Waterer' ● 'Nevada'
● 'Queen of Denmark'
● 'Sarah van Fleet'

Rosa x *odorata* 'Pallida'

planting bare-rooted roses

The basic planting method is the same for all roses (see below). On arrival, unpack the plants, check their condition and, if the roots are dry, stand plants in a bucket of water for an hour or two. If you cannot plant them immediately, heel them in to keep their roots moist until you are ready (see page 61). If the weather is very wet or cold, plants can stay heeled in until February without injury.

planting a bare-rooted rose

1 **Before planting,** tidy and trim plants to size. Prune each stem back to three to five buds long (climbers and ramblers to about 1.2m/4ft) and remove any dead wood and weak growth. Trim 5–8cm (2–3in) off the end of each main root.

2 **After placing** the rose in the prepared site, check that the rose is at its original depth, with the bud joint (the bulge immediately above the roots) just below surface level. The hole should be large enough to take the roots comfortably when they are evenly spread out over a small mound of soil.

3 **Carefully replace** the excavated soil over the roots, a little at a time, shaking the plant from time to time to ensure soil fills all air pockets between the roots.

4 **When the hole is** completely filled, firm all round the plant using hands or feet, and level the surface.

Support standard roses with a 5 x 5cm (2 x 2in) treated wooden stake, driven in before refilling the hole to avoid root damage. The top of the stake should reach the lowest rose branch. Use rose ties to hold the stem firmly to its support.

The splendid hips of *Rosa* 'Fru Dagmar Hastrup' can be gathered now and used to raise new roses in winter.

success with roses

Roses will thrive for many years if you prepare the ground well, plant carefully and then foster their positive health.

● **roses prefer slightly acid soils.** Chalky soils and overliming can result in deficiencies of vital nutrients, indicated by yellowing leaves and weak growth. If you garden on chalk choose old shrub roses (damask and hybrid musk), as they are fairly lime-tolerant.

● **cultivate soil thoroughly** and deeply (see page 149). Roses like heavy soils, but these sometimes drain badly. Correct poor drainage before planting as waterlogging is lethal (see page 152). Improve light soils (see opposite) to prevent summer drought.

● **buy strong plants** with plenty of roots and healthy stems.

● **choose disease-resistant varieties** if you prefer not to spray.

● **plant with care:** too deep or shallow planting, inadequate firming, dry or damaged roots, overcrowding and planting under trees all lead to problems.

● **prune for open growth,** so air can circulate, but avoid heavy pruning on shrub and floribunda roses. Clear away all prunings.

● **feed with** a high-potash rose fertiliser. Avoid high-nitrogen feeds, which encourage soft growth that is vulnerable to pests and diseases.

looking ahead . . .
☑ WINTER In late winter prune climbing roses.
☑ Move pots of roses for forcing into the greenhouse.
☑ EARLY SPRING Remove winter protection from young plants.
☑ Prune bush roses.
☑ Finish planting bare-rooted roses.

there is still time to . . .

● **take hardwood cuttings** up to the end of October, and root in a spare bed outdoors (see Late Summer).

● **prune rambler roses** and weeping standards, which are ramblers grafted on tall stems (see Late Summer).

● **dig over** new rose beds.

spacing roses

MINIATURES	30cm (12in)
PATIO	45cm (18in)
HYBRID TEAS	45cm (18in)
FLORIBUNDAS	60–75cm (24–30in)
SHRUB ROSES	1.2–1.5m (4–5ft)
CLIMBERS AND RAMBLERS	2.4m (8ft)
STANDARDS	1.8m (6ft)

Rose varieties vary in vigour so you may need to adjust these guidelines; check catalogue descriptions before planting.

climbers

Virginia creeper (*Parthenocissus quinquefolia*) in its full autumn glory is trained up a bamboo support, with japanese anemones (*Anemone* x *hybrida* 'Whirlwind') at its feet.

The main jobs this season lay the foundations for trouble-free performance next year, and include tying in plants and checking that supports are sound. When the weather is fair, autumn is also a good time to plant new climbers and to continue to take hardwood cuttings.

now is the season to . . .

■ **check plant ties** and tie in any new shoots before the autumn gales.

■ **inspect layers and cuttings** and pot up those that are well rooted (see below).

■ **cut back herbaceous climbers,** such as golden hop and the perennial pea, to ground level once growth has died back. Pull up annual climbers that have been killed by the frost.

■ **trim self-clinging climbers** if necessary, to keep growth well away from window frames and downpipes. Trim back all climbers where growth is encroaching into guttering.

■ **prune late flowering clematis,** such as *C. tangutica* and *C. viticella*, which are growing through conifers and evergreens, once they have finished flowering. Cut back to 60–90cm (2–3ft) to reveal the full beauty of the host plant in winter.

checking layered climbers

1 Gently loosen the soil from under the layer. If plenty of roots have developed, use secateurs to sever the layer from the parent plant. If only a few, poorly developed roots are revealed, replace the soil and re-peg the stem securely.

2 Plant the severed layer in potting compost, in a pot that will just accommodate the roots; a 10–13cm (4–5in) pot is usually adequate. After watering well, stand the pot in a coldframe or greenhouse, or under a cloche over winter.

■ **plant hardy climbers** and wall shrubs in well-prepared ground (see below).

■ **water newly planted climbers** if dry spells occur and give established plants a twice-weekly soaking.

and if you have time . . .

■ **take hardwood cuttings.**

■ **treat wooden supports** and repair if necessary (see page 43).

■ **weed and mulch** around established plants.

propagation

Check semi-ripe cuttings taken in summer. Carefully up-end the pot, with your fingers spread over the compost, and gently slide it off. Pot up any well-rooted cuttings individually into 8cm (3in) pots and grow them on in a greenhouse or indoors on a cool, well-lit windowsill. Leave poorly rooted cuttings to develop further.

Layers started last spring are likely to have rooted by now (see opposite).

planting hardy climbers and wall shrubs

Plant new climbers while the soil is warm and moist. In these favourable conditions the plant can concentrate on building up a good root system rather than trying to make top growth at the same time.

The exceptions to autumn planting are evergreens and climbers that are on the borderline of hardiness in cold areas. Such plants include California lilac (*Ceanothus*), *Clematis armandii*, *Cytisus battandieri* and *Trachelospermum*, all of which are best planted in spring.

Before planting, clear all weeds and prepare the ground thoroughly by digging in plenty of well-rotted manure or compost. This is particularly important if the site is at the base of a wall where the soil tends to be poorer and drier than elsewhere in the garden. Dig a hole about 45cm (18in) away from the base of the wall, and at least twice the size of the rootball. Mix a bucketful of well-rotted manure or compost into the excavated soil. Plant climbers other than clematis (see below) so that the top of the rootball is at soil level. Where possible, put up any essential supports in advance of planting to avoid damage to the new plant.

After planting mulch the soil with a layer of chipped bark or cocoa shells at least 5cm (2in) deep. This will help to insulate the roots from the worst of frosts, reduce water loss, and suppress weeds.

planting clematis against a wall

1 **Remove the pot** and if the roots are spiralling around the rootball, tease them loose with your fingers.

2 **Place the clematis in the hole**, spreading out any loose roots, and position it so that the top of the rootball is 10cm (4in) below ground level. Then back-fill round the rootball, firm and water.

3 **Spread out the plant's stems** and tie them to several short bamboo canes, stuck into the soil at an angle to the wall. Do this for all climbers whether they are self-clinging or not.

climbers/2

using supports

Most climbers and all wall shrubs need some form of support. The two best options are trellis or wires run through vine eyes. There is also netting made of plastic or wire, but this is rarely used because it is less attractive in appearance.

trellis

Trellis is an extremely adaptable material to use in all sorts of sites around the garden. It instantly transforms any surface as it is decorative in its own right even before the climbing plants become established. Most trellis is made of wood and comes in many different designs, styles and prices.

● **basic 'squared' trellis** is the most economical and comes in 1.8m (6ft) lengths in panel widths from 30cm–1.8m (1–6ft).
● **more decorative styles** include panels with concave or convex tops, diamond lattice and panels open in the centre.
● **criss-crossed willow stems** suit an informal or cottage garden, but expanding willow trellis is not very durable and may last only a couple of years.
● **mount trellis to support climbers** on walls and fences.
● **mount panels** between stout fence posts to act as a free-standing screen around a patio, as a divider within the garden or along the boundary instead of a solid fence.
● **fix trellis on top of low walls** or fences to raise their height, to create privacy or to expand the growing area for plants.

erecting trellis on walls and fences

Whatever the design, the most important point when putting up trellis is to incorporate battens or blocks of wood to create a 3–5cm (1–2in) space between the trellis and the wall or fence to which it is fixed. This gap is essential not only to allow room for plant stems to twine around the trellis, but also to allow air to circulate, which helps to prevent diseases. Birds often take advantage of the gap to build their nests.

wire supports

Strong galvanised wire running through vine eyes provides an inexpensive alternative to trellis on walls and fences, and is especially useful where you plan to cover large areas with climbing plants or wall shrubs.

● **on walls (1)** use flat vine eyes hammered into the mortar.
● **on fences (2)** fix screw-type vine eyes to timber posts.
● **run the wires (3)** horizontally along the mortar lines of a brick wall so they are hardly visible. Space horizontal wires approximately 30cm (12in) apart and vertical wires 1.8m (6ft) apart.
● **strain the wires between the vine eyes (4)** and tighten using pliers, or fit tension bolts to make sure there is no slack.

Ivy and virginia creeper cover a wooden trellis.
As both are self-clinging, they do not need to be tied in.

Decorative vines such as this *Parthenocissus* make an unusual, eye-catching subject for an autumn hanging basket.

maintaining supports

Check wooden supporting posts of trellis and other plant supports, paying particular attention to the structure at soil level as this is where rotting is most likely to occur. Rather than buying a replacement, it is sometimes possible to saw off the rotten part and insert the post into a metal post holder, hammered into the hole occupied by the old post. Otherwise, sink a concrete spur into a hole dug next to the existing post, and bolt the two together.

easy-access solutions

Growing climbing plants on certain sites can be a problem if the structure requires occasional maintenance, such as a wooden fence or shed that needs treating with wood preservative every couple of years. The solution is either to put up hinged trellis panels (see below) or to grow climbers that are herbaceous and die down every autumn, or that tolerate hard pruning (see box, above left).

It is also worth considering annual climbers such as sweet peas.

mounting trellis

If the trellis is flimsy, mount it on battens all round. Fix top and bottom battens on the wall and secure trellis to them. Sturdy trellis should not need battens (see below).

looking ahead . . .

☑ LATE SPRING Plant out rooted layers that have overwintered under cover.
☑ EARLY SPRING Check semi-ripe cuttings and pot up once they are well rooted.

mounting hinged trellis

1 Screw a wooden batten to the wall along the top and bottom of the area to be covered by trellis.

2 Using hinges, join the lower edge of the trellis panel to the bottom batten mounted on the wall.

3 Join the top battens on trellis and wall with stout hooks and eyes so that, when access is required, you can unhook the panel and lower it to the ground, plants and all.

shrubs & trees

Many shrubs and trees look spectacular in autumn, with late flowering species in bloom and brilliant foliage tints as the season closes. In the midst of this dramatic display, take time to think about planting, renovating and propagating new plants for the years ahead.

now is the season to . . .

■ **continue watering regularly** in a dry autumn. Concentrate on shrubs and hedges planted less than a year ago, and trees planted up to two years ago.

■ **water container-grown shrubs** and trees in dry weather, but gradually reduce the frequency as autumn advances.

■ **keep on top of the weeds,** especially fast-growing annuals like bittercress, which still have time to flower and spread their seeds.

■ **pot up rooted cuttings** and overwinter in a coldframe or cool greenhouse.

■ **move rooted layers** to their permanent sites (see opposite).

■ **transplant rooted** hardwood cuttings, taken last autumn, to their new homes.

■ **protect new plants,** especially young evergreens, from cold winds.

■ **leave faded flowerheads** on hydrangeas to protect their young shoots from severe weather until early spring.

■ **prepare planting sites** for new hedges (see page 46).

■ **plant new evergreen shrubs,** trees and hedges between early and mid-autumn for best results, but wait until next spring if your garden is cold or exposed.

■ **start planting new deciduous trees,** shrubs and hedges in prepared sites (see page 46).

■ **prune long shoots** of late-summer and early autumn flowering shrubs (see opposite).

■ **begin renovating** neglected deciduous hedges in late autumn (see opposite).

■ **propagate new shrubs** and hedges from hardwood cuttings (see opposite).

and if you have time . . .

■ **collect ripe seeds** from trees and shrubs for sowing now, if exposure to frost is necessary for germination, or to store until spring.

■ **net holly branches** laden with berries to protect them from birds until Christmas.

Evergreen hedges, such as privet, should be given a last trim now. Those that are overgrown are best left until spring.

The leaves of *Nyssa sylvatica* turn red and gold before they fall. Use a wire lawn rake or electric blower to clear them from the lawn.

propagation

This is the time to take hardwood cuttings of shrubs and check those taken last year, as they take about a year to root. You can move those that have rooted well to their growing positions, but some shrubs are slow to root and may need to be left a little longer.

taking hardwood cuttings

Hardwood cuttings are 20–30cm (8–12in) portions of ripe, firm stems that have grown this year, either cut just below a bud or pulled from the main stem with a thin strip, or heel, of old bark.

● **first trim any ragged edges** from the heel, then root the cuttings in a sheltered position. (For evergreen cuttings, remove leaves from the lower portion.)

● **dig a V-shaped trench** about 10cm (4in) deep, and fill with equal amounts of soil and grit.

● **push the cuttings** into this mixture, upright and about 15cm (6in) apart, so that only 5–8cm (2–3in) is visible above the surface.

● **firm gently with your foot,** water if the soil is dry and leave until next autumn.

For a hedge, plant hardwood cuttings in threes where they are to grow. Planting through thick plastic insulates the soil and keeps it moist.

moving layers

Layers produced from flexible shoots pegged into the soil in spring or last autumn should have rooted firmly by now. Young shoots are the most visible indication of success, but to be certain gently pull at the layer to test whether there is any resistance.

● **transplant a layer** with plenty of well-developed roots to its permanent prepared site by cutting the branch joining it to the parent plant, then lifting it carefully with a fork.

● **on cold, inhospitable soils** it may be prudent to sever the layer now, but leave it in place and move it next spring.

● **unrooted or poorly rooted** layers can be left for another year without harm.

pruning late shrubs

Late flowering shrubs such as *Buddleja davidii*, caryopteris, leycesteria and brachyglottis were traditionally pruned immediately after flowering, but experience shows that early spring is often a safer time with less risk of frost damage if a warm autumn stimulates new growth. Leaving top growth in place over winter also protects plants and benefits wildlife. So just shorten long shoots that might be damaged by strong winds now, and complete the pruning in early spring.

renovating neglected hedges

You can cut back overgrown deciduous hedges, such as beech, hornbeam and hawthorn, to restore their shape and fill in bare patches (see left). Use hedge shears and do this any time between late autumn and the end of winter during frost-free weather. Feed the hedge in early spring to support new growth.

renovating a beech hedge

1 **Prune the hedge evenly** all over using hedge shears. Trim it to 10–15cm (4–6in) less than the ultimate finished surface to allow room for dense re-growth.

2 **To reduce the size** more severely, cut back one side now and wait for a year before you cut the other side.

The pink and orange seed capsules of *Euonymus europaeus* 'Red Cascade' make it one of the most conspicuous small trees in autumn.

shrubs & trees/2
planting trees and shrubs

Dig over sites for new shrubs, trees and hedges well before planting if you can, so that the ground has a month or two in which to settle. If you have no opportunity of preparing the whole area in advance, you can plant immediately after digging individual sites (see below).

To prepare a site for a new hedge, mark out the position by digging a trench 60cm (2ft) wide, with the planting line down its centre. Prepare the ground several weeks in advance or immediately before planting. As you refill the trench after planting, loosen the soil on the sides, especially in heavy soil, to prevent it from becoming a drainage channel for the surrounding ground.

planting a container-grown tree or shrub
Mark out the planting position and dig a hole large enough to allow for 10cm (4in) of planting mixture (see below) beneath and all round the rootball.

● Thoroughly water the plant and stand it in the hole to check its position before carefully removing the container.

● Fill in around the rootball with planting mix, firming it as you go with your fists or a trowel handle, and level the surface.

● For trees, position a stake on the lee side (the side away from the prevailing wind) and drive it in at an angle of 45 degrees to avoid damaging the rootball. Secure the tree with an adjustable tie.

preparing for planting

1 Mark out a circle, about 1–1.2m (3–4ft) across, if you are planting in lawn or a grassed area.

2 Lift the turf and fork out any perennial weeds, then dig the area to the depth of a spade blade. Stack this topsoil to one side. Use a fork to loosen the subsoil and work in some garden compost or leaf-mould. Chop up any turf and lay this grass side down in the hole.

3 Prepare a planting mixture in the following way. Mix in a bucket 2.5 litres (½ gallon) each of well-rotted manure and garden compost (or leaf-mould), plus 100g (4oz) each of seaweed meal and bone meal, and fork this into the heap of excavated topsoil.

4 Before planting the tree or shrub add enough of the planting mix to raise the plant to the right depth.

staking container-grown and bare-rooted trees

A short stake is adequate for sturdy and short-stemmed trees. For bare-root trees, drive the stake in vertically to come a third of the way up the trunk; secure with a tie.

For container-grown trees, drive in a short stake at an angle after planting, so that it misses the rootball and can be attached about 45cm (18in) above the ground.

Alternatively, drive in two short upright stakes 60cm (2ft) apart on opposite sides of the trunk, join with a horizontal batten and attach to the tree with an adjustable tie.

looking ahead . . .
☑ WINTER Prune and shape deciduous shrubs and trees.
☑ EARLY SPRING Feed hedges that have been renovated.
☑ Renovate overgrown shrubs.
☑ Prune late flowering shrubs.
☑ LATE SPRING Plant evergreen trees and shrubs.
☑ Prune hydrangeas.

staking trees

Young trees need staking until their new roots have anchored them securely in the ground (see above). For trees with tall slender trunks or large heads of evergreen foliage, drive in a long stake so the top reaches the lowest branch and secure with one or two tree ties. Use ties with cushioning between tree and stake, or pad the contact point with a wad of sacking.

there is still time to . . .

● **prepare sites** for new trees and shrubs. Plant deciduous species between autumn and spring, but leave evergreens until spring if you cannot plant them by mid-autumn.
● **take semi-ripe cuttings** of evergreens in early autumn and root in a coldframe. Suitable plants include privet, laurel, lavender and lonicera.

planting a bare-rooted tree or shrub

1 **Dig out a hole** large enough to take the roots comfortably when spread out, and check the depth so the soil mark on the stem is at ground level. For trees, drive in a vertical stake 8–10cm (3–4in) off-centre and on the lee side, away from the prevailing wind.

2 **Hold the plant** upright in position, spread a few trowels of planting mix (see 3, opposite) over the roots, and gently shake the plant up and down to settle the mix in place. Repeat and firm the plant lightly with your fist.

3 **Half-fill the hole** and gently tread firm. Check the plant is still at the correct depth and adjust if necessary by adding or removing soil.

4 **Back-fill the hole,** firm again and level the surface. Attach a tree to its support with an adjustable tie fixed near the top of the stake.

alpine gardens

It is time to start tidying alpine beds and borders, even though some plants are still in flower. The most important tasks are clearing away fallen leaves, topping up the gravel mulch and protecting vulnerable plants from winter wet.

now is the season to . . .

■ **clear up fallen leaves** regularly.

■ **control weeds** as necessary. Hoe annual weeds to prevent them producing a late batch of seeds. Dig out perennial weeds, or spot treat them with weedkiller to reduce the amount of disturbance to your plants.

■ **replenish gravel mulch** on alpine beds and borders, tucking it carefully around stems. A layer at least 2–3cm (1in) deep will allow rain to drain away quickly, keeping the stems dry.

■ **protect vulnerable plants** from winter wet (see opposite).

■ **trim back straggly plants** or those that have begun to encroach on less vigorous neighbours. Alpines like aubrieta and gold dust (*Aurinia*) often look bare at the base, so cut them back in September to encourage new growth.

■ **continue to plant new alpines** in mild weather and sheltered gardens so they will have time to establish before winter.

■ **propagate new alpines** from cuttings and divide large clumps (see right).

■ **collect seeds** from late-summer-flowering alpines, such as some of the dwarf alliums and gentians, and sow immediately in pots of gritty compost.

propagation

Seeds sown in autumn usually germinate well, especially if you ensure good drainage. Use clay pots filled with gritty compost and sow the seeds thinly. Cover them with a thin layer of compost topped by a 5mm (¼in) layer of grit, but for very fine seeds cover with grit only. Stand the pots in a coldframe where the seeds will benefit from being chilled by winter frosts in a process known as stratification.

dividing alpines

Use this method not only to make more plants but also as a means of controlling them. Divide every three years or so.

● Lift and divide plants like campanulas, spring-flowering gentians, violas and sedum, then replant immediately to increase plant numbers.

● Discard the old central portion and replant only the young, outer sections.

● Trim back long, straggly shoots to about 5cm (2in) to help reduce wilting.

Many rosette-forming plants, such as *Sempervivum* 'Silverine', can be propagated from rooted offsets which can be replanted to fill gaps.

An autumn-flowering gentian (*Gentiana x stevenagensis*) brings a splash of colour to an alpine bed. The flowered stems will later die back to semi-evergreen overwintering rosettes.

alpines **to propagate by root cuttings**
- *Ancyclus depressus* • erodium • geranium • morisia
- *Primula denticulata*

taking cuttings

Creeping willows and other woody alpines are easily raised from small hardwood cuttings (see page 45). Insert them in pots of gritty compost and stand in a coldframe.

● **multiply mossy saxifrages** by pulling off individual rosettes. Trim the base and remove any old leaves. Insert the rosettes in clay pots filled with gritty alpine compost and stand them in a coldframe to root over winter.

● **root individual leaves** of *Ramonda myconi* by pushing the base into small pots of gritty alpine compost. Stand them in a coldframe to root over winter.

● **taking root cuttings** in the dormant period is a means of raising some alpine plants, often those with short stems that make conventional cuttings awkward to handle.

taking root cuttings

● Carefully dig up the plants and wash the roots.

● Cut one or two roots into 2–5cm (1–2in) sections. Fill a half-sized seed tray with a mix of equal parts John Innes No. 1 compost and horticultural grit to within 2–3cm (1in) of the rim.

● Lay the cuttings horizontally on the surface of the compost, about 5cm (2in) apart, and cover them with a layer of grit.

protecting vulnerable plants from wet

Alpines can cope with almost any amount of cold, provided their roots and leaves are kept dry, but they will deteriorate rapidly if subjected to cold damp conditions; plants with grey, silver or hairy leaves are particularly vulnerable. Any protection must allow free airflow, because if the plants are too confined they will be harmed by condensation.

● **place an extra layer of grit** around the base of moisture-sensitive plants, such as lewisias (see top right).

Cover low-growing plants with a wire mesh or bamboo cage, or an upturned hanging basket, to prevent falling leaves settling and causing the plants to rot. Clear leaves from the mesh at regular intervals.

adding a layer of grit

1 **Hold back the leaves** with your hand before applying a gravel mulch around individual plants, or cover the plant with an upturned pot. This avoids the laborious task of picking gravel off the leaves.

2 **Spread the mulch** around the stem, tucking it carefully under the leaves, to keep the stem dry and prevent it from rotting at soil level.

keeping alpine beds tidy

3 **Trim back** the straggly growth of trailing alpines to 8–10cm (3–4in) to encourage bushy new growth. Do this in early autumn, so that any new growth will harden before the first frosts.

1 **Carefully remove** fallen leaves with a hand fork.

2 **Using secateurs,** cut off all dead flowerheads to improve the look of the bed.

water gardens

Vital autumn tasks for ponds or water features include cutting back dying plants and netting the pond against falling leaves. These jobs need doing as soon as possible and take very little time, so do not put them off or you are likely to store up problems for the future.

now is the season to . . .

■ **give top priority** to netting ponds to keep out fallen leaves. If they blow into the pond, they will rot down and pollute the water. Stretch a fine nylon net over the entire pond and secure it at the edges with bricks or short canes. Make sure the net is kept taut or birds could become entangled.

■ **cut back dying foliage** and clear pond debris (see right).

■ **protect fish** from herons (see opposite).

■ **empty container ponds** and store them for the winter. Move any pond plants or fish to a temporary reservoir in the protection of a greenhouse or conservatory.

■ **divide overgrown marginal plants** in the same way as perennials (see page 31). If your garden is in a cold area, delay this job until spring. Divide bog garden plants if they are several years old and have formed large clumps, but take care not to puncture the liner as you work.

■ **reduce the amount of food** you give fish as temperatures drop. In winter they will live off their reserves.

■ **remove submersible pumps** and store over winter; drain and insulate external pumps (see opposite).

■ **transfer tender floating aquatic plants** to a frost-free place for winter (see opposite).

The handsome floating aquatic, water hawthorn (*Aponogeton distachyos*), will flower until the first autumn frost then must be cut back.

clearing up the pond

● **scoop out** the worst of the debris that builds up through the year in early autumn, before toads settle down to hibernate in the bottom of the pond.

● **pull out blanketweed** by hand or by winding the long filaments round a cane.

● **use a net** or an old kitchen sieve to scoop out any detritus. Pile blanketweed and debris on a plastic sheet spread beside the pond, and leave it for a couple of days so creatures can return to the water, before adding it to the compost heap.

Use a net to remove dead leaves and other debris from the pond surface.

● **cut back the foliage** of marginal plants and water lilies as they die back. You need to do this regularly, as dead leaves rot down quickly and will pollute the water.

● **for marginal plants with hollow stems,** take care not to cut below the water level or the stems will fill with water and the plants may die.

● **oxygenating plants** that have formed lots of growth will need thinning. To do this, cut out surplus growth if you can, otherwise use a garden rake to pull some out of the pond, but be careful not to puncture the liner. Leave the prunings by the pond for a couple of days so water creatures can crawl back to the water.

protecting fish against herons

Herons can become much more of a problem from autumn to spring when there is less plant cover to protect fish. First give the fish some secure hiding places, such as short lengths of drainpipe, then put in place some form of heron deterrent.

Placing a length of drainpipe in the pond will give fish a place to hide from predators.

● **the safest,** but not the most attractive means of protection, is to cover the pond with a net, which has the added value of catching fallen leaves (see below).

● **stretch a wire** at a height of 15cm (6in) just back from the pond's edge. This will trip and frighten a heron when it lands near the pond and attempts to walk to the edge.

● **another option** is to buy a movement-detecting bird scaring device.

overwintering floating plants

Floating aquatic plants that are frost-tender, such as water hyacinth (*Eichhornia crassipes*), need to overwinter under cover. Take out a clump and place it in a bowl of water with a layer of soil in the bottom. Keep the bowl in a light place at a minimum temperature of 10°C (50°F): the windowsill of a cool room is ideal. Fruits of the annual water chestnut (*Trapa natans*) can be treated the same way. Hardy floating plants like fairy moss and water soldier survive by sinking to the bottom of the pond for the winter.

pump care

External pumps should be drained and insulated with bubble plastic for the duration of winter. Submersible pumps are best removed from the pond and stored over winter in a shed or garage. This is vital if the pump is in water less than 45cm (18in) deep as there is danger of it becoming frozen and damaged in a severe winter.

● Disconnect the pump and cover the connector with a stout plastic bag, tying it securely in place.

● Remove the filter, and clean both it and the pump in fresh water. Once it is dry, pack the pump away until spring.

● If your pump remains in water through winter, run it for a short time every two weeks.

looking ahead . . .

☑ WINTER If you have fish or wildlife in your pond, keep an area of water ice-free by floating a tennis ball in the water.

☑ EARLY SPRING Reconnect pumps.

netting a pond

1 Buy a piece of netting big enough for your pond and anchor one side of it to the pond's edge, using short stakes or tent pegs knocked into the ground.

2 Unroll the netting carefully, lifting it over plants in the pond.

3 Secure the netting round all sides, using stakes or burying its edge beneath large stones.

patios & containers

Keep the colour going in your containers until the first hard frosts, then plant some seasonal displays to cheer the gloom of winter. Now is also the time to plant spring bulbs, and to tuck up tender plants so they can flourish again next summer.

now is the season to . . .

■ **clear out hanging baskets** and other containers of annual plants once flowering has finished. Compost the remains unless they show signs of pests or diseases, in which case remove or burn them. In particular, watch out for the cream grubs of vine weevil in the compost (see page 28).

■ **store containers** that are not frost-proof in a shed or garage after cleaning.

■ **move frost-tender perennials** and shrubs under cover before the first frost. Keep them in a greenhouse or conservatory that is heated sufficiently to remain frost-free.

■ **plant up containers** for autumn colour (see below).

■ **plant bulbs** for spring flowers (see opposite).

■ **check containers** every couple of days and water the compost sparingly if necessary.

and if you have time . . .

■ **plant up containers** for winter colour.

planting containers in autumn

Planting containers at this time of year means paying even more attention than usual to good drainage, for compost that is soggy and poorly drained is liable to freeze solid in winter and kill or damage the plants, particularly bulbs. For this reason, avoid using potting compost containing water-retaining gel. You should also mass plants closely together to ensure a full display as there will be little growth between now and spring. Bear in mind the following:

● Put in a layer of drainage material about 5cm (2in) deep. Pieces of broken pots, or 'crocks', are ideal, but large stones or chunks of broken polystyrene trays are also suitable.

Lay fine plastic netting over the top of polystyrene pieces or crocks, then fill with compost.

● Lay fine plastic netting over the top of the crocks to prevent the spaces becoming clogged with compost.

● Part-fill the container with a free-draining compost. Then pack in the plants closely and so they are at the same depth as they were growing previously.

● Leave at least a 1cm (½in) gap between the top of the compost and the rim to allow room for watering.

● Firm the compost lightly and water well. Stand the container on pot feet or pieces of tile so that excess water drains away freely.

plants for autumn colour

Seasonal plants for autumn are often overlooked, yet they give a generous display right up until the frosts arrive, and even longer in a sheltered spot or an unheated porch or conservatory. Get the most value from your autumn pots and hanging baskets by planting early. A blend of flowers, fruits

Chrysanthemums in pots will keep the patio colourful and cheerful through autumn. Move them under cover well before the first frosts.

Dismantle container displays once flowering is finished. Put annual plants on the compost heap and move tender perennials to a frost-free place such as the greenhouse.

and foliage ensures a tremendous show of colour and to achieve this don't be afraid to use some plants more usually grown indoors.

- **florists' cyclamen,** the type sold as houseplants, bear masses of flowers in white, pink, red and purple, often with the bonus of scent.
- **winter cherry** (*Solanum capsicastrum*) has small, bright orange fruits.
- **frost-tender heathers** (*Erica gracilis*) bear white, pink or red flowers. These look lovely with ornamental cabbages or kale with frilled leaves patterned in shades of pink, purple, cream and green.
- **winter-flowering pansies** will bloom during mild spells in winter and again in spring.
- **chrysanthemums,** the quintessential flower of autumn, make a glorious show of colourful blooms in a wide range of colours.

bulbs for spring flowers

Bulbs liven up the patio in spring like nothing else, and autumn is the time to get planting. Daffodils, small narcissi and early flowering bulbs like crocuses need to go in as soon as possible, preferably by the end of September so they have enough time to establish a good root system. Tulips, on the other hand, are best planted in late autumn to avoid several diseases that could strike if the bulbs have been sitting in the compost for longer.

To create a really eye-catching display, plant different bulbs in layers in a deep container at least 30cm (12in) deep and 30cm (12in) across. A pot this size will accommodate 8–10 daffodils bulbs, 10–12 tulips or 15–18 crocuses.

Protect pots from the worst of the winter frost and rain in a coldframe or unheated greenhouse. Otherwise, stand them in a sheltered spot against the house wall, and tuck bubble plastic, straw or leaves around the pots to protect them from frost. Give the warmest spot to hyacinths as they are most likely to suffer from the cold.

PROTECTION TIP Make a cover of chicken wire to sit on top of large containers to protect newly planted bulbs against cats and squirrels.

planting bulbs in a large container

1 **Prepare your pot** with a layer of crocks topped with around 5–8cm (2–3in) potting compost, then place the largest bulbs, usually tulips or daffodils, so their tops will be covered by 15cm (6in) of compost. Space them closely but so they do not touch, and cover them with a little compost.

2 **Position medium-sized bulbs** between the tulips, and add more compost. Finish off with small bulbs like crocus, dwarf narcissi or muscari, then cover with a 5cm (2in) layer of compost. Water after planting, then periodically.

Tulips make a spectacular display in late spring. Tall cultivars need a sheltered spot.

lawns

Autumn is the best time to repair damaged turf and prepare your lawn to withstand winter. The grass needs mowing less frequently as temperatures drop, but there are fallen leaves and wormcasts to sweep up.

now is the season to . . .

■ **rake up fallen leaves** regularly (see opposite).

■ **mow grass less frequently** and raise the height of the cutting blade.

■ **scatter wormcasts** by brushing the lawn with a stiff broom or a besom before you mow (see opposite).

■ **apply autumn fertilisers,** which are high in phosphates and potash. This slows down the topgrowth of the grass and encourages better root development. Choose a day when the grass is dry and the soil is moist, especially where powder or granular formulations are used, so that they fall off the grass blades and onto the soil.

■ **make repairs** to damaged lawns by reseeding bare patches and renewing broken edges (see page 56–7).

■ **aerate the lawn** if drainage is poor or moss is a problem; top-dress to relieve compaction (see opposite and page 56).

■ **make a last effort** to eradicate moss and weeds before winter sets in (see opposite).

■ **sow new lawns or lay turf** on soil well prepared in advance (see Late Spring). The relatively warm moist soil and the likelihood of air temperatures dropping as winter approaches, mean that root development is rapid and leaf growth is slow and steady, so a new lawn laid in autumn will be well established in time for next spring.

■ **look out for toadstools** and other fungi. This is the time of year they are visible, even though they may be present in the soil all year round. Most are harmless and just feed on organic matter in the soil, but brush them off if you wish.

This autumn border, featuring *Phormium tenax* 'Variegatum' and *P.* 'Cream Delight', is set off by the crisply edged, immaculately maintained lawn.

mowing

Grass continues to grow while the soil is still relatively warm and moist, but with the first frosts it starts to show signs of slowing down; it is only when the soil temperature drops below 5–7°C (41–45°F) that the grass stops growing for the winter. Before that time, it helps to leave the grass longer to protect the base of the plants from early frosts. Once it shows no signs of growth, cease mowing until the spring.

● **mow less frequently:** once a week should be sufficient.

● **raise the cutting blade** to 2–4cm (1–1½in)

● **remove all grass clippings** as they will encourage the development of moss and worm activity.

MOWING TIP If the grass is too wet to cut and you have a hover mower, remove the blades (or put the mower on its highest setting) and run it over the lawn to 'blow dry' the grass. Then you can mow.

Gather the leaves into a pile with a lawn rake and stack them in a corner of the garden, to rot down into leaf-mould.

clearing leaves from the lawn

If leaves are allowed to accumulate on the lawn or are left in drifts or piles for more than four or five days, the grass will suffer. Moss is encouraged by the dark moist conditions under the leaves, and leaves left lying about will also promote worm activity (see right).

Rake up the leaves and use them to make leaf-mould (see page 145). You can also use your mower to help clear leaves and mow the grass at the same time: a light covering of leaves can be chopped by the mower and collected in the grass box. Add the mixed leaves and grass to the compost heap.

clearing moss and weeds

● **where weeds occur** throughout the lawn, apply a combined weed and autumn feed compound.

● **if few weeds are present,** spot-treat them or paint the centre of each rosette carefully with weedkiller.

Use a weedkiller 'pen' to paint a chemical onto the centre of individual lawn weeds.

Rake out dead moss using a metal-tined lawn rake.

● **to control moss,** first cut the grass short to expose the patches of moss, then apply a mosskiller such as lawn sand. Wait until the moss turns brown, which shows it is dead, before raking it out. If any moss patches appear to recover, treat them again within about three weeks.

● **lawn sand helps** to control spreading weeds such as clover, speedwells, trefoils and silver weeds. All will be severely weakened by frequent applications when the leaves are wet.

wormcasts

Worms are very useful in the garden, recycling dead plant material, aerating the soil and improving its structure, but unfortunately they make disfiguring casts on lawns, especially in autumn when they come up to pull fallen leaves and grass clippings into the soil. If you do not disperse the casts on lawns, the mower or your feet will flatten them, smothering the underlying grass. Wormcasts also contain weed seeds brought up from below ground level, and these will germinate when exposed to daylight.

The worms that form casts tend to prefer alkaline, or limy, soil, so by using an acidic fertiliser such as sulphate of ammonia in spring and summer, the number of worms will gradually reduce as the soil turns more acidic. The worms will move to surrounding borders to carry on their useful work.

Disperse wormcasts with a besom before mowing the lawn.

lawns/2

repairs

Lawns are subjected to much wear and tear through the summer months. This may be due to natural causes, such as drought, but people walking and playing games, and pets, will also take their toll. Rather than allowing damaged areas to deteriorate further, it is best to deal with them in early autumn, when the lawn is little used. This gives the grass plenty of time to recover before next summer.

relieving compaction

The main cause of many lawn problems is soil compaction, usually caused by regular activity or traffic on the lawn pressing air out of the soil. The resulting lack of air causes grass to die from the roots up, leaving sparse or bald patches, unless you take steps to alleviate compaction.

● Spike the lawn with a border fork every 15–20cm (6–8in) to a depth of 15cm (6in). Even better is to use a hollow-tine spiker, which allows more air round the grass roots as it takes out small plugs of turf, which can be swept up and composted.

● Fill the holes by brushing in a top-dressing (see above right) to encourage new roots to form.

top-dressing mixture

suitable for a clay or poorly drained soil
- 1 part peat or peat alternative
- 2 parts loam or good quality topsoil
- 4 parts horticultural sand

levelling bumps and hollows

Bumps and hollows can develop as the ground settles, with regular foot traffic, and if machinery runs over the same route. Such areas need levelling, with soil added or removed to re-establish the level (see below). Never use a roller to level a lawn, as this will only increase the problem.

dealing with bare patches

Bare patches may be due to weeds smothering the grass or something left lying on it; eventually the grass will die due to lack of light. Spills of concentrated fertiliser or other chemicals may 'burn' the grass, killing it off in patches. These areas can be re-seeded to restore the lawn to its original condition (see Early Spring).

levelling an uneven lawn

1 With a half-moon edging iron, cut two lines through the turf in the form of a cross with its centre in the middle of the affected area.

2 Use a spade to cut horizontally under the grass at a depth of about 5cm (2in). Then roll back the sections of turf with your spade to expose the soil, and loosen the surface with a fork.

3 To level a hump scrape away enough soil to make the area level with its surroundings. For a hollow, fill the depression with good quality topsoil and gently firm until the level is fractionally higher than the surrounding area.

4 Replace the rolled-back turf and firm it gently, using the back of a rake. It should be fractionally higher than the surrounding lawn as it will settle slightly over time.

- First go over the area with a spring-tined lawn rake. Rake vigorously to drag out all the old dead grass, including pieces of dead root, and to score the soil surface.
- Use a garden fork to break up the surface and ease soil compaction. Jab the tines 2–3cm (1in) into the soil.
- Rake the soil to a depth of about 1–2cm (½–¾in) to create a fine seedbed. Sow grass seed evenly over the area, at a rate of about 30g per m² (1oz per sq yd), and lightly rake it in.

repairing broken lawn edges

The most vulnerable areas of a lawn are the edges, which can easily become ragged or damaged by walking or mowing. If left alone, damaged edges will gradually crumble away and spoil the overall look of the lawn. Eventually you will need to re-cut the lawn, reducing its area. Far better is to repair damage in the early stages (see below). The repair should be invisible within six weeks.

Choose a fine day in autumn to carry out a grand clear-up of the lawn and to tackle all the repair jobs that need doing before the onset of winter.

repairing a lawn edge

1 **Place a wooden plank** on the lawn to act as a guide and, using a half-moon edging iron, cut out a section of turf behind the damaged edge.

2 **Use a spade** to cut horizontally under the turf at a depth of about 5cm (2in), severing the grass roots.

3 **Lift the section of turf** and rotate it 180 degrees; this will place the damaged area within the lawn and leave a neat edge. Firm the turf until it is just higher than the surrounding lawn, as it will settle over winter.

4 **Fill the gap** around the damaged area with fine garden soil and firm. Sow grass seed and water it in. If the weather is dry, lay a piece of horticultural fleece over the seeded area to prevent it from drying out and to encourage rapid germination, when the fleece is removed.

fruit

As the harvest draws to a close for another year, it is time to start tidying up and planting new fruit while conditions are still pleasant outdoors. Peaches and cane fruits need pruning, and it is worth taking some hardwood cuttings of gooseberries and currants.

harvesting **now**

• apples • apricots • blackberries • blackcurrants • figs • grapes • medlars • nectarines • peaches • pears • plums • quince • raspberries • alpine and perpetual strawberries

now is the season to . . .

■ **harvest fruit** as it ripens. Gather everything by the end of October or just before the first frost, and carefully store those varieties that keep well. Check fruit in store regularly (see opposite).

■ **prune fan-trained peaches** before the end of September and take measures against peach leaf curl (see page 60).

■ **finish preparing the ground** for new fruit by clearing weeds, digging the planting sites, and working in plenty of garden

compost or rotted manure (see Late Summer and page 142). Dig in green manures sown after strawberries were lifted in early summer.

■ **protect fruit trees** by fixing grease bands around their trunks (see opposite).

■ **start planting new fruit** if the soil is in a workable condition (see page 142).

■ **protect bare roots** of new fruit plants by 'heeling' them in a spare piece of ground if you can't plant immediately (see page 61).

■ **pot up strawberries** in 13cm (5in) pots for early

Clear fallen leaves and fruits, and burn or thoroughly compost them to defeat overwintering pests and disease spores.

fruiting under glass and stand outside until late November, then bring under glass (see Winter).

■ **dig up and divide rhubarb** for replanting in fresh ground (see page 60), but leave this until the spring on heavy soils.

■ **take hardwood cuttings** of healthy bush fruits and root them in the open (see page 60).

■ **start winter pruning** apples and pears in November when crops have been picked and leaves have fallen (see Winter).

and if you have time . . .

■ **remove the roof netting** from fruit cages to allow birds to clear many of the pests remaining on plants or hibernating at ground level, and to reduce the risk of snow damage.

storing apples and pears

1 Wrap individual fruits loosely in a sheet of newspaper.

2 Place wrapped fruits in a single layer in a shallow wooden or cardboard box.

Alternatively, apples store well in plastic bags, pierced to allow them some air; keep no more than three in each bag. Store in a cool place and check regularly for signs of rotting.

storing apples and pears

Although ideally apples and pears are left on the tree until ripe enough to pick easily, late-maturing varieties are best cleared by the end of October or early November, and stored. This applies particularly to pears such as 'Docteur Jules Guyot' and 'Beurré Hardy', which should be brought indoors to continue ripening before the weather deteriorates.

storage times for late apples and pears

APPLES

'Annie Elizabeth'	December–May *
'Ashmead's Kernel'	December–March
'Blenheim Orange'	November–January
'Bramley's Seedling'	November–March *
'Crispin' (syn. 'Mutsu')	November–February
'Golden Noble'	October–January *
'Howgate Wonder'	November–February *
'Orleans Reinette'	December–February
'Ribston Pippin'	November–January
'Spartan'	November–January
'Sturmer Pippin'	December–April
'Sunset'	November–December
'Suntan'	December–March

PEARS

'Catillac'	December–April *
'Joséphine de Malines'	December–January
'Packham's Triumph'	November–December
'Winter Nelis'	November–January

* cooking varieties

An **espalier-trained pear** forms an effective divider in part of a larger garden. Prune once all the fruits have been cropped.

● **for long storage,** keep apples and pears in an airy, cool but frost-free place (see Late Summer).

● **pears benefit from slightly warmer conditions** than apples, and ripen best at about 10°C (50°F). As pears spoil quickly, check them every two or three days to see if they are ready to eat by gently pressing the stalk end for signs of softening.

● **inspect all stored fruit** regularly. Remove any that show signs of damage or disease and use immediately or discard.

preventing fruit tree problems

Trap winter moths by fixing grease bands round the trunks of apple, pear, plum and cherry trees. If left untreated these insects will cause extensive damage to the leaves, blossom and shoots. A barrier of insecticidal grease applied in October will trap the wingless female moths as they emerge late in autumn and winter and climb the tree to lay their eggs.

● **spread the grease** directly onto the bark or onto a strip of paper 10cm (4in) wide, fixed to form a continuous band around the trunk; prepared grease bands are also available.

● **tree stakes** provide an alternative route for the moths, so grease these too.

● **check occasionally** that the bands are still sticky, and leave in place until April.

Wrap a prepared grease band around the trunk to prevent damage by winter moths.

bitter pit

Bitter pit is a disorder of apples that renders the fruit inedible. It is the result of calcium deficiency, which causes dark sunken pits on the skin and brown bitter spots within the flesh, especially on the fruit of young trees. Most apple trees outgrow the problem, but useful preventative measures include watering regularly and mulching in dry weather. If a soil test shows the pH is lower than 6.5, lime around the tree (see page 148).

fruit/2

pruning and propagation

Cane fruits and trained peaches will need pruning in autumn, while bush fruit and rhubarb can be propagated.

renewing your rhubarb

Although rhubarb is perennial and seems to thrive even when neglected, it does benefit from regular division and replanting in fresh soil once every four or five years. If your soil is light, divide rhubarb crowns in late autumn, but wait until the following spring if you garden on heavy ground.

Dig up a crown of rhubarb and cut it into segments.

• Dig up a complete crown and cut it vertically with a spade into segments, each with two or three fat dormant buds at the top. Alternatively, use a spade to split the crown where it is growing, then lift each division separately.

• Discard the old central portion of the crown as well as any rotten pieces.

• Replant the healthy outer portions about 1–1.2m (3–4ft) apart, in soil that has been deeply dug and enriched with plenty of rotted manure.

• Leave surplus segments exposed on the surface for six to eight weeks. Then you can force them in the greenhouse for an extra early crop (see Winter).

peaches

• **protect late varieties,** such as 'Bellegarde', which may not finish cropping before the first frosts. If low temperatures are forecast, cover unharvested fruit with fine netting or fleece, which will also help to deter birds.

• **prune fan-trained trees** as soon as cropping ends by cutting out the fruited sideshoots back to young low shoots, and tie these in as replacements. Also cut out any dead, broken or old exhausted branches. To avoid disease problems in the future, complete this pruning by the end of September and protect all cuts with wound paint.

• **if peach leaf curl** has been a problem in previous seasons, take steps to prevent its recurrence by spraying trees with copper fungicide just as the leaves are about to fall. Gather up the leaves and burn them. Protecting plants with a polythene screen during winter is a further precaution (see Winter).

cane fruits

• **cut back fruited summer raspberry canes** to ground level, if not done earlier, and tie in the new canes as replacements.

Trim very tall canes to 15cm (6in) above the top training wire, or bend the tops down and tie them to the wire.

• **continue harvesting autumn raspberries** until frost finishes the crop. Cover the plants with a layer or two of fleece on cold nights to help to extend the harvest for a week or two.

• **prune blackberries and hybrid berries** by cutting out fruited canes at ground level. In mild areas, fan out the young, replacement canes and tie these to the wires (see Late Summer).

• **in cold gardens,** bundle the young canes together and tie them on the lowest wire, then fan them out in spring.

• **sever rooted tip layers** of blackberry and hybrid berries taken in summer, and transplant into their growing positions.

Tie young blackberry canes together over winter.

taking cuttings of bush fruit

Take hardwood cuttings from gooseberry and currant bushes as soon as the leaves have fallen (see below). The cuttings root slowly and should be left undisturbed until next autumn. when they can be moved to their final positions.

taking cuttings of blackcurrants

1 **Select strong, straight** stems of this year's growth on healthy plants. Cut the base just below a leaf joint and remove the thin growing tip to leave a cutting about 30cm (12in) long. For gooseberries and red and white currants, rub off all but the top four or five buds. For blackcurrants, leave all buds intact.

2 **Dig a long slit trench** with a spade in a sheltered area of weed-free ground. Push in the cuttings about 10cm (4in) deep and 15cm (6in) apart, and firm with your foot. On heavy soil, cover the bottom of the slit with 5cm (2in) of sharp sand before inserting the cuttings.

Autumn-fruiting raspberries trained decoratively on wires.
This makes them easier to harvest and to prune.

strawberries

You can still plant summer-fruiting strawberries (see Late Summer), but with only a short time to get established they will not crop well in the first summer and it is usual to remove their first flush of flowers next spring to help the plants to build up strength.

● **larger pot-grown strawberry plants** and cold-stored runners (often sold as '60-day' or '80-day' plants) will produce a small crop of fruit next summer but should not be forced during their first year.

● **in a dry autumn,** continue watering summer-planted strawberries regularly until there is substantial rainfall.

● **perpetual strawberries** often continue fruiting until the first frosts, or a little after if you protect plants with cloches or fleece. Do not cut plants down after fruiting, but simply tidy them by removing all mulching material and weeds, and lightly fork over the soil between plants. Transplant runners to a new bed and these will give a full crop next year.

caring for bare-rooted plants

To give new fruit plants the best start you should plant them early in the dormant season, in well-prepared ground that is not frozen or waterlogged. Plant bare-rooted trees and bushes as soon as they are delivered (see page 142); if soil or weather conditions are unsuitable, make sure the roots are kept covered to prevent them from drying out. Well-packed plants will be safe for several days if stored undisturbed in a cool, frost-free place.

Where the delay is likely to be longer, 'heel in' the trees or bushes in a spare piece of ground in a sheltered part of the garden:

● **dig a shallow trench** large enough to take the roots. Unpack the plants soon after delivery and lay them at a shallow angle so that they are safe from wind damage; cover the roots with soil excavated from the trench.

● **alternatively, gather the plants** into a sheltered corner and heap damp straw or autumn leaves over their roots.

looking ahead . . .

☑ EARLY SPRING Fan out young canes of blackberries and hybrid berries.
☑ Remove grease bands.
☑ Remove the first flush of flowers from late planted strawberries.

there is still time to . . .

● **order new fruit soon** for autumn and early winter planting, before choice varieties are sold out (see Late Summer).

vegetables

With many crops approaching maturity it is time to harvest and store your produce before frost strikes.
Plan for next year as you clear the ground; thorough preparations made now will improve
plant growth and yields in future.

now is the season to . . .

■ **harvest crops regularly** and store excess produce (see below and page 64).

■ **clear crops** after harvest. Put any green waste or crop residue onto the compost heap unless affected by pests and disease, in which case they should be burned or disposed of in the dustbin.

■ **dig over and manure the soil** as it is cleared of crops. This is particularly important on heavy soils, which will benefit from being broken down by winter frosts. By leaving the soil in ridges it will also keep drier through the winter.

■ **plan, sow, plant and prepare** for next year, once the ground is clear and cultivated. Then you can start off next year's crops, or leave the soil vacant so the frost can help to improve its structure.

■ **earth up winter brassicas** to prevent wind rock.

■ **remove supports** used for climbing crops and detach remnants of the spent plants. Then sort, bundle and store the supports somewhere dry until next year.

■ **continue to hoe regularly** to kill weed seedlings as they emerge.

■ **remove and burn** the stems of maincrop potatoes if they are affected by potato blight.

peas and beans

Continue to harvest peas, french beans and runner beans as they become ready, or leave some for drying. Sow broad beans and early peas for cropping next spring to summer.

● **sow early cultivars of peas** under cloches to be ready for picking in early summer. The cloches will be essential for winter protection after the seedlings have emerged.

● **sow broad beans** to crop from late spring to early summer. Longpod cultivars are the hardiest.

● **harvest maincrop peas** for using fresh when the seeds have swollen and the pods are still green (see Late Summer).

● **for dried peas and beans cut the plants** off at ground level when the seeds are visibly swollen. Allow the vines to hang on the support and dry out before harvesting the pods.

SOIL IMPROVEMENT TIP Leave the roots of peas and beans in the ground after the crop has finished: they contain high levels of nitrogen, which will benefit a follow-on crop of brassicas (see Winter).

cabbages, cauliflowers and other brassicas

Some jobs need doing at the start of autumn, while others are better left until the end of the season.

in early autumn:

● **use up summer and autumn cabbages.** Harvest these less hardy crops that will not store for long periods before cutting the hardier winter cabbages.

● **transplant spring cabbages** into their cropping site (see opposite). In order to achieve a succession, sow more seed under cloches ready to transplant in early spring. Where headed cabbages and loose-leaved spring greens are both required, plant the cabbages closer together in the rows. Then remove alternate plants to eat as spring greens and leave the others to form a head.

sowing early peas and beans

1 Sow peas in a block after taking out a spade-width of soil. Sow in three rows, staggering the spacing. Cover with cloches.

2 Sow broad beans 15cm (6in) apart in rows 60cm (2ft) apart, to overwinter and crop in summer.

3 On exposed sites, protect young broad bean plants with fleece, or grow them under cloches.

harvesting now

- beetroot • carrots • celeriac • celery • chinese cabbage
- florence fennel • french and runner beans • jerusalem artichokes • kale • leeks • lettuces and salad leaves • maincrop potatoes • marrow • onions • parsnips • peas • pumpkins and squash • salad radish • salsify • scorzonera • spinach and spinach beet • spring onions • summer and autumn cauliflowers • summer, autumn and winter cabbages • swedes • turnips

The blue-green foliage of leeks shows up well in front of the flowering evening primrose and lavatera. Young box plants will grow to form a low edging, while at the end of the row is a standard euonymus.

- **sow summer cauliflowers** under the protection of a cloche or in modular trays in a coldframe.

Net young brassica plants, especially in cold weather, against attack by wood pigeons.

- **earth up the soil** around the stems of cabbages, cauliflowers and brussels sprouts, to help to prevent them from rocking in the wind and loosening their roots in wet soil conditions.
- **sow turnips** for a leafy crop of greens, or turnip tops, but choose a hardy variety such as 'Green Stone Top'.
- **transplant chinese cabbage** and chinese broccoli sown in trays in late summer. Plant them out under the protection of cloches or low polythene tunnels.
- **sow texsel greens** early under similar protection as a cut-and-come-again crop for late autumn and early winter. Keep sowings well watered to ensure swift germination and rapid early growth. Cut leaves in five to six weeks when they are about 25cm (10in) high.

in late autumn:

- **cut and store winter cabbages** of the Dutch winter-white type. They will keep in a cool, frost-free place with good air circulation for up to three weeks.
- **harvest Savoy and 'January King'** cabbages as required. These are hardy enough to stand over winter in the garden.
- **protect spring cabbages** with cloches or fleece when long periods of frost are forecast.

- **cover chinese cabbages** with low polythene tunnels, cloches or fleece during cold weather as they can only withstand very light frost.
- **protect cauliflowers** by drawing up the outer leaves and tying them to cover the curd when frosty weather is forecast. It is the rapid thaw on mild sunny days that damages the curd rather than the cold weather itself.

looking ahead . . .

☑ WINTER Protect new seedlings of peas and broad beans with cloches or fleece.

☑ Protect crops from attack by birds, as food becomes scarce.

☑ EARLY SPRING Transplant autumn-sown spring cabbages.

transplanting spring cabbages

1 **Space young cabbages** 30cm (12in) apart in rows 30cm (12in) apart and plant very firmly.

2 **To test for firmness,** tug an indivdual leaf; the plant should remain bedded in the soil. If it becomes dislodged, plant again more firmly.

vegetables/2

onions, roots and salad crops

Autumn is the ideal time to clean up the vegetable garden and make a fresh start for next year. As the various crops come to the end of their production cycles, dispose of their debris as you harvest, rather than leaving remnants *in situ* where they could harbour pests and diseases. This also leaves the soil clear for digging.

onions

● **finish lifting bulb onions** as soon as possible. Leave them on the ground or in trays to allow the skins to cure in the sun, but bring them inside if persistent rain threatens and before the first frost.

● **store the onions** after the tops have died and dried off. Clean off any soil and all withered roots, twist off the old dead leaves and hang in strings or nets, or simply place on open trays in a cool, airy and frost-free place.

HARVESTING ONIONS TIP In a wet season, if the onion tops are slow to die down, bend the leaves over just above the swollen part, or neck. This speeds the dying down process.

If your soil is heavy, plant garlic cloves on top of a ridge for improved drainage.

Harvest leeks when you need them by digging them up with a garden fork.

● **plant garlic cloves now,** as they need at least two months of cold weather in order to grow well, and a longer growing season produces larger bulbs the following year.

● **plant sets** (small bulbs) of the hardier types of onion, but only if your soil is light and free draining.

● **harvest leeks** with a garden fork as you need them; they are hardy enough to stand through the coldest winter months.

root crops

There are various ways in which you can extend the harvest of your root crops. Many can be stored in or out of the ground to last through the coming months and still taste good. The method you choose will depend on the amount of excess produce you have and how long you wish to store it (see also Late Summer).

● **cover carrots and parsnips** in the row with loose straw, after the foliage has died down. In this way you can store them in the ground over winter, but keep a watch for mice hiding in the straw and eating the roots.

● **harvest maincrop carrots** and store in sand (see opposite).

● **earth up florence fennel** once the stem bases begin to swell and protect with cloches to extend the harvesting season.

● **dig up beetroot** as soon as the foliage starts to die down and store in clamps or boxes of moist sand (see opposite).

● **lift maincrop potatoes** as the foliage dies down. If possible, leave the tubers on the soil surface for a few hours to allow the skins to harden.

Ripen pumpkins after harvesting by leaving them on the ground, where the sun can 'cure', or harden, their skins.

- **store large quantities of potatoes** in a 'clamp' outdoors (see below). The straw and soil casing will insulate the tubers and protect them from frost.
- **lift salsify** and store in boxes of damp sand in a cool shed.
- **lift and store turnips** in clamps, or cover them in the row with loose straw where they will keep until Christmas.
- **cover scorzonera roots** in the row with loose straw and lift as required.

building a clamp

A clamp is a protective casing in which to store potatoes and other root crops outdoors during inclement weather. It is important to choose a well-drained site for a clamp, or the potatoes, or other roots, may become waterlogged and rot. Choose a north-facing position, so that the clamp has a cool, even temperature, which encourages the tubers to stay in good condition.

Spread straw over the soil, about 20cm (8in) thick, and pile the potatoes on this base. Cover the tubers thickly with more straw and top this with a 10cm (4in) layer of soil, taken from around the clamp to leave a drainage 'moat'. Pull some wisps of straw through the top to make a ventilation chimney, then pat firm the earthen sides with the back of a spade. Other roots like beetroots, carrots, celeriac and turnips can also be stored in a clamp after you have removed any leafy tops.

salads and tender crops

- **cut down tomato plants** and hang them in a cool dry shed or greenhouse to allow the remaining fruits to ripen.
- **sow seeds of winter lettuce** and winter spinach under fleece or cloches at 14-day intervals to ensure a continuity of crop.
- **cover spinach plants** with cloches or a polythene tunnel to extend the harvesting season into early winter.
- **cut and harvest marrows** before the first frosts. They will store for several months laid on open trays in a cool, frost-free place with a good flow of air.
- **harvest pumpkins and squash** and leave them outdoors to ripen their skins.
- **leave dead sweetcorn** stems in place on exposed sites to provide some wind protection for those crops that remain.

Grow young winter lettuce plants in a soil bed under the protection of a coldframe.

perennial crops

- **cut asparagus stalks** down to ground level, and burn.
- **prune jerusalem artichoke** stems to the ground and compost, or cut and lay them over the row of tubers as winter protection and to make lifting easier in frosty weather.

storing carrots in sand

1 After harvesting the carrots, wash off the dirt and cut off the feathery tops.

2 Store in single layers in boxes, alternating with layers of damp sand.

3 Cover with a final layer of sand and store in a cool, frost-free shed.

herbs

Although many herbs are still providing useful pickings
for the kitchen, the emphasis in the herb garden
now is on clearing, tidying and planting.
Make sure that herbs in pots for winter use are
healthy and growing strongly.

now is the season to . . .

■ **continue harvesting** the leaves of basil, mint and rosemary,
and the stems or roots of horseradish, liquorice and orris for
immediate use or storage (see opposite).

■ **pot up selected herbs,** including self-sown parsley, early in
the season for winter use. Later on, bring a batch indoors for
growing on a windowsill (see below).

■ **extend the picking season** of outdoor herbs, such as parsley,
as temperatures fall, by covering them with cloches or fleece.

■ **insulate potted herbs** outdoors or bring them under cover if
frost threatens. Before the first frost, move under glass
tender herbs such as lemon verbena, pineapple sage and
french lavender.

Bronze fennel can be cut down
in autumn. Or you might leave
the stems to be frost enhanced.

■ **continue clearing** old
growth and spent
flowerheads, but leave some
of the more decorative for
foraging birds. Top-dress
bare soil with garden
compost.

■ **scorch beds of mint**
affected by rust with a flame
gun or a small fire of straw
and kindling, to kill the
spores and sterilise the soil.

■ **dig the site** for a new herb
garden and leave rough over
winter for spring planting.

■ **start planting hardy perennials** such as mint and comfrey
(see opposite).

■ **make final sowings of chervil and lamb's lettuce** in a
coldframe, spent growing bag or cool greenhouse border.

■ **lift and divide large clumps of perennial herbs** such as
fennel, tarragon, lemon balm and lovage (see opposite).

■ **plant evergreen herbs,** such as box, curry plant or lavender,
to edge beds and borders on light soils and in mild gardens;
elsewhere, especially on heavy or cold ground, planting is
best done in April or late summer.

■ **check layers of thyme and rosemary** pegged down in early

summer as well as leggy plants 'dropped' in spring or winter
(see Winter), and separate the young plants if they have
rooted. If not, re-peg and look again in early spring.

and if you have time . . .

■ **take hardwood cuttings** of elderberries to root outdoors.
Once rooted, plant them as traditional guardians of herbs and
herb gardens.

■ **cut back chives** as the leaves brown and start to die down.

■ **sow seed of umbellifers** such as angelica, caraway and lovage
in a coldframe or greenhouse.

potting up winter supplies

If you have not already potted up plants of basil, chives,
parsley, small tarragons, marjoram and mint from the garden
for winter use, do so as soon as you can. Keep them in the
greenhouse or a lightly shaded place outdoors, sheltered from

Divide clumps of chives and
pot up ready to bring them
indoors for winter use.

Mint is one of the herbs that
can be potted up in autumn for
use during winter.

Hyssop is a semi-evergreen shrub with aromatic leaves. Its dark blue flowers are attractive to birds and butterflies.

cold winds, and water them if necessary. Before moving plants indoors, check carefully for signs of aphids or other pests; a precautionary spray of insecticidal soap will help to control pest numbers.

Augment herb supplies by exploring garden centres for end-of-season bargains. Young plants of thyme, sage, rosemary and salad burnet are a good size for indoor windowsills, before planting out next spring.

dividing herbs

Every three to four years, lift and divide vigorous clump-forming herbs to control and rejuvenate their growth (see below). Do this early in autumn in mild, protected areas, otherwise wait until March or April.

herbs to divide
- comfrey • fennel
- liquorice • lovage
- saponaria • sorrel
- tansy • tarragon
- variegated lemon balm

planting hardy herbs

Plant new perennial herbs in September, while the soil is still relatively warm. Water the plants and allow them to drain before planting them in prepared sites (see Late Summer); large plants can be cut into two or more portions using a sharp knife.

- **dig a hole large enough** to accommodate the roots comfortably. Fork over the soil in the bottom and mix in a little potting compost.
- **loosen any tightly wound roots** before planting. Make sure that the top of the rootball is at surface level and replace the excavated soil.
- **firm gently and water** if conditions are dry.

harvesting and drying roots

Dig up roots when growth has ceased and plants are dormant. Lift them carefully with a spade or fork to avoid damage, wash off the soil, remove any top growth and cut off thin, fibrous roots.

Small roots of arnica, angelica, liquorice and marshmallow dry well whole, but larger ones, such as dandelions, horseradish, lovage, orris and sweet cicely, are better split lengthways and sliced. Dry the roots in a microwave on full power in 30-second bursts, or in a conventional oven set at 50°C (120°F), until they are light and fragile. Allow the roots to cool, then store them in airtight tins.

there is still time to . . .
- **gather seed heads** to dry for kitchen use or to sow in spring.
- **prepare new herb borders** for planting during late autumn.

dividing lemon balm

1 **Cut back** old top growth close to the ground, then ease out the clump by inserting a digging fork all round the outside and levering upwards.

2 **Use a spade to chop** the clump into smaller segments. You may find it easier to split very large clumps *in situ* and then fork up the segments.

3 **Replant** only the young outer sections in fresh soil, then firm. Water in dry weather.

looking ahead . . .
☑ EARLY SPRING Check again to see whether layers and 'dropped' herbs have rooted.
☑ Divide herb clumps growing in cold gardens.
☑ SUMMER Layer herbs.
☑ LATE SUMMER Plant herb hedges such as santolina.

the greenhouse

With shortening days and falling temperatures, the greenhouse offers a safe haven from conditions outdoors. Make preparations now for an influx of tender plants that need to share frost-free space with rooting cuttings and fresh sowings.

now is the season to . . .

■ **reduce watering** and feeding as growth slows. Stop damping down, only water in the mornings and avoid wetting foliage to prevent fungal diseases, which thrive in a damp atmosphere.

■ **open ventilators on mild days,** but keep them closed during frost or fog.

■ **harvest remaining crops** as they mature, and clear out exhausted plants.

■ **allow permanent plants** a little more space, to improve the movement of air between them.

■ **remove shade netting and paint** and wash down the outside of the glass. Shield young seedlings from very bright sunshine with sheets of newspaper or a layer of fleece.

■ **pot up seedlings** of annuals and other plants sown in late summer.

■ **pot up well-rooted cuttings** of tender perennials and other plants propagated in late summer.

■ **sow hardy annuals,** prick out into trays and overwinter in a coldframe for early flowers next year.

■ **sow sweet peas** in deep pots or paper tubes (see opposite).

■ **sow winter lettuces** for spring cutting and leaf lettuce as a seedling crop for winter use (see below).

■ **pot up lilies** in deep pots for flowering in their containers or for transplanting outdoors in spring.

Plump, healthy-looking lily bulbs are ready for potting up. They can be moved outdoors in spring, left in their pots or transplanted to beds.

■ **make space** for tender perennials lifted from outdoors.

■ **dry bulbs and tubers** ready for their winter rest (see page 35).

■ **stop watering cacti** to keep them dry and safe from frost.

■ **pot up some hardy perennials** such as astilbes, aquilegias, dicentras and hellebores, to flower early indoors.

■ **prune climbers** under glass (see opposite).

■ **check for pests,** especially whitefly and red spider mite, and spray with insecticide. It is too late to introduce biological controls, which are only effective in warm conditions.

■ **pick off fading leaves,** dead flowers and any sign of decay or mould, to reduce the risks from fungal diseases.

Scrub out containers before storing or re-using them.

■ **clean and sort pots.** Clean out gutters and water butts or tanks when leaves have finished falling (see page 70).

■ **from November,** bring in batches of potted strawberries for forcing in a well-lit position.

■ **bring potted spring bulbs** into light and warmth once they have shoots about 5cm (2in) high.

■ **move potted herbs inside** for winter supplies (see page 66).

■ **in late autumn insulate** the greenhouse (see page 71), and test heaters before they are needed. If you plan to install heating, decide on the kind of plants you wish to grow and the temperature regime they prefer.

■ **make repairs** to greenhouse and coldframes before winter.

sowing winter lettuce

Choose a suitable variety, such as 'Arctic King', green or red 'Parella' or the greenhouse iceberg-type 'Kelly's'. Sow seeds in pots and prick out seedlings into trays. About six weeks later plant the lettuces in a greenhouse border or coldframe, or keep them in trays in a coldframe for planting outdoors under cloches in late winter.

For earlier harvest under cover, sow mixed lettuces or misticanza (a lettuce, chicory and endive mixture) in rows in a greenhouse border or deep box, and cut the leaves with

sowing sweet peas in paper tubes

1 **Fold a sheet of newspaper** or pages from an old telephone directory to make a long strip about 10cm (4in) wide. Roll this round a rolling pin or thick piece of dowel and fasten with sticky tape. Then slide off the paper tube.

2 **Pack the tubes** in a seed tray so they stand upright. Use a plastic funnel to fill them with compost and sow two seeds in each tube, about 1cm (½in) deep. Stand the tray in a little water until the top of the compost is moist.

3 **When seedlings** have four pairs of leaves, remove the weaker plant and pinch out the tip of the other to encourage strong sideshoots to develop.

scissors when 8–10cm (3–4in) high. Several harvests are possible during the winter.

sweet peas from seed

For top-quality blooms sow sweet peas in deep pots of moist soil-based seed compost during mid-October. Stand the pots in a coldframe or unheated greenhouse, and ventilate well in mild weather. Keep the seedlings in a coldframe until March, when they can be planted out.

You can also raise sweet peas in home-made paper tubes (see above). This method avoids any root disturbance because you keep the tubes in the tray over winter and plant them intact; the paper will disintegrate in the soil.

pruning climbers under glass

Tender climbers such as passionflowers, stephanotis and *Plumbago auriculata* can make a lot of new growth during summer, and you can cut this back in October or November to admit more light to the greenhouse and improve air circulation around the plant's stems. You should check the specific pruning requirements for each species, but in general you can cut out some of the older stems, thin new growth and shorten it to fit

the space available, then remove any weak shoots. This should leave a well-spaced arrangement of branches, which you tie securely to their supports.

The fast-growing evergreen climber *Allamanda cathartica* is frost tender and best grown in a greenhouse. Its golden trumpet-shaped flowers appear from late summer to early autumn.

preparing for winter

The autumn clean-up in preparation for overwintering tender plants is a good opportunity to wash pots and cloches. Used plant containers can be a source of disease if they are left in a dirty condition under the greenhouse staging. Water butts and gutters also benefit from a scrub so they do not become a source of damping-off disease and other problems. Don't forget to wash the outside of the glass – this is particularly important as light levels fall and you fix up winter insulation.

cleaning greenhouse equipment

- **examine your containers.** You can sometimes mend cracks and breaks in large clay pots with strong waterproof glue, with a tight wire hoop round the outside for reinforcement. Discard broken, cracked and brittle plastic containers. Repair wooden trays and boxes with slats, perhaps from an old fence panel or pallet.
- **scrub pots and trays** in warm soapy water with added horticultural disinfectant. Use a stiff washing-up brush to get well into the corners and under rims, where pests often hide. There is no need to scrape chalky deposits from clay pots, but do remove all traces of green algae.
- **dry containers** thoroughly before packing away according to size. Keep clay and plastic pots separate. Paint wooden trays with diluted horticultural disinfectant or a wood preservative.
- **plastic labels** are re-useable. If you soak them in a container filled with a diluted bleach solution they will be easy to scrub clean with a scourer or wire-wool pad. Rinse and spread out to dry.
- **drain water tanks** and rain butts and scrub the insides with warm soapy water and disinfectant. Rinse very well before re-filling.
- **clear leaves** from roof gutters and clean with disinfectant as a precaution against disease.

CLEANING TIP Clean and wash coldframes and cloches now, before their main season of use.

The cup-and-saucer vine (*Cobaea scandens*) grows rapidly in greenhouse conditions and needs support (left). Its greenish cream flowers gradually turn purple.

Remove leaves from gutters that supply water butts.

By late autumn you should insulate the greenhouse, even though late crops such as this cucumber 'Pepinex' are still to be harvested.

insulating the greenhouse

About 80 per cent of the heat in a greenhouse is lost through the glass, but you can reduce this dramatically by insulating the inside during the coldest months, from late September or October until April.

Double glazing is the most efficient way to conserve heat, but it is expensive and only a serious option for a conservatory that is also used as a living area. A far cheaper method is to line the greenhouse inside with a skin of clear polythene sheeting, pinned to the glazing bars or attached with special plastic clips to leave a 2–3cm (1in) air gap. This can save 30 per cent of the heat lost. By using bubble plastic for lining, the saving increases to 40 per cent. Thicker materials save even more heat, but reduce light levels proportionally. An effective compromise is to use thick triple-layer bubble plastic with large bubbles for the lower half of the walls, and thinner material above bench level.

Instead of insulating the roof, install a thermal screen above head height to pull across on horizontal wires at night and on cold days. Use fleece, clear woven plastic or a similar porous material to reduce condensation, which is sometimes a problem with polythene-sheet insulation.

VENTILATING TIP Remember to trim and fix insulation materials around ventilators so that these can be opened during mild weather.

there is still time to . . .

- **pot up spring bulbs** for early flowers indoors.
- **clean the greenhouse** before it fills up with tender plants.
- **bring in tender plants** that have stood outdoors during summer before the frost comes, but first scrub the pots and spray the plants with insecticide.

looking ahead . . .

☑ WINTER Bring in strawberries and more potted bulbs for forcing.
☑ Plant out winter lettuces under cloches.
☑ EARLY SPRING Plant out sweet peas and hardy annuals.
☑ LATE SPRING Remove insulation.

the healthy garden

There are many clearing up and cultivation tasks that need doing before winter, all of them essential to maintain the good health of your plants. From now on, be prepared for frosty nights, and don't forget to feed the birds as the weather deteriorates.

autumn checklist

Use this checklist to make sure you do not overlook any important autumn jobs.

Clear dead and dying plant growth from borders and put it on the compost heap.

● **start removing dead plant** remains from borders and vegetable beds, and clear weeds for composting.
● **rake up leaves,** particularly those fallen on alpines and herbs which cannot stand damp conditions, and stack for leaf-mould (see page 145).
● **net ponds** to prevent any fallen leaves from fouling the water.
● **give hedges** a final trim.
● **raise the cutting height** of lawn mowers for the last cuts.
● **sow or turf** new lawns.
● **finish harvesting fruit,** and check supplies in store.
● **gather vegetables** and store any excess.

● **start planting new roses,** hardy climbers, shrubs, trees and perennials while the ground is still warm.
● **begin winter digging,** especially on heavy soils that are best left rough and exposed to frost.
● **finish cleaning the greenhouse,** coldframes and cloches. Wash and dry pots and trays, and store neatly.
● **prick out and pot up seedlings** and rooted cuttings.
● **insulate the greenhouse,** and prepare plants inside for colder weather.
● **move outdoor containers** under cover before hard weather, or insulate them where they stand.
● **drain and roll up hosepipes** and clean out water butts. Drain and insulate taps if severe frost threatens.
● **repair fences, gates, decking** and other wooden structures while the timber is dry.
● **order seeds** (see opposite).
● **continue to check plants for problems,** especially diseases (see right).

preparing for frost

Plan ahead so you are ready to protect plants if a sharp frost suddenly occurs after a long, warm autumn.
● **do not feed plants** with high-nitrogen fertiliser during autumn, as this encourages soft growth vulnerable to injury.
● **choose hardy varieties** of winter vegetables and grow them in the warmest part of the garden.
● **in very cold areas,** only grow fruit that ripens early, so you can harvest it before conditions deteriorate.
● **mulch plants of borderline hardiness** with straw, leaves or crumpled newspapers held in place with wire netting.
● **shield young and tender shrubs** with windbreaks of plastic mesh or sacking.
● **do not tidy perennials** too thoroughly, because dead growth will insulate roots and trap a covering of fallen leaves.
● **keep a supply of newspapers,** old curtains, blankets or fleece to cover coldframes, cloches and vulnerable plants outdoors.

FROST TIP Check plants after a hard frost, especially those recently planted, and firm them in if they have been forced out of the soil.

seasonal problems

Pest attacks diminish during autumn, but many diseases thrive in damp, mild conditions. There is still time to spray with fungicide if you notice symptoms of rust, mildew or black spot, but sensible precautions have longer-term impact.
● **clear leaves** and other plant debris unless needed for frost protection.
● **part prune shrubs** or thin out congested stems to improve the air circulation.
● **gather fallen fruits** and put them out for the birds in a corner, well away from plants. Pick rotten or mummified fruits and remove or burn.
● **ventilate plants under glass** whenever possible, and water only when absolutely necessary, preferably early in the day.

Pick mummified tree fruits as soon as you see them, but do not compost them.

Squirrel-proof bird feeders such as these are filled with seeds and nuts and suspended in trees.

Enjoy the flowering of colourful annuals, such as these variegated trailing nasturtiums, until the first frost causes them to collapse.

seed catalogues

Order seed catalogues early and take time to read them, noting what you would like to grow and where. It makes sense to rely on familiar favourites, but why not try a few novelties or alternative varieties as well? Seeds that have been specially prepared for easier germination – primed, chitted and coated – can help to ensure success. Remember that if you can't provide the necessary heat for raising tender plants, many seed catalogues offer seedlings or plug plants that relieve you of tricky germination procedures.

looking after birds

Many birds are useful allies in your efforts to control plant pests. As the weather deteriorates, they will appreciate a regularly supply of food, either on a bird table safe from cats and squirrels, or in feeders suspended among branches; balls

of fat mixed with seeds are popular with small birds. As further encouragement, introduce bird boxes into your garden now as shelter over winter and before the main nesting season starts in March.

bonfire guidelines

First, ask yourself: do you really need a bonfire? You can compost most soft plant remains, stack leaves to make leaf-mould, and often shred woody material (see page 145). If you do have a bonfire, follow these safety rules:

● **site it well away** from buildings, fences and other combustible structures.

● **keep it small** or use an incinerator to confine it.

● **have a hosepipe** or buckets of water handy in case you need to douse the flames.

● **wear gloves,** stout footwear and other protective clothing.

● **use a fork** to add material to the fire.

● **keep children** at a safe distance; shut pets indoors.

● **afterwards** allow the remains to cool, then add the potash-rich ash to the compost heap in layers.

Dry materials thoroughly before burning them in a hot incinerator.

Fresh blooms of dahlias, nerines, japanese anemones, fuchsia and autumn crocus mingle with glowing rose hips, cotoneaster berries and structural seed heads, just as leaves turn yellow, red, orange and purple. This crescendo of colour and texture at the end of the growing season provides the grand finale of the gardening year. The ingredients are easy to assemble. Choose shrubs and trees like the japanese maples and liquidambars for their autumn leaf tints. Plant clumps of swaying grasses in a tapestry of late flowering perennials. Plan surprises, like the dazzling orange lanterns of physalis, or the turquoise berries and fiery red calyces of clerodendrum. Then stand back and enjoy the show.

Physalis alkekengi var. franchetii

plant selector

perennials

Many perennials continue to flower well into autumn. A few of these non-woody but durable plants are evergreen, but most are herbaceous, that is they die down in winter. Plant in the dormant season, preferably in autumn or early spring.

purple, blue and violet

1 Aconitum carmichaelii 'Arendsii'
Aconite, Monkshood

The glossy, dark green fingered leaves contribute to borders throughout spring and summer. In early autumn branching spires of rich blue helmeted flowers are carried on sturdy stems. All parts are highly toxic if ingested. Hardy.

Height: 1.2m (4ft) **Spread:** 35cm (14in)

Site: Partial shade, sun. Moist but well-drained soil

Use: Lightly shaded or sunny border, woodland garden

Good companions: Aconitum 'Spark's Variety', Anemone x hybrida 'Whirlwind', Viburnum x bodnantense 'Dawn'

2 Liriope muscari
Lilyturf

The dense clumps of evergreen grassy leaves may look a little untidy, but the spikes of knobbly violet-blue flowers, which never fully open, are eye-catching in autumn. Hardy.

Height: 30cm (12in) **Spread:** 45cm (18in)

Site: Sun, partial shade. Well-drained soil

Use: Ground cover, sunny or lightly shaded border

Good companions: Aster x frikartii 'Mönch', Echinacea purpurea 'White Lustre', x Solidaster luteus 'Lemore'

3 Penstemon 'Raven'

In late summer and autumn, this tall slender-stemmed hybrid bears numerous red-purple, broad tubular flowers with a white throat. A taller and tougher hybrid is 'Blackbird', which has black-purple, narrow tubular flowers. Good for cutting. Not fully hardy.

Height: 75cm (2ft 6in) **Spread:** 45cm (18in)

Site: Sun, partial shade. Fertile well-drained soil

Use: Sunny or lightly shaded border

Good companions: Aster amellus 'Veilchenkönigin', Penstemon 'Evelyn', Sedum 'Herbstfreude'

4 Tricyrtis formosana
Toad lily

Wiry stems set with glossy, near-oval leaves carry intriguing upturned waxy flowers. These are pale

'Versicolor', *Hydrangea* 'Preziosa', *Viburnum* x *bodnantense* 'Dawn'

6 Chrysanthemum 'Emperor of China'
Rubellum Group chrysanthemum

In autumn the foliage of this hybrid is suffused with crimson as the flowering season reaches its climax. The quilled petal-like ray-florets are silvery pink but with a glow of deep crimson in the centre of the flowerhead. Hardy.

Height: 1.2m (4ft) **Spread:** 60cm (2ft)
Site: Sun. Well-drained soil
Use: Sunny border
Good companions: *Anaphalis triplinervis* 'Sommerschnee', *Fuchsia magellanica* 'Versicolor', *Geranium wallichianum* 'Buxton's Variety'

7 Gaura lindheimeri 'Siskiyou Pink'

At first this gives the impression of being a lightweight perennial, but over weeks in late summer and autumn graceful stems carry clouds of small pink flowers. Hardy.

Height and spread: 60cm (2ft)
Site: Sun. Well-drained soil
Use: Gravel garden, sunny border
Good companions: *Allium hollandicum* 'Purple Sensation', *Eryngium* x *tripartitum*, *Erysimum* 'Bowles' Mauve'

8 Geranium sanguineum
Bloody cranesbill

The species and its cultivars make tidy clumps of finely cut leaves that are brightened throughout summer and autumn by an almost unflagging succession of cupped flowers. The usual colour is magenta-pink; 'Album' is pure white; and var. *striatum* is pale pink with dark veining. Hardy.

Height: 25cm (10in) **Spread:** 30cm (12in)
Site: Sun, partial shade. Well-drained soil
Use: Front of sunny or lightly shaded border, raised bed, rock garden

Good companions: *Gladiolus* 'The Bride', *Lavandula angustifolia* 'Hidcote', *Origanum laevigatum* 'Herrenhausen'

9 Penstemon 'Stapleford Gem'

From midsummer to early autumn, sometimes later, the erect stems of this large-leaved hybrid carry outward-facing, lipped tubular flowers. Their colour is a subtle blend of mauve-blue and pink, with purple lines in the pale throat. Hardy.

Height: 60cm (2ft) **Spread:** 45cm (18in)
Site: Sun, partial shade. Well-drained soil
Use: Sunny or lightly shaded border
Good companions: *Aster* x *frikartii* 'Mönch', *Caryopteris* x *clandonensis* 'Heavenly Blue', *Penstemon* 'Evelyn'

10 Physostegia virginiana 'Vivid'
False dragonhead, Obedient plant

The pink or white tubular flowers cluster in short spikes on square stems. They are 'obedient' in that, if moved, they stay in their new position. The plant has running roots and makes dense clumps. The flowers of this cultivar are bright purple-pink. Good as a cut flower. Hardy.

Height: 45cm (18in) **Spread:** 30cm (12in)
Site: Sun, partial shade. Moist, well-drained soil
Use: Sunny or lightly shaded border
Good companions: *Anemone* x *hybrida* 'Honorine Jobert', *Galtonia candicans*, *Phlox paniculata*

11 Sanguisorba obtusa
Burnet, Japanese burnet

In late summer and early autumn the grey-green leaves, which are composed of numerous leaflets, are topped by fluffy 'bottlebrush' spikes of rich mauve-pink flowers. Hardy.

Height and spread: 60cm (2ft)
Site: Sun, partial shade. Moist, well-drained soil
Use: Sunny or lightly shaded border
Good companions: *Astilbe* x *arendsii* 'Irrlicht', *Veronica gentianoides*, *Viola cornuta* Alba Group

12 Schizostylis coccinea 'Sunrise'
Kaffir lily

The grassy clumps of this rhizomatous perennial are almost evergreen. In autumn and early winter slender spires thrust up through the blade-like leaves bearing salmon-pink cup-shaped flowers. 'Major' has bright red flowers. Good as a cut flower. Not fully hardy.

Height: 60cm (2ft) **Spread:** 30cm (12in)
Site: Sun. Moist but well-drained soil
Use: Sunny border
Good companions: *Anemone* x *hybrida* 'Honorine Jobert', *Aster novi-belgii* 'Heinz Richard', *Diascia rigescens*

---

mauve-purple heavily speckled with red-purple. Hardy.

Height: 75cm (2ft 6in) **Spread:** 45cm (18in)
Site: Partial shade. Humus-rich and moist but well-drained soil
Use: Shaded border, woodland garden
Good companions: *Asplenium scolopendrium*, *Helleborus foetidus* Wesker Flisk Group, *Hosta sieboldiana* var. *elegans*

pink and mauve

5 Anemone x hybrida 'September Charm'
Japanese anemone

Branched wiry stems rise from a handsome base of dark divided leaves to carry upward-facing flowers. These are purple on the outside with pink inner petals around yellow stamens. Distinguished and long flowering. Hardy.

Height: 75cm (2ft 6in) **Spread:** 45cm (18in)
Site: Sun, partial shade. Humus-rich and moist but well-drained soil
Use: Sunny or lightly shaded border
Good companions: *Fuchsia magellanica*

pink and mauve (continued)

1 Sedum 'Herbstfreude'
Ice plant

The clump of fleshy grey-green leaves is attractive long before the small starry flowers, which are clustered in flat heads, open in early autumn. These are pink at first then darken to orange-red. Red-brown seed heads follow and add interesting texture to the winter garden. Hardy.

Height and spread: 60cm (2ft)
Site: Sun. Well-drained soil
Use: Gravel garden, sunny border
Good companions: *Caryopteris* x *clandonensis* 'Heavenly Blue', *Festuca glauca* 'Elijah Blue', *Stipa gigantea*

2 Sedum 'Vera Jameson'
Stonecrop

In late summer and early autumn arching purple stems, clothed with fleshy purple-pink leaves, carry heads of pink starry flowers. Hardy.

Height: 25cm (10in) **Spread:** 45cm (18in)
Site: Sun. Well-drained soil
Use: Front of sunny border, raised bed
Good companions: *Eryngium alpinum*, *Gaura lindheimeri* 'Siskiyou Pink', *Knautia macedonica*

bronze and maroon

3 Galax urceolata
Wandflower

In autumn and winter the toothed, nearly heart-shaped evergreen leaves are burnished bronze. Slender spires of tiny white flowers are borne in late spring or early summer. Hardy.

Height: 30cm (12in) **Spread:** 1m (3ft)
Site: Partial shade. Lime-free, humus-rich, moist but well-drained soil
Use: Ground cover, lightly shaded border, woodland garden
Good companions: *Disanthus cercidifolius*, *Hamamelis* x *intermedia* 'Pallida', *Rhododendron luteum*

4 Ophiopogon planiscapus 'Nigrescens'
Black lilyturf

This produces creeping clumps of near-black grassy leaves, which are usually relieved by a hint of green at the base. Shiny black berries, which follow on from tiny mauve flowers, mature in autumn and last into winter. Hardy.

Height: 20cm (8in) **Spread:** 30cm (12in)
Site: Sun, partial shade. Humus-rich, moist but well-drained soil
Use: Front of border
Good companions: *Galanthus elwesii*, *Saxifraga fortunei*, *Tiarella wherryi*

5 Panicum virgatum 'Rubrum'
Switch grass

The ribbon-like leaves of this deciduous perennial grass turn from green to light yellow then bronze in autumn, coinciding with airy sprays of tiny similarly coloured seed heads. Good for cutting. Hardy.

Height: 1.2m (4ft) **Spread:** 75cm (2ft 6in)
Site: Sun. Well-drained soil
Use: Sunny border
Good companions: *Berberis thungergii* f. *atropurpurea*, *Eryngium alpinum*, *Sedum* 'Herbstfreude'

red and russet

6 Canna 'Assaut'
Indian shot plant

The hybrid cannas are impressive foliage plants with large paddle-like leaves, which in late summer and autumn are topped by spikes of brightly coloured broad-petalled flowers. In the case of 'Assaut' the leaves are brown-purple and the flowers intense orange-scarlet. Half hardy.

General care: Plant out in early summer. In frost-prone areas, lift the rhizomatous perennials before the first frost, remove leaves and stems and store in frost-free conditions in boxes of barely moist compost. Plant while dormant in spring (see Late Spring).

Height: 2m (6ft) **Spread:** 60cm (2ft)

Site: Sun. Fertile, moist soil
Use: Formal bedding, moist border
Good companions: *Lobelia* 'Queen Victoria', *Musa basjoo*, *Ricinus communis* 'Impala'

7 Imperata cylindrica 'Rubra'

In a hot summer this grass produces spikes of silvery flowers, but its main ornamental value is the red stain that extends down from the tips of the erect leaf blades in summer and early autumn. Not fully hardy.

Height: 50cm (20in) **Spread:** 30cm (12in)
Site: Sun, partial shade. Moist, well-drained soil
Use: Sunny or lightly shaded border
Good companions: *Ceratostigma willmottianum*, *Geranium sanguineum*, *Phlox paniculata* 'Fujiyama'

8 Iris foetidissima
Gladwyn iris, Stinking iris

It is only when the evergreen strap-shaped leaves are crushed that this plant gives off an unpleasant smell. The beardless flowers, mauve with

touches of yellow, do not count for much in early summer, but the seedpods split in autumn to show their bright orange contents. Var. *citrina* flowers freely and has large pods. All parts can be harmful if ingested. Good for cutting. Hardy.

Height: 60cm (2ft) **Spread:** 45cm (18in)
Site: Sun, shade. Well-drained, even poor, soil
Use: Shady border, underplanting for trees and shrubs, wild garden, woodland
Good companions: *Euphorbia characias* subsp. *wulfenii*, *Pachysandra terminalis*, *Vinca minor*

9 Kniphofia triangularis
Red hot poker, Torch lily

From a clump of narrow grassy leaves rise slender wiry stems that terminate in a cluster of narrow tubular flowers of intense scarlet paling to yellow at the mouth.

Height: 75cm (2ft 6in) **Spread:** 45cm (18in)
Site: Sun, partial shade. Moist, well-drained soil
Use: Sunny or lightly shaded border
Good companions: *Agapanthus* 'Lilliput', *Galtonia candicans*, *Schizostylis coccinea* 'Sunrise'

10 Canna 'King Midas'
Indian shot plant

This hybrid has erect, dark green paddle-like leaves and in late summer and early autumn orange-marked, rich yellow flowers. Half hardy.

General care: Plant out in early summer. In frost-prone areas, lift the rhizomatous perennials before the first frost, remove leaves and stems and store in frost-free conditions in boxes of barely moist compost. Plant while dormant in spring (see Late Spring).

Height: 2m (6ft) **Spread:** 60cm (2ft)
Site: Sun. Fertile, moist soil
Use: Formal bedding, moist border
Good companions: *Canna* 'Assaut', *Dahlia* 'Bishop of Llandaff', *Dahlia* 'Zorro'

11 Chrysanthemum 'Mary Stoker'
Rubellum Group chrysanthemum

From late summer this bushy, woody-based clump-forming perennial bears sprays of long-lasting flowerheads. The orange-yellow, petal-like ray-florets radiate from a boss that is green at first then yellow. Good for cutting. Hardy.

Height: 75cm (2ft 6in) **Spread:** 60cm (2ft)
Site: Sun. Well-drained soil
Use: Sunny border
Good companions: *Anemone* x *hybrida* 'September Charm', *Aster ericoides* 'Pink Cloud', *Penstemon* 'Stapleford Gem'

12 Helenium 'Sonnenwunder'
Helen's flower

Branching stems carry clear yellow flowerheads with yellow-brown centres. The sprays are long lasting and good for cutting. Hardy.

Height: 1.5m (5ft) **Spread:** 60cm (2ft)
Site: Sun. Fertile and moist but well-drained soil
Use: Sunny border
Good companions: *Helenium* 'Moerheim Beauty', *Miscanthus sinensis* 'Silberfeder', *Rudbeckia fulgida* var. *deamii*

1 Helianthus 'Lemon Queen'
Sunflower

This perennial has running roots and needs
staking, but for several weeks from late summer
the branched stems bear numerous lemon-yellow
daisy-like flowerheads. Good for cutting. Hardy.
Height: 2m (6ft) **Spread:** 1.2m (4ft)
Site: Sun. Moist but well-drained soil
Use: Back of sunny border
Good companions: *Aster amellus*
'Veilchenkönigin', *Echinacea purpurea* 'White
Lustre', *Helenium* 'Sonnenwunder'

2 Kniphofia 'Prince Igor'
Red hot poker, Torch lily

Majestic, incandescent red hot poker with erect
stems set with red-orange tubular flowers,
making giant 'torches' that last from early to mid-
autumn. Hardy.
Height: 2m (6ft) **Spread:** 1m (3ft)
Site: Sun. Moist but well-drained soil
Use: Sunny border
Good companions: *Agapanthus* 'Blue Giant',
Cortaderia selloana 'Sunningdale Silver',
Miscanthus sinensis 'Silberfeder'

3 Molinia caerulea subsp. arundinacea 'Windspiel'
Purple moor grass

This deciduous grass forms a clump of flat leaves
through which rise erect stems bearing purple
flowerheads. By autumn these are full of tiny
seeds and the whole plant is honey tinted.
Height: 1.8m (6ft) **Spread:** 50cm (20in)
Site: Sun, partial shade. Moist but well-drained
soil, preferably acid
Use: Sunny or lightly shaded border, waterside,
woodland garden
Good companions: *Alchemilla mollis*, *Epimedium
x versicolor* 'Sulphureum', *Miscanthus sinensis*
'Zebrinus'

4 Physalis alkekengi var. franchetii
Chinese lantern, Japanese lantern

A rather untidy plant with running roots and
insignificant flowers, but the orange papery
'lanterns' that enclose inedible scarlet berries are
brightly decorative and suitable for drying. All
parts can cause stomach upset if ingested and
contact can cause skin reactions. Hardy.
Height: 60cm (2ft) **Spread:** 1m (3ft)
Site: Sun, partial shade. Well-
drained soil
Use: Sunny or lightly shaded border
Good companions: *Cotoneaster
conspicuus* 'Decorus', *Helleborus
argutifolius*, *Rosa glauca*

5 Rudbeckia fulgida var. deamii
Black-eyed susan

Bushy perennial with pointed leaves and hairy
stems that branch to carry numerous daisy-like
flowerheads. The orange-yellow, petal-like ray-
florets radiate from the brown-black eye. Hardy.
Height: 75cm (2ft 6in) **Spread:** 45cm (18in)
Site: Sun, partial shade. Moist but well-drained
soil
Use: Sunny or lightly shaded border, wild garden
Good companions: *Chrysanthemum* 'Mary
Stoker', *Helenium* 'Moerheim Beauty',
Miscanthus sinensis 'Silberfeder'

6 Rudbeckia 'Herbstsonne'
Coneflower

In late summer and early autumn, tall leafy
branching stems carry masses of bright yellow

daisy-like flowers. The petal-like ray-florets droop
to form a wide skirt around the central green
cone. Excellent for cutting. Hardy.
Height: 2m (6ft) **Spread:** 1m (3ft)
Site: Sun, partial shade. Moist, well-drained soil
Use: Back of border
Good companions: *Kniphofia* 'Prince Igor', *Molinia
caerulea* subsp. *arundinacea* 'Windspiel',
Rudbeckia fulgida var. *deamii*

cream and white

7 Anaphalis margaritacea
Pearl everlasting

In late summer and early autumn, spreading
clumps of dull green leaves, woolly and white
underneath, are topped by clusters of long-lasting,
white daisy-like flowers. The leaves of the shorter
var. *yedoensis* are outlined in white. Hardy.
Height and spread: 60cm (2ft)
Site: Sun, partial shade. Moist, well-drained soil

Use: Ground cover, sunny or lightly shaded border

Good companions: *Anemone hupehensis* 'Hadspen Abundance', *Anemone* x *hybrida* 'Honorine Jobert', *Hydrangea macrophylla* 'Blue Wave'

8 Anemone x hybrida 'Honorine Jobert'
Japanese anemone

A star of the autumn garden, but can be invasive. Wiry branching stems rise above lobed dark leaves and bear a long succession of white flowers with yellow stamens. Hardy.

Height: 1.2m (4ft) **Spread:** Indefinite

Site: Sun, partial shade. Humus-rich and moist but well-drained soil

Use: Sunny or lightly shaded border

Good companions: *Anemone hupensis* 'Hadspen Abundance', *Anemone* x *hybrida* 'September Charm', *Aster novi-belgii* 'Heinz Richard'

9 Cimicifuga simplex Atropurpurea Group [syn. Actaea]
Bugbane, Cohosh

In early to mid-autumn sinuous slender stems carry 'bottlebrushes' of small, sweetly scented cream flowers. The stems and deeply cut leaves develop their rich purple best in full sun. Hardy.

Height: 1.5m (5ft) **Spread:** 60cm (2ft)

Site: Sun, partial shade. Humus-rich, moist soil

Use: Moist border

Good companions: *Anemone* x *hybrida* 'Honorine Jobert', *Astilbe* 'Professor van der Wielen', *Astrantia major* 'Claret'

10 Cortaderia selloana
Pampas grass

This evergreen grass makes a substantial clump of arching leaves. In late summer stout stems carry long-lasting, silky cream plumes, which are good for drying. 'Aureolineata' has yellow-margined leaves, which become more pronounced as they age. Hardy.

Height: 2.2m (7ft) **Spread:** 1.5m (5ft)

Site: Sun. Well-drained soil

Use: Specimen clump, sunny border

Good companions: *Buddleja davidii* 'Black Knight', *Lavandula* x *intermedia* Dutch Group, *Verbena bonariensis*

11 Echinacea purpurea 'White Lustre'
Coneflower

Stiff upright plant with branching stems that carry flowerheads nearly 15cm (6in) across. Each flower consists of a glistening orange-brown central cone and drooping, greenish white, petal-like ray-florets. Other cultivars have purple or crimson ray-florets. Hardy.

Height: 1m (3ft) **Spread:** 45cm (18in)

Site: Sun. Humus-rich, well-drained soil

Use: Sunny border

Good companions: *Centaurea hypoleuca* 'John Coutts', *Deschampsia cespitosa* 'Goldschleier', *Liatris spicata*

12 Saxifraga fortunei
Saxifrage

Deciduous or semi-evergreen species with lobed and toothed round leaves that are deep green on the surface, red on the underside. In late autumn branching stems suspend showers of white starry flowers above the foliage. Each flower has one petal longer than the others. Hardy.

Height and spread: 35cm (14in)

Site: Partial, full shade. Humus-rich and moist but well-drained soil

Use: Shady border

Good companions: *Alchemilla mollis*, *Helleborus foetidus* Wester Flisk Group, *Sarcococca hookeriana* var. *digyna*

3 Euphorbia seguieriana subsp. niciciana
Milkweed, Spurge

For many weeks in late summer and early autumn this spurge adds a fresh note with heads of lime-green flowers over blue-grey leaves. All parts can be harmful if ingested and contact with the sap can cause skin reactions. Hardy.
Height: 50cm (20in) **Spread:** 45cm (18in)
Site: Sun. Well-drained soil
Use: Gravel garden, sunny border
Good companions: *Bergenia* 'Ballawley', *Stipa gigantea*, *Verbascum* Cotswold Group 'Gainsborough'

4 Kniphofia 'Green Jade'

In late summer and early autumn, stout stems rise up through the arching leaves of this evergreen perennial to carry a 'torch' of green buds. When fully open, the tubular flowers are white. Hardy.
Height: 1.2m (4ft)
Spread: 60cm (2ft)
Site: Sun, partial shade. Humus-rich and moist but well-drained soil
Use: Sunny or lightly shaded border
Good companions: *Helenium* 'Sonnenwunder', *Pennisetum alopecuroides* 'Hameln', *Rudbeckia* 'Herbstonne'

5 Pachysandra terminalis

This evergreen perennial makes a dense cover of glossy leaves arranged in neat rosettes. In autumn, small inedible white fruits follow insignificant but scented white flowers, borne in spring. Tolerant of dry shade. Hardy.
Height: 20cm (8in) **Spread:** Indefinite
Site: Shade, sun. Moist but well-drained soil
Use: Ground cover, woodland garden
Good companions: *Geranium macrorrhizum*, *Helleborus foetidus*, *Lunaria annua*

6 Pennisetum alopecuroides 'Hameln'
Fountain grass

This evergreen grass makes a dense clump of linear arching leaves. It is transformed in autumn when fuzzy caterpillar-like flowerheads weigh down their thin stems. The flowerheads are green at first then pale brown. Not fully hardy.
Height: 1m (3ft) **Spread:** 1.2m (4ft)
Site: Sun. Moist but well-drained soil
Use: Sunny border
Good companions: *Cosmos atrosanguineus*, *Kniphofia* 'Percy's Pride', *Sanguisorba obtusa*

cream and white (continued)

1 Scabiosa caucasica 'Miss Willmott'
Pincushion flower, Scabious

Like its blue counterparts, this scabious flowers over many weeks in late summer and early autumn. The pincushion effect referred to in its common name is produced by protruding styles at the centre of the greenish white to cream flowerheads. Excellent for cutting. Hardy.
Height: 1m (3ft) **Spread:** 50cm (20in)
Site: Sun. Well-drained soil. Good on lime
Use: Sunny border, wild garden
Good companions: *Eryngium alpinum*, *Lavandula angustifolia* 'Hidcote', *Verbascum* 'Helen Johnson'

green

2 Euphorbia schillingii
Milkweed, Spurge

This spurge has attractive foliage, with a central white vein highlighting the dark green of the leaves. Lime-yellow bracts, which remain ornamental from mid-summer through to mid-autumn, cup the relatively insignificant but specialised flowers. All parts of this plant can be harmful if ingested and contact with the sap can cause allergic skin reactions. Hardy.
Height: 1m (3ft) **Spread:** 30cm (12in)
Site: Partial shade, sun. Moist but well-drained soil
Use: Lightly shaded or sunny border, woodland garden
Good companions: *Aconitum* 'Ivorine', *Epimedium* x *versicolor* 'Sulphureum', *Helleborus argutifolius*

asters

The asters include some of the most useful perennials for autumn borders as they flower profusely in a wide range of colours, often yellow centred. The daisy-like blooms are long lasting on the plant or cut. All of the following are hardy but vary in their requirements.

1 Aster amellus 'King George'
This makes a rather dull clump of narrow hairy leaves in spring and summer, but in autumn it bears large violet-purple flowerheads.
Height: 45cm (18in) **Spread:** 40cm (16in)
Site: Sun. Well-drained soil. Good on lime
Good companions: *Eryngium alpinum*, *Lavandula angustifolia* 'Hidcote', *Verbascum* 'Helen Johnson'

2 Aster novae-angliae 'Andenken an Alma Pötschke'
New England aster
In late summer and the first half of autumn sprays of bright reddish pink flowerheads top a stiff clump of foliage. Other New England asters are mainly mauve, pink or white.
Height: 1m (3ft) **Spread:** 75cm (2ft 6in)
Site: Sun, partial shade. Moist but well-drained soil
Good companions: *Gaura lindheimeri* 'Siskiyou Pink', *Penstemon* 'Blackbird', *Sedum spectabile* 'Brilliant'

3 Aster lateriflorus 'Horizontalis'
In mid-autumn this stiff-stemmed bushy plant bears masses of white starry flowerheads with fluffy pink centres.
Height: 60cm (2ft) **Spread:** 30cm (12in)
Site: Partial shade. Moist but well-drained soil

Good companions: *Aconitum carmichaelii* 'Arendsii', *Anemone* x *hybrida* 'Whirlwind', *Geranium* x *magnificum*

4 Aster ericoides 'Pink Cloud'
Over several weeks in autumn this bushy perennial with needle-like leaves produces a mass of small, pale pink flowers.
Height: 1m (3ft) **Spread:** 30cm (12in)
Site: Sun. Well-drained soil
Good companions: *Bergenia* 'Ballawley', *Geranium* 'Johnson's Blue', *Verbena bonariensis*

5 Aster pringlei 'Monte Cassino'
Erect branching stems, which are set with tiny narrow leaves, are liberally sprinkled with white starry flowerheads throughout autumn.
Height: 1m (3ft) **Spread:** 30cm (12in)
Site: Partial shade, sun. Moist but well-drained soil
Good companions: *Anaphalis triplinervis* 'Sommerschnee', *Phlox paniculata* 'Fujiyama', *Tradescantia* Andersoniana Group 'Osprey'

6 Aster novi-belgii 'Kristina'
Michaelmas daisy, New York aster
In late summer and early autumn the dense 'cushion' of dark green leaves is almost hidden by white semi-double flowerheads.
Height: 30cm (12in) **Spread:** 45cm (18in)
Site: Sun, partial shade. Fertile and moist but well-drained soil
Good companions: *Anemone* x *hybrida* 'September Charm', *Aster novi-belgii* 'Heinz Richard', *Phlox paniculata* 'Eventide'

7 Aster amellus 'Veilchenkönigen'
This makes a neater plant than 'King George', with smaller flowerheads of intense violet carried on stiff stems.
Height: 40cm (16in) **Spread:** 30cm (12in)
Site: Sun. Well-drained soil. Good on lime
Good companions: *Aster ericoides* 'Pink Cloud', *Delphinium* Belladonna Group 'Cliveden Beauty', *Echinacea purpurea* 'White Lustre'

annuals & biennials

These short-lived plants often give good value over many weeks.
If deadheaded regularly in summer, many continue to flower and brighten
beds and borders in autumn until stopped by frosts.

purple, blue and violet

1 Anagallis monellii
Blue pimpernel

Evergreen perennial commonly grown as an
annual raised from cuttings. In summer and early
autumn, low branching stems clothed with
narrow pointed leaves carry small saucer-shaped
flowers of intense blue. Not fully hardy.
General care: Buy young plants in early summer
or take cuttings between late spring and early
summer and overwinter under glass.
Height: 15cm (6in) **Spread:** 40cm (16in)
Site: Sun. Moist but well-drained soil
Compost: Soil-based (John Innes No. 2) or soil-less
Use: Container, front of sunny bed or border
Good companions: *Cosmos bipinnatus* 'Sea
Shells', *Heliotropium arborescens* 'Marine',
Nicotiana Domino Series

2 Convolvulus tricolor 'Royal Ensign'

Bushy then sprawling short-lived perennial grown
as an annual. The funnel-shaped flowers, borne
from midsummer to early autumn, are vivid deep
blue with a yellow-and-white centre. Hardy.
General care: Sow seed *in situ* or in pots in
mid-spring.
Height: 30cm (12in) **Spread:** 35cm (14in)
Site: Sun. Well-drained soil
Compost: Soil-based (John Innes No. 1)
Use: Container, front of sunny bed or border
Good companions: *Cleome hassleriana* 'Rose
Queen', *Delphinium grandiflorum* 'Blue Butterfly',
Salvia viridis 'Oxford Blue'

3 Heliotropium arborescens 'Marine'
Cherry pie, Heliotrope

Short-lived shrub usually grown as an annual. This
compact cultivar has dark, deeply veined leaves
and large heads of small, violet-blue flowers
during summer and early autumn. Half hardy.
General care: Sow seed under glass at
16–18°C (61–64°F) in mid-spring.
Height: 45cm (18in) **Spread:** 35cm (14in)
Site: Sun. Moist but well-drained soil
Compost: Soil-based (John Innes No. 3) or soil-less
Use: Container, formal bedding, sunny border
Good companions: *Lobelia erinus* 'Crystal

Palace', *Verbena* 'Imagination', *Viola* x *wittrockiana*
'Jolly Joker'

4 Isotoma axillaris

Perennial usually grown as an annual. It forms a
mound of dark green, slender narrow-lobed
leaves and bears a profusion of scented, blue
starry flowers in summer and autumn. Tender.
General care: Sow seed under glass at
16–18°C (61–64°F) in mid-spring.
Height and spread: 30cm (12in)
Site: Sun, partial shade. Well-drained soil
Compost: Soil-based (John Innes No. 2)
Use: Container, sunny bed or border
Good companions: *Pelargonium* 'Bird Dancer',
Petunia Fantasy Series, *Scaevola aemula* 'Blue
Wonder'

5 Pennisetum villosum
Feathertop

Deciduous perennial grass usually grown as an
annual. In late summer and early autumn soft
'bottlebrush' plumes weigh down arching stems
above the loose tuft of narrow leaf blades. The
plumes are greenish white at first but age to
purple. Not fully hardy.
General care: Sow seed under glass at
13–18°C (55–64°C) in early spring.
Height and spread: 60cm (2ft)
Site: Sun. Well-drained soil
Use: Sunny bed or border
Good companions: *Eryngium* x *tripartitum*, *Gaura
lindheimeri*, *Sedum* 'Herbstfreude'

6 Salvia farinacea 'Victoria'
Mealy sage

Short-lived perennial grown as an annual. In
summer and autumn mealy stems carry spikes of
small flowers clear of glossy green foliage. Stems
and flowers are intense purple-blue. Half hardy.
General care: Sow seed under glass at
16–18°C (61–64°F) in mid-spring.
Height: 60cm (2ft) **Spread:** 30cm (12in)

Site: Sun. Moist but well-drained soil
Compost: Soil-based (John Innes No. 2) or soil-less
Use: Container, sunny bed or border
Good companions: *Cosmos bipinnatus* 'Sea
Shells', *Lobelia erinus* 'Crystal Palace', *Verbena*
'Imagination'

7 Verbena rigida

Perennial with toothed lance-shaped leaves
grown as an annual as it is too tender to survive
winters except in favoured coastal gardens. Tight
clusters of fragrant purple-violet flowers are borne
in summer and early autumn. Not fully hardy.
General care: Sow seed at 18–20°C (64–68°F)
under glass in early spring.
Height: 50cm (20in) **Spread:** 40cm (16in)
Site: Sun. Moist but well-drained soil
Use: Sunny border
Good companions: *Cosmos bipinnatus* Sensation
Series, *Dahlia* 'Porcelain', *Nicotiana* Domino Series

pink and mauve

8 Begonia semperflorens Organdy Series
Wax begonia

Fibrous-rooted perennial usually grown as a bedding annual. It has glossy, dark green or bronze foliage and sprays of pink, red or white flowers from early summer to mid-autumn. Tender.

General care: Sow seed under glass at 16°C (61°F) in late winter or early spring or take cuttings from overwintered plants in spring.

Height and spread: 15cm (6in)

Site: Sun. Well-drained soil

Compost: Soil-based (John Innes No. 2) or soil-less

Use: Container, formal bedding

Good companions: *Bassia scoparia* f. *tricophylla*, *Brachyscome iberidifolia* Splendour Series, *Dianthus chinensis* Baby Doll Series

9 Callistephus chinensis Princess Series
China aster

Numerous dwarf and taller cultivars of china aster flower in late summer and autumn. The semi-double flowerheads of the tall Princess Series, in a range of colours that includes shades of pink, red, purple and white, have quilled and incurved petal-like ray-florets. Half hardy.

General care: Sow seed under glass at 16°C (61°F) in early spring or *in situ* in mid-spring.

Height: 60cm (2ft) **Spread:** 30cm (12in)

Site: Sun. Moist, well-drained soil. Good on lime

Use: Sunny border, formal bedding

Good companions: *Dahlia* 'Porcelain', *Fuchsia* 'Leonora', *Heliotropium arborescens* 'Marine'

10 Cosmos bipinnatus 'Sea Shells'

Erect annual with feathery foliage. Tall wiry stems support large starry flowerheads, the florets of which are rolled into tubes. The colour range includes pink, red and white. Half hardy.

General care: Sow seed under glass in mid-spring or *in situ* in late spring.

Height: 1m (3ft) **Spread:** 45cm (18in)

Site: Sun. Moist but well-drained soil

Use: Sunny border, formal bedding

Good companions: *Alcea rosea* 'Nigra', *Clarkia amoena* Satin Series, *Nicotiana* Domino Series

11 Lavatera trimestris 'Silver Cup'
Mallow

Erect and bushy annual with somewhat coarse lobed leaves. Pink funnel-shaped flowers, which are heavily veined in a darker shade, are borne in profusion during summer and early autumn. Suitable for cutting. Hardy.

General care: Sow seed *in situ* in early autumn or mid-spring.

Height: 75cm (2ft 6in) **Spread:** 40cm (16in)

Site: Sun. Well-drained soil

Use: Formal bedding, sunny bed or border

Good companions: *Centaurea cyanus*, *Consolida ajacis* Giant Imperial Series, *Xeranthemum annuum*

12 Petunia 'Purple Wave'
Multiflora petunia

The multiflora petunias are bushy hybrid perennials grown as annuals. They produce trumpet-shaped flowers, up to 5cm (2in) across, in great profusion in summer and early autumn. Those of 'Purple Wave' are an intense magenta. Half hardy.

General care: Sow seed under glass at 13–18°C (55–64°F) in early spring.

Height: 45cm (18in) **Spread:** 75cm (2ft 6in)

Site: Sun. Well-drained soil

Compost: Soil-based (John Innes No. 1)

Use: Container, formal bedding, front of sunny border

Good companions: *Brachyscome iberidifolia* Splendour Series, *Pelargonium* 'L'Elégante', *Verbena* 'Silver Anne'

pink and mauve (continued)

1 Xeranthemum annuum

Annual with silver-green leaves and wiry upright branching stems that carry papery, single or double daisy-like flowerheads through summer and early autumn in shades of pink, red, purple or white. Suitable for cutting and drying. Half hardy.

General care: Sow seed under glass at 16°C (61°F) in early spring.

Height: 60cm (2ft) **Spread:** 35cm (14in)

Site: Sun. Well-drained soil

Use: Sunny bed or border

Good companions: *Brachyscome iberidifolia* Splendour Series, *Dianthus chinensis* Baby Doll Series, *Nigella damascena* 'Miss Jekyll'

red and russet

2 Arctotis x hybrida 'Flame'
African daisy

The hybrid African daisies are perennials usually grown as annuals, many easily raised from seed. They have felted silver-green leaves and produce flowerheads in a wide range of colours from mid-summer to early autumn. 'Flame' is raised annually from cuttings and bears a profusion of vivid orange-red flowers. Tender.

General care: Buy plants in early summer or take cuttings in summer and overwinter young plants under glass.

Height: 45cm (18in) **Spread:** 30cm (12in)

Site: Sun. Moist but light, well-drained soil

Compost: Soil-based (John Innes No. 2) with added grit

Use: Container, formal bedding, front of border

Good companions: *Ageratum houstonianum*, *Layia platiglossa*, *Viola* x *wittrockiana* 'Jolly Joker'

3 Bassia scoparia f. tricophylla
Burning bush, Summer cypress

Fast-growing annual that forms a cone-shaped bush packed with narrow leaves. In summer these are light green but in late summer or autumn they turn deep purplish red. The green flowers are insignificant. Half hardy.

General care: Sow seed under glass at 16°C (61°F) in early to mid-spring or *in situ* in late spring.

Height: 75cm (2ft 6in) **Spread:** 45cm (18in)

Site: Sun. Well-drained soil

Compost: Soil-based (John Innes No. 2)

Use: Container, formal bedding, sunny border

Good companions: *Antirrhinum* Sonnet Series, *Cleome hassleriana* 'Rose Queen', *Nigella damascena* 'Miss Jekyll'

4 Dahlia 'Figaro Red'
Dwarf bedding dahlia

Low-growing dahlia raised annually from seed with a long flowering season if regularly deadheaded. The Figaro Series includes plants with double or semi-double flowerheads in a range of colours. Half hardy.

General care: Sow seed under glass at 16°C (61°F) in early spring. Deadhead regularly.

Height and spread: 40cm (16in)

Site: Sun. Fertile, humus-rich, well-drained soil

Compost: Soil-based (John Innes No. 2) or soil-less

Use: Container, formal bedding

Good companions: *Amaranthus caudatus* 'Viridis', *Canna* 'Assaut', *Fuchsia* 'Lady Thumb'

5 Helianthus annuus 'Velvet Queen'
Sunflower

Sunflowers are fast-growing annuals with stout stems bearing large daisy-like flowerheads. 'Velvet Queen' is moderately tall with red-brown velvet florets surrounding the darker brown centre. Suitable for cutting. Hardy.

General care: Sow seed under glass at 16°C (61°F) in late winter or *in situ* in mid-spring.

Height: 1.5m (5ft) **Spread:** 45cm (18in)

Site: Sun. Moist, well-drained soil. Good on lime.

Use: Sunny bed or border

Good companions: *Layia platiglossa*, *Nicotiana* 'Lime Green', *Rudbeckia hirta* 'Rustic Dwarf'

6 Impatiens New Guinea Group
Balsam, Busy lizzie

These sub-shrubby hybrid perennials are usually grown as annuals raised from seed or from cuttings for their brightly coloured flowers and colourful foliage, which may be red, bronze or variegated yellow. 'Spectra' includes soft and intense colours, sometimes bicoloured. Tender.

General care: Buy plants in early summer or take cuttings from overwintered plants in spring.

Height: 35cm (14in) **Spread:** 30cm (12in)

Site: Partial shade. Humus-rich and moist but well-drained soil

Compost: Soil-based (John Innes No. 2) or soil-less

Use: Conservatory or greenhouse minimum 10°C (50°F), container, formal bedding

Good companions: *Begonia* 'Orange Cascade', *Fuchsia* 'Gartenmeister Bonstedt', *Solenostemon* 'Crimson Ruffles'

yellow and orange

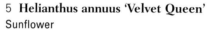

7 Bidens ferulifolia

Short-lived perennial usually grown as an annual. The sprawling stems, which are lightly clothed with finely divided leaves, carry numerous small, yellow daisy-like flowerheads throughout summer and early autumn. Not fully hardy.

General care: Sow seed under glass at 13–18°C (55–64°F) in mid-spring, or take cuttings from overwintered plants in spring.

Height: 30cm (12in) **Spread:** 1m (3ft)

Site: Sun. Well-drained soil

Compost: Soil-based (John Innes No. 2) or soil-less

Use: Container, sunny bed or border

Good companions: *Helichrysum petiolare*, *Petunia* Surfinia Series, *Scaevola aemula*

8 Cosmos sulphureus 'Sunset'

Upright annual with narrow-lobed leaves and long-stemmed flowerheads produced freely from mid-summer until the first frosts. The usual colour is yellow but 'Sunset' is rich orange. Tender.

General care: Sow seed under glass at 16°C (61°F) in mid-spring.

Height: 50cm (20in) **Spread:** 35cm (14in)

Site: Sun. Moist but well-drained soil

Use: Sunny bed or border

Good companions: *Nicotiana langsdorffii*, *Nicotiana* 'Lime Green', *Viola* x *wittrockiana* 'Baby Lucia'

9 Layia platyglossa
Tidy tips

Bushy annual with narrow grey-green leaves. In summer and the first half of autumn it produces numerous daisy-like flowers that have white-tipped, yellow petal-like ray-florets and rich yellow centres. Cut flowers are long lasting. Hardy.

General care: Sow *in situ* in autumn or spring.

Height: 45cm (18in)

Spread: 25cm (10in)

Site: Sun. Moist but well-drained soil

Use: Sunny bed or border

Good companions: *Molucella laevis*, *Nemesia* 'Carnival', *Zinnia* 'Envy'

10 Limonium sinuatum Forever Series
Statice

Perennial usually grown as an annual with stiffly branching winged stems that are rough to the touch. In late summer and early autumn these carry sprays of tiny flowers that are surrounded by colourful papery bracts in yellow, white, blue or pink. Suitable for cutting and drying. Not fully hardy.

General care: Sow seed under glass at 13–18°C (55–64°F) in spring.

Height: 60cm (2ft) **Spread:** 40cm (16in)

Site: Sun. Well-drained soil

Use: Sunny bed or border

Good companions: *Antirrhinum* Sonnet Series, *Bidens ferulifolia*, *Brachyscome iberidifolia* Splendour Series

11 Rudbeckia hirta 'Rustic Dwarf'
Black-eyed susan

Short-lived branching perennial or biennial usually grown as an annual. The stems and leaves are bristly. The large flowerheads are composed of dark centres surrounded by petal-like ray-florets in shades of yellow, bronze or chestnut; sometimes they are bicoloured. Suitable for cutting. Hardy.

General care: Sow seed under glass in early to mid-spring.

Height: 60cm (2ft) **Spread:** 35cm (14in)

Site: Sun, partial shade. Moist but well-drained soil

Compost: Soil-based (John Innes No. 2)

Use: Container, formal bedding, sunny or lightly shaded border

Good companions: *Cosmos sulphureus* 'Sunset', *Nicotiana langsdorffii*, *Verbena* 'Peaches and Cream'

12 Scabiosa stellata 'Paper Moon'

In summer this hairy annual bears pale mauve-blue flowerheads on wiry stems. The intriguing yellowish seed heads that follow are up to 8cm (3in) across and composed of tightly clustered, cup-shaped papery bracts with maroon centres. The seed heads are suitable for drying. Hardy.

General care: Sow *in situ* in mid-spring.

Height: 45cm (18in) **Spread:** 25cm (10in)

Site: Sun. Well-drained soil

Use: Sunny bed or border

Good companions: *Lagurus ovatus*, *Papaver rhoeas* 'Mother of Pearl', *Salvia viridis* 'Oxford Blue'

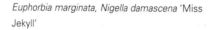

yellow and orange (continued)

1 Tagetes Zenith Series
Afro-French marigold

Bushy annual hybrid with deeply cut leaves and yellow, orange or bicoloured double flowerheads throughout summer and early autumn. Half hardy.

General care: Sow seed under glass at 21°C (70°F) in early spring.

Height: 30cm (12in) **Spread:** 25cm (10in)

Site: Sun. Well-drained soil

Compost: Soil-based (John Innes No. 2) or soil-less

Use: Container, formal bedding, front of sunny border

Good companions: *Euphorbia marginata, Lagurus ovatus, Tagetes tenuifolia* 'Lemon Gem'

2 Tithonia rotundifolia 'Goldfinger'
Mexican sunflower

Compact bushy annual that in late summer and autumn produces orange flowerheads. Half hardy.

General care: Sow under glass in mid-spring at 15°C (59°F) or *in situ* in late spring.

Height: 75cm (2ft 6in) **Spread:** 25cm (10in)

Site: Sun. Well-drained soil

Use: Sunny bed or border

Good companions: *Bidens ferulifolia, Tagetes* Zenith Series, *Tropaeolum* Alaska Series

cream and white

3 Lagurus ovatus
Hare's tail

This annual grass forms a tuft of pale grey-green leaves. Fluffy oval flowerheads age from greenish white, often tinged purple, to buff-cream. Hardy.

General care: Sow seed *in situ* in mid-spring.

Height: 40cm (16in) **Spread:** 30cm (12in)

Site: Sun. Well-drained soil

Use: Border, gravel garden

Good companions: *Eschscholzia californica,*

Euphorbia marginata, Nigella damascena 'Miss Jekyll'

4 Nicotiana sylvestris
Tobacco plant

Short-lived perennial usually grown as an annual. Stout stems rise from large basal leaves and carry scented, white long-tubed flowers. Half hardy.

General care: Sow seed under glass at 18°C (64°F) in mid-spring.

Height: 1.2m (4ft) **Spread:** 50cm (20in)

Site: Sun, partial shade. Fertile and moist but well-drained soil

Use: Sunny or lightly shaded border

Good companions: *Amaranthus caudatus* 'Viridis', *Molucella laevis, Nicotiana* 'Lime Green'

green

5 Amaranthus caudatus 'Viridis'
Love-lies-bleeding, Tassel flower

Bushy annual with large, heavily veined, light

green leaves. In summer and autumn dangling tassels are packed with tiny green flowers that fade to cream. Half hardy.

General care: Sow seed under glass at 20°C (68°F) in mid-spring.

Height: 1.2m (4ft) **Spread:** 75cm (2ft 6in)

Site: Sun. Humus-rich, moist but well-drained soil

Compost: Soil-based (John Innes No. 2)

Use: Conservatory or greenhouse minimum 7°C (45°F), container, formal bedding, sunny border

Good companions: *Amaranthus caudatus, Dahlia* 'Claire de Lune', *Dahlia* 'Moor Place'

6 Nicotiana langsdorffii
Tobacco plant

Short-lived perennial grown as an annual. From a rosette of large sticky basal leaves rise branching stems that carry sprays of pale green flowers in late summer and early autumn. Half hardy.

General care: Sow seed under glass at 18°C (64°F) in mid-spring.

Height: 1.2m (4ft) **Spread:** 45cm (18in)

Site: Sun, partial shade. Fertile and moist but well-drained soil

Use: Sunny or lightly shaded border

Good companions: *Impatiens* New Guinea Group hybrids, *Nicotiana sylvestris, Viola × wittrockiana* Clear Crystal Series

bulbs

Perennials with underground organs are a very varied group, encompassing true bulbs, corms, tubers and rhizomes. Many bloom in spring or summer, but others flower in autumn after a period of summer dormancy.

purple, blue and violet

1 Crocus banaticus

This crocus produces blue-purple flowers in early autumn. Hardy.

General care: Plant in late summer with the top of the corm about 10cm (4in) deep.

Height: 10cm (4in) **Spread:** 5cm (2in)

Site: Sun. Well-drained soil

Use: Raised bed, rock garden, sunny border

Good companions: *Campanula poscharskyana* 'Stella', *Crocus tommasinianus*, *Juniperus squamata* 'Blue Star'

2 Crocus speciosus

Darkly veined, pale to deep mauve-blue goblets, supported by long pale tubes, appear before the leaves. Increases steadily. The form 'Albus' is white. Hardy.

General care: Plant in late summer with the top of the corm about 10cm (4in) deep.

Height: 10cm (4in) **Spread:** 5cm (2in)

Site: Sun. Well-drained soil

Use: Raised bed, rock garden, underplanting for shrubs, wild garden

Good companions: *Anemone blanda*, *Colchicum* 'The Giant', *Crocus tommasinianus*

pink and mauve

3 Amaryllis belladonna

Red-purple flowering stems support funnel-shaped flowers that are usually bright pink. The fan of strap-shaped leaves emerges later and persists through winter. Not fully hardy.

General care: Plant in late summer with the top of the bulb just covered by soil.

Height: 75cm (2ft 6in) **Spread:** 15cm (6in)

Site: Sun. Well-drained soil

Use: Base of sunny wall, warm border

Good companions: Best grown uncrowded by other plants

4 Colchicum 'Rosy Dawn'

Autumn crocus, Naked ladies

In autumn, this hybrid produces up to six white-centred, lightly chequered mauve-pink flowers. The large leaves emerge in spring. Hardy.

General care: Plant in summer or early autumn with the top of the corm about 10cm (4in) deep.

Height: 15cm (6in) **Spread:** 20cm (8in)

Site: Sun, partial shade. Well-drained soil

Use: Front of border, planting in grass, underplanting for shrubs and trees

Good companions: *Galanthus elwesii*, *Helleborus hybridus*, *Tiarella wherryi*

5 Colchicum 'The Giant'

Autumn crocus, Naked ladies

White-throated, rich mauve-pink goblet-shaped flowers, faintly chequered inside, emerge before the large leaves, which develop in spring. Hardy.

General care: Plant in summer or early autumn with the top of the corm about 10cm (4in) deep.

Height: 20cm (8in) **Spread:** 10cm (4in)

Site: Sun, partial shade. Well-drained soil

Use: Front of border, planting in grass, underplanting for shrubs and trees

Good companions: *Colchicum speciosum* 'Album', *Crocus speciosus*, *Crocus tommasinianus*

6 Crinum × powellii

The stems support heads of up to ten fragrant, pink, flared trumpet-shaped flowers, which emerge from a base of bright green, strap-shaped leaves. 'Album' is white. Not fully hardy.

General care: Plant in spring with the tip of the bulb's neck above ground. Leave established clumps undisturbed. Dry mulch in winter.

Height: 75cm (2ft 6in) **Spread:** 30cm (12in)

Site: Sun. Well-drained soil but with a plentiful supply of moisture in summer

Use: Warm border

Good companions: *Agapanthus* 'Lilliput', *Passiflora caerulea*, *Solanum crispum* 'Glasnevin'

pink and mauve (continued)

1 Crocus kotschyanus

In late summer or early autumn, mauve flowers are borne on slender white tubes before the leaves develop. Inside the flowers there are orange dots at the base. Hardy.

General care: Plant in summer with the top of the corm about 8cm (3in) deep.

Height: 8cm (3in) **Spread:** 5cm (2in)

Site: Sun. Well-drained soil

Use: Front of border, raised bed, rock garden

Good companions: Crocus chrysanthus 'Zwanenburg Bronze', Euphorbia myrsinites, Muscari botryoides 'Album'

2 Cyclamen hederifolium
Sowbread

Although the first flowers often appear in late summer, the main season is early autumn, when well-established tubers, which can be more than 15cm (6in)

across, may produce as many as 50 blooms. These have swept-back twisted petals, usually a shade of pink but sometimes white. The leaves are normally marbled and remain attractive from autumn to early summer. Hardy.

General care: Plant in the first half of summer, just after the leaves have died down. Set the corm indented side (from which the roots grow) uppermost just below the surface of the soil and cover with leaf-mould. Mulch with leaf-mould in summer.

Height: 10cm (4in) **Spread:** 15cm (6in)

Site: Partial shade, sun. Well-drained soil

Compost: Soil-based (John Innes No. 1) with added leaf-mould and grit

Use: Container, raised bed, rock garden, underplanting for shrubs, woodland garden

Good companions: Crocus tommasinianus, Galanthus nivalis, Primula vulgaris

3 Nerine bowdenii

Stiff stems bear three to nine glistening pink flowers, which have narrow wavy-edged petals. The flowers open before the strap-shaped leaves develop and are good for cutting. Best at the foot of a sunny wall. 'Mark Fenwick' is a vigorous selection. Hardy.

General care: Plant in early spring with the neck of the bulb just below the surface of the soil. Leave established clumps undisturbed for best flowering display.

Height: 50cm (20in) **Spread:** 10cm (4in)

Site: Sun. Well-drained soil

Use: Sunny border

Good companions: Myrtus communis subsp. tarentina, Origanum laevigatum 'Herrenhausen', Passiflora caerulea

4 Sternbergia lutea

The rich yellow flowers, which are goblet-shaped and lustrous, show up well against the glossy dark green of the grass-like leaves. These do not reach their full length, up to 30cm (12in), until spring. Best planted at the foot of a sunny wall. Not fully hardy.

General care: Plant in late summer with the top of the bulb about 10cm (4in) deep.

Height: 15cm (6in) **Spread:** 8cm (3in)

Site: Sun. Well-drained soil

Use: Sunny border, rock garden

Good companions: Euphorbia myrsinites, Sedum spathulifolium 'Cape Blanco', Sempervivum tectorum

5 Colchicum speciosum 'Album'
Autumn crocus, Naked ladies

The usual flower colour of the species is pink-mauve and 'Atrorubens' is a fine red-purple form. These are excellent autumn plants, but this white cultivar, with its elegant weather-resistant goblets supported on green-tinted tubes, is outstandingly beautiful. The large lance-shaped leaves appear in spring. Hardy.

General care: Plant in summer and early autumn with the top of the corm about 10cm (4in) deep.

Height: 15cm (6in) **Spread:** 20cm (8in)

Site: Sun, partial shade. Well-drained soil

Use: Front of border, planting in grass, underplanting for shrubs and trees

Good companions: Geranium macrorrhizum, Helleborus argutifolius, Vinca minor 'La Grave'

6 Leucojum autumnale
Autumn snowflake

The tuft of grassy leaves starts to develop in late summer or early autumn, at the same time as the flower stems. The stems carry one, occasionally several, white bell-shaped flowers that are tinged pink. Hardy.

General care: Plant in late summer with the top of the bulb about 8cm (3in) deep.

Height: 20cm (8in) **Spread:** 5cm (2in)

Site: Sun. Moist but well-drained soil

Use: Sunny border, raised bed, rock garden

Good companions: Alchemilla conjuncta, Hebe cupressoides 'Boughton Dome', Saxifraga 'Peter Pan', Viola 'Molly Sanderson'

dahlias

Dahlias make a colourful show in moist beds and borders from late summer until first frost. The flowerheads vary in shape and size, from neat pompoms and daisies to huge shaggy domes, in pastels, vibrant tones and deep velvety hues. Lift these half-hardy tuberous perennials after frost has blackened the foliage and overwinter in cool, dry frost-free conditions.

1 Dahlia 'Claire de Lune'
Collerette dahlia
This belongs to a group with flowers that have an outer row of petal-like ray-florets around a 'collar' of shorter florets and a central disc. Here the ray-florets and collar are pale yellow and the disc is orange-yellow.
Height: 1m (3ft) **Spread:** 60cm (2ft)
Good companions: *Dahlia* 'Bishop of Llandaff', *Dahlia* 'David Howard', *Tagetes tenuifolia* 'Lemon Gem'

2 Dahlia 'Peach Cupid'
Miniature ball dahlia
This belongs to a group with small ball-shaped flowerheads packed with incurved petal-like florets arranged in a spiral. Here the blooms are warm pink and open from midsummer.
Height: 1.2m (4ft) **Spread:** 75cm (2ft 6in)
Good companions: *Dahlia* 'Porcelain', *Penstemon* 'Blackbird', *Penstemon* 'Stapleford Gem'

3 Dahlia 'Yellow Hammer'
Dwarf bedding dahlia
This bronze-foliaged dahlia bears orange-centred, yellow single flowerheads and is suitable for containers or as a bedding plant.
Height: 50cm (20in) **Spread:** 40cm (16in)
Good companions: *Canna* 'King Midas', *Dahlia* 'Bishop of Llandaff', *Dahlia* 'David Howard'

4 Dahlia 'Bishop of Llandaff'
Peony-flowered dahlia
The bright red flowerheads consist of two or more rings of flat petal-like ray-florets and a central disc of conspicuous yellow anthers. The purple-black foliage is highly ornamental.
Height: 1m (3ft) **Spread:** 60cm (2ft)
Good companions: *Canna* 'Assaut', *Cosmos antrosanguineus*, *Dahlia* 'Zorro'

5 Dahlia 'Zorro'
Giant decorative dahlia
This is a deep red example of a group with double flowerheads that have no central disc but are composed of layers of blunt-tipped, slightly twisted petal-like ray-florets.
Height: 1.2m (4ft) **Spread:** 60cm (2ft)
Good companions: *Amaranthus caudatus*, *Cosmos atrosanguineus*, *Gladiolus callianthus* 'Murieliae'

6 Dahlia 'David Howard'
Miniature decorative dahlia
The orange double flowerheads are composed of layers of blunt-tipped, slightly twisted petal-like ray-florets. The blooms are about 8cm (3in) across and there is no central disc.
Height: 1m (3ft) **Spread:** 60cm (2ft)
Good companions: *Dahlia* 'Bishop of Llandaff', *Dahlia* 'Claire de Lune', *Dahlia* 'Yellow Hammer'

7 Dahlia 'Porcelain'
Water lily dahlia
This is a small-flowered example of a group that bears shallowly cup-shaped double flowerheads composed of relatively few rounded, broad, petal-like ray-florets. The white flowerheads are tinted purple-mauve.
Height: 1.2m (4ft) **Spread:** 60cm (2ft)
Good companions: *Dahlia* 'Peach Cupid', *Dahlia* 'White Moonlight', *Penstemon* 'Evelyn'

8 Dahlia 'White Moonlight'
Miniature semi-cactus dahlia
This belongs to a group with double flowerheads, in which the pointed petal-like ray-florets are rolled under for up to half their length, giving them a quilled appearance. The pure white flowers are up to 20cm (8in) across.
Height: 1.2m (4ft)
Spread: 60cm (2ft)
Good companions: *Dahlia* 'Kiwi Gloria', *Dahlia* 'Peach Cupid', *Dahlia* 'Porcelain'

climbers

Climbers twine, cling with aerial roots or clasp with tendrils. Trained on architectural supports or other plants, they assert the vertical dimension of the garden. Plant in the dormant season.

red and russet

1 Parthenocissus quinquefolia
Virginia creeper

Vigorous, woody-stemmed self-clinging climber grown for its foliage, which turns from green to brilliant crimson in autumn. Inconspicuous greenish flowers in late spring or early summer are followed by inedible blue-black berries. Hardy.
General care: To prevent shoots invading gutters and covering windows, cut back in winter or early spring to about 1.2m (4ft) from vulnerable areas.
Height and spread: 18m (60ft)
Site: Sun, partial shade. Well-drained soil
Use: Large mature tree climber, wall
Good companions: *Hedera colchica* 'Dentata', *Vitis coignetiae*, *Vitis vinifera* 'Purpurea'

2 Parthenocissus tricuspidata 'Veitchii'
Boston ivy

Vigorous, woody-stemmed self-clinging climber. The three-lobed leaves, smaller than those of the typical Boston ivy, open purple-red and become more richly coloured in autumn. Hardy.
General care: Cut back shoots in winter or early spring to about 1.2m (4ft) from vulnerable areas.
Height and spread: 18m (60ft)
Site: Sun, shade. Well-drained soil
Use: Large mature tree climber, wall
Good companions: *Ilex* x *altaclarensis* 'Camelliifolia', *Prunus lusitanica*, *Taxus baccata*

3 Rosa 'Crimson Shower'
Rambler rose

The pliant stems of this deciduous rambler are well furnished with glossy, bright green leaves. Clusters of crimson semi-double flowers are borne from midsummer to early autumn. Hardy.
General care: Prune between late winter and early spring, cutting up to a third of the oldest stems to near ground level and reducing sideshoots to three or four buds.
Height: 5m (15ft) **Spread:** 2.5m (8ft)
Site: Sun. Humus-rich, moist but well-drained soil
Use: Arbour, arch, wall
Good companions: *Clematis* 'Alba Luxurians', *Rosa* 'Aimée Vibert', *Trachelospermum jasminoides*

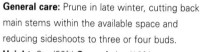

4 Vitis 'Brant'
Vine

The boldly lobed leaves of this vigorous woody vine colour splendidly in autumn, turning bronze-red. The edible red-purple grapes are sweet if there has been enough sun to ripen them. Hardy.
General care: Prune in late winter, cutting back main stems within the available space and reducing sideshoots to three or four buds.
Height: 6m (20ft) **Spread:** 4m (12ft)
Site: Sun, partial shade. Well-drained soil. Good on lime
Use: Pergola, wall
Good companions: *Clematis rehderiana*, *Lonicera* x *brownii* 'Dropmore Scarlet', *Rosa* Golden Showers

5 Vitis coignetiae
Japanese crimson glory vine, Vine

Vigorous deciduous vine with stout woody stems. The dark green, often huge, heart-shaped leaves, with a reddish felted underside, turn vivid red in autumn. Inconspicuous green flowers in spring are followed by inedible black grapes. Hardy.
General care: Prune in late winter, cutting back main stems within the available space and reducing sideshoots to three or four buds.
Height: 6m (20ft) **Spread:** 4m (12ft)
Site: Sun, partial shade. Well-drained soil. Good on lime
Use: Pergola, wall
Good companions: *Clematis montana* var. *rubens* 'Elizabeth', *Lonicera* x *americana*, *Vitis vinifera* 'Purpurea'

yellow and orange

6 Celastrus orbiculatus
Oriental bittersweet, Staff vine

Vigorous deciduous twiner with yellow autumn leaves and showy yellow berries. Hardy.
General care: To control growth on a pergola or wall, prune in late winter or early spring.
Height: 12m (40ft) **Spread:** 8m (25ft)
Site: Sun, partial shade. Well-drained soil
Use: Pergola, tree climber, wall
Good companions: *Clematis montana*, *Vitis coignetiae*, *Wisteria sinensis*

These deciduous clematis are hardy twining climbers that flower from late summer into early autumn. All do well on lime but need rich, well-drained soil. Grow in sun or partial shade, but with the base shaded. Most can be pruned in late winter or early spring, cutting all growths back to a pair of strong buds 30–60cm (1–2ft) above the ground.

1 Clematis 'Gipsy Queen'
Large-flowered clematis

The velvety single flowers, 15cm (6in) across, are violet-purple with deep red anthers.

Height: 3m (10ft) **Spread:** 1.5m (5ft)

Good companions: *Clematis* 'Ernest Markham', *Rosa* 'Crimson Shower', *Rosa* 'Madame Alfred Carrière'

2 Clematis 'Etoile Rose'
Texensis Group clematis

Small-flowered clematis ideal for growing through shrubs. The nodding urn-shaped flowers are deep pink with silver margins. Dies back to ground level in winter.

Height: 3m (10ft) **Spread:** 2m (6ft)

Good companions: *Choisya ternata*, *Clematis* 'Lasurstern', *Rosa* 'Pink Perpétué'

3 Clematis 'Ernest Markham'
Large-flowered clematis

The vivid red flowers with cream-brown anthers are produced most freely in full sun. For a flowering season from early summer to mid-autumn, prune in late winter, trimming half the stems lightly and cutting back the remaining stems to a pair of buds 30–60cm (1–2ft) above ground level.

Height: 5m (15ft) **Spread:** 2.5m (8ft)

Good companions: *Clematis* 'Jackmanii', *Jasminum officinale*, *Solanum laxum* 'Album'

4 Clematis 'Abundance'
Viticella Group clematis

Small-flowered clematis that bears darkly veined, wine-red flowers with greenish yellow anthers from midsummer to late autumn.

Height: 3m (10ft) **Spread:** 2m (6ft)

Good companions: *Ceanothus* x *delileanus* 'Topaze', *Clematis* 'Gillian Blades', *Rosa* 'Madame Grégoire Staechelin'

5 Clematis rehderiana

Vigorous twiner with elegantly divided foliage. It bears sprays of nodding, straw-yellow, bell-shaped flowers that have a sweet but light scent. Flowers most freely in full sun.

Height: 6m (20ft) **Spread:** 3m (10ft)

Good companions: *Rosa* 'Bobbie James', *Vitis* 'Brant', *Wisteria floribunda* 'Multijuga'

6 Clematis 'Bill MacKenzie'

The nodding yellow single flowers have red anthers. They are borne in profusion over a long season and are followed by fluffy seed heads.

Height: 6m (20ft) **Spread:** 2.5m (8ft)

Good companions: *Rosa banksiae* 'Lutea', *Vitis* 'Brant', *Wisteria floribunda* 'Multijuga'

7 Clematis 'Huldine'
Viticella Group clematis

Vigorous twiner with slightly cupped flowers, about 10cm (4in) across. Their upper surface is clean white, the underside tinted mauve.

Height: 4m (12ft) **Spread:** 2m (6ft)

Good companions: *Buddleja crispa*, *Clematis* 'Warszawska Nike', *Rosa* 'Parade'

shrubs & trees

In autumn, late flowering trees and shrubs have to compete with others that have brilliantly coloured foliage, which shows up well against sombre evergreens. Plant in the dormant season, preferably in autumn or early spring.

purple, blue and violet

1 Callicarpa bodinieri var. giraldii 'Profusion'
Beauty berry

Deciduous shrub with narrow toothed leaves that are bronze-purple when young. Small mauve-pink flowers in midsummer are followed by tight clusters of inedible violet-purple berries. Hardy.

General care: In late winter or early spring cut back the previous season's growth.

Height and spread: 2.5m (8ft)

Site: Sun, partial shade. Well-drained soil

Use: Sunny or lightly shaded border

Good companions: *Fuchsia magellanica* 'Versicolor', *Lonicera* x *purpusii* 'Winter Beauty', *Rosa glauca*

2 Caryopteris x clandonensis 'Kew Blue'

Grey-green-leaved aromatic deciduous shrub with clusters of deep blue flowers borne on erect stems from late summer to early autumn. Hardy.

General care: In early to mid-spring cut stems back to a low framework.

Height: 1m (3ft) **Spread:** 1.5m (5ft)

Site: Sun. Well-drained soil. Good on lime

Use: Sunny border

Good companions: *Eryngium* x *tripartitum*, *Erysimum* 'Bowles' Mauve', *Lilium candidum*

3 Ceanothus 'Autumnal Blue'
California lilac

The bright glossy foliage of this evergreen hybrid shows off large sprays of sky-blue flowers in late summer, autumn and occasionally spring. Hardy.

General care: Trim in early to mid-spring.

Height and spread: 3m (10ft)

Site: Sun. Well-drained soil

Use: Sunny border, warm wall

Good companions: *Myrtus communis* subsp. *tarentina*, *Rosa* 'Parade', *Vitis* 'Brant'

4 Clerodendrum trichotomum var. fargesii

Deciduous bushy shrub or small tree that bears sprays of fragrant white flowers in late summer and autumn. These emerge from the red-tinged

base of the calyces, which are retained even when the berries ripen to a startling blue.

Height and spread: 5m (15ft)

Site: Sun. Humus-rich, moist but well-drained soil

Use: Sunny border

Good companions: *Fargesia nitida*, *Hydrangea macrophylla* 'Blue Wave', *Hydrangea paniculata* 'Unique'

5 Hebe 'Autumn Glory'

Spreading evergreen shrub with purplish stems and dark green leaves outlined with purplish red. Bears spikes of mauve-blue tubular flowers in late summer and autumn. Not fully hardy.

Height: 60cm (2ft) **Spread:** 1m (3ft)

Site: Sun, partial shade. Moist but well-drained soil

Compost: Soil-based (John Innes No. 2)

Use: Container, sunny or lightly shaded border, raised bed, rock garden

Good companions: *Euonymus fortunei* 'Emerald Gaiety', *Fuchsia* 'Riccartonii', *Hydrangea macrophylla* 'Blue Wave'

pink and mauve

6 Calluna vulgaris 'Peter Sparkes'
Ling, Scots heather

The single species of heather, a low evergreen shrub with scale-like leaves, has given rise to a very large number of cultivars. The spikes of small single or double flowers remain colourful over several months in late summer and autumn. 'Peter Sparkes' has double pink flowers. Hardy.

General care: Clip over in early to mid-spring.

Height: 40cm (16in) **Spread:** 50cm (20in)

Site: Sun. Lime-free, humus-rich soil

Compost: Ericaceous

Use: Container, front of sunny border, ground cover, heather garden, wild garden

Good companions: *Erica carnea* 'King George', *Erica* x *darleyensis* 'Furzey', *Pinus mugo* 'Mops'

7 Euonymus europaeus 'Red Cascade'
Spindle tree

Deciduous shrub or small tree often bare at the

base but with a bushy head. Inconspicuous until autumn, when leaves turn red and branches arch over with the weight of scarlet-pink capsules, which split to reveal orange seeds. Hardy.
Height: 3m (10ft) **Spread:** 2.5m (8ft)
Site: Sun, partial shade. Well-drained soil. Good on lime
Use: Border, wild garden
Good companions: *Acanthus mollis* Latifolius Group, *Berberis darwinii*, *Cotoneaster lactaeus*

8 Fuchsia 'Alice Hoffman'

Upright deciduous shrub with dense purple-green foliage. Throughout summer and autumn pink semi-double flowers, with a pink-veined white 'skirt', dangle from stem tips. Not fully hardy.
General care: Cut stems down to the base in early spring.
Height and spread: 50cm (20in)
Site: Sun, partial shade. Moist, well-drained soil
Compost: Soil-based (John Innes No. 3)
Use: Container, sunny or lightly shaded border
Good companions: *Fuchsia* 'Riccartonii',

Hydrangea 'Preziosa', *Viburnum* x *bodnantense* 'Dawn'

9 Fuchsia 'Mrs Popple'

This upright deciduous hybrid fuchsia blooms profusely throughout summer and early autumn. The tube and long sepals are glossy red, the petals violet-purple and the long stamens and style are crimson. Not fully hardy.
General care: Cut stems down to the base in early spring.
Height and spread: 1m (3ft)
Site: Sun, partial shade. Moist, well-drained soil
Compost: Soil-based (John Innes No. 3)
Use: Container, sunny or lightly shaded border
Good companions: *Ceratostigma willmottianum*, *Fuchsia* 'Alice Hoffman', *Hydrangea macrophylla* 'Madame Emile Mouillère'

10 Hibiscus syriacus 'Woodbridge'

Upright deciduous grey-stemmed shrub that bears lobed dark green leaves, and from late summer to mid-autumn pink flowers with dark centres. Suitable for training as a standard. Hardy.
Height: 3m (10ft) **Spread:** 2m (6ft)
Site: Sun. Humus-rich and moist, well-drained soil
Use: Sunny border
Good companions: *Anemone hupehensis* 'Hadspen Abundance', *Penstemon* 'Evelyn', *Veronica gentianoides*

11 Rosa 'English Miss'
Floribunda rose

Throughout summer and early autumn this compact deciduous bush carries large sprays of scented, pale pink fully double flowers. Hardy.

General care: Prune between late winter and early spring, cutting main stems back to a height of about 30cm (12in) and shortening sideshoots to two or three buds.
Height: 75cm (2ft 6in) **Spread:** 60cm (2ft)
Site: Sun. Fertile and moist but well-drained soil
Use: Formal bedding, sunny border
Good companions: *Geranium macrorrhizum*, *Stachys byzantina* 'Silver Carpet', *Veronica peduncularis* 'Georgia Blue'

12 Rosa 'Felicia'
Hybrid musk rose

The arching stems of this vigorous deciduous bush bear sprays of scented, apricot-tinted light pink flowers in early summer then intermittently, often with a strong flush in autumn. Hardy.
General care: Prune in late winter to early spring, removing about a third of stems; select the oldest and cut back main stems by up to a third and sideshoots by half.
Height and spread: 1.5m (5ft)
Site: Sun. Reasonably fertile and moist but well-drained soil
Use: Hedge, sunny bed or border
Good companions: *Nepeta* 'Six Hills Giant', *Rosa* 'Buff Beauty', *Viola riviniana* Purpurea Group

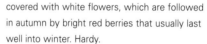

red and russet

1 Amelanchier canadensis
Shadbush

In autumn the foliage of this deciduous shrub or small tree turns brilliant orange and red. In spring it produces white starry flowers, which are followed by edible blue-black fruits. Hardy.

Height: 7m (23ft) **Spread:** 2m (6ft)

Site: Sun, partial shade. Moist but well-drained soil, preferably lime-free

Use: Specimen tree

Good companions: *Acer griseum, Cornus florida* 'Cherokee Chief', *Sorbus hupehensis*

2 Cercidiphyllum japonicum
Katsura tree

Deciduous tree with heart-shaped leaves that are bronze when young, green in summer then shades of red, pink and yellow in autumn. There are tiny red flowers in spring. Hardy.

Height: 20m (65ft) **Spread:** 12m (40ft)

Site: Sun, partial shade. Humus-rich and moist but well-drained soil, preferably lime-free

Use: Specimen tree, woodland garden

Good companions: *Acer pensylvanicum* 'Erythrocladum', *Hamamelis* x *intermedia* 'Diane', *Picea breweriana*

3 Cotinus 'Flame'
Smoke bush

Deciduous large shrub or small tree with light green, rounded leaves that turn brilliant orange-red in autumn. Tiny pink flowers in summer are followed by inedible purple-pink fruits that form smoke-like plumes. Hardy.

General care: To promote the growth of large leaves, cut stems down to near ground level in early spring.

Height: 6m (20ft) **Spread:** 5m (15ft)

Site: Sun, partial shade. Moist, well-drained soil

Use: Canopy in border, specimen

Good companions: *Cotoneaster frigidus* 'Cornubia', *Ilex aquifolium* 'Handsworth New Silver', *Philadelphus* 'Belle Etoile'

4 Cotoneaster conspicuus 'Decorus'

This small-leaved evergreen shrub forms a mound of arching stems. In early summer these are covered with white flowers, which are followed in autumn by bright red berries that usually last well into winter. Hardy.

Height: 1.5m (5ft) **Spread:** 2.5m (8ft)

Site: Sun, partial shade. Well-drained soil

Use: Bank, ground cover, raised bed, large rock garden

Good companions: *Euonymus alatus* 'Compactus', *Prunus lusitanica, Pyracantha* 'Orange Glow'

5 Crataegus persimilis 'Prunifolia'
Hawthorn

Broad-headed deciduous tree armed with strong thorns. The glossy green leaves turn orange and red in autumn. In late spring there are clusters of small white flowers, which are followed by bright red haws that last into winter. Hardy.

Height: 8m (25ft) **Spread:** 10m (33ft)

Site: Sun, partial shade. Well-drained soil

Use: Canopy in border, specimen tree, woodland garden

Good companions: *Crocus speciosus, Galanthus nivalis, Primula vulgaris*

6 Disanthus cercidifolius

Rather spidery, slightly fragrant flowers are borne in autumn, but the value of this deciduous shrub lies in the blue-green foliage, which in autumn turns shades of yellow, red and purple. Hardy.

Height and spread: 3m (10ft)

Site: Sun, partial shade. Lime-free, moist but well-drained soil

Use: Canopy in border, woodland garden

Good companions: *Erythronium californicum* 'White Beauty', *Fothergilla major* Monticola Group, *Kirengeshoma palmata*

7 Euonymus alatus 'Compactus'
Winged spindle

This is a compact form of a dense-growing deciduous shrub, the twigs of which often develop corky wings. It makes little impact until autumn when the leaves turn brilliant shades of deep pink and red, and purplish capsules split open to reveal scarlet seeds. Hardy.

Height: 1m (3ft) **Spread:** 1.5m (5ft)

Site: Sun, partial shade. Well-drained soil

Use: Hedge, sunny or lightly shaded border

Good companions: *Cotoneaster salicifolius* 'Rothschildianus', *Helleborus argutifolius, Prunus lusitanica*

8 Fuchsia 'Riccartonii'

Vigorous deciduous shrub with neat pointed leaves that are dark green with a bronze tint. Throughout summer and autumn there are showers of small red flowers with purple petals. In mild climates specimens can exceed the dimensions given here. Not fully hardy.

General care: Cut stems back to a low framework in early spring.

Height: 2.5m (8ft) **Spread:** 1.5m (5ft)

Site: Sun, partial shade. Moist but well-drained soil

Use: Hedge, sunny or lightly shaded border

Good companions: *Daphne bholua* 'Jacqueline Postill', *Hydrangea aspera* Villosa Group, *Spiraea japonica* 'Anthony Waterer'

9 Fuchsia 'Snowcap'

Upright deciduous hybrid fuchsia that blooms freely from midsummer to mid-autumn. The semi-double flowers are red with a 'skirt' of pink-veined white petals. Not fully hardy.

General care: Cut stems down to the base in early spring.

Height: 1m (3ft) **Spread:** 75cm (2ft 6in)

Site: Sun, partial shade. Moist but well-drained soil

Compost: Soil-based (John Innes No. 3)

Use: Container, sunny or lightly shaded border

Good companions: *Exochorda macrantha* 'The Bride', *Fuchsia* 'Leonora', *Hydrangea macrophylla* 'Ayesha'

10 Gaultheria mucronata 'Mulberry Wine'

Evergreen shrub making a dense thicket covered with small lustrous leaves. When this female clone is grown close to a male plant the small, white urn-shaped flowers, which are borne in late spring and early summer, are pollinated. The long-lasting berries that form ripen from magenta to deep purple-red in autumn. Hardy.

General care: Remove suckers to limit spread.

Height and spread: 1.2m (4ft)

Site: Partial shade. Lime-free, moist soil

Use: Heather garden, peat bed, rock garden, woodland garden

Good companions: *Acer palmatum* 'Corallinum', *Leucothoe* 'Scarletta', *Rhododendron* 'Praecox'

11 Hydrangea 'Preziosa'
Mophead hydrangea

Deciduous shrub with purple-tinted stems and young leaves, which also take on attractive tints in autumn. The heads of sterile flowers, which in summer are red-pink or, on acid soils, mauve-blue, deepen to purple-red in autumn. Hardy.

General care: Deadhead and in early to mid-spring cut out up to a quarter of old stems.

Height and spread: 1.5m (5ft)

Site: Sun, partial shade. Moist but well-drained soil

Compost: Soil-based (John Innes No. 3)

Use: Container, sunny or lightly shaded border, woodland garden

Good companions: *Fuchsia* 'Riccartonii', *Hydrangea paniculata* 'Unique', *Viburnum opulus* 'Roseum'

12 Liquidambar styraciflua 'Worplesdon'
Sweet gum

Deciduous tree of broadly conical shape grown principally for its foliage. The fingered leaves, which have five to seven lobes and are dark green in summer, turn purple-red and orange-yellow in autumn. In winter the corky bark of some twigs can be a feature. Hardy.

Height: 25m (80ft) **Spread:** 12m (40ft)

Site: Sun. Moist but well-drained soil, preferably lime-free

Use: Specimen tree, woodland garden

Good companions: *Acer cappadocicum* 'Aureum', *Acer grosseri* var. *hersii*, *Hamamelis* x *intermedia* 'Pallida'

red and russet (continued)

1 Malus 'John Downie'
Crab apple

Young specimens of this deciduous tree are narrow and upright but older plants tend to spread. In late spring white flowers open from pink buds. The crimson-flushed yellow crab apples that follow are highly ornamental. Hardy.

Height: 10m (33ft) **Spread:** 6m (20ft)
Site: Sun. Moist but well-drained soil
Use: Canopy in border, specimen tree
Good companions: *Colchicum* 'Rosy Dawn', *Galanthus nivalis*, *Narcissus* 'Actaea'

2 Metasequoia glyptostroboides
Dawn redwood

Fast-growing, deciduous conical conifer with bright green, feathery foliage that turns russet and gold before falling. Mature trees may exceed the dimensions given. Hardy.

Height: 25m (80ft) **Spread:** 5m (15ft)
Site: Sun. Humus-rich, moist but well-drained soil
Use: Specimen tree, waterside
Good companions: *Fargesia murieliae*, *Gunnera manicata*, *Salix alba* subsp. *vitellina* 'Britzensis'

3 Prunus sargentii
Sargent's cherry

Round-headed deciduous tree that is very attractive in mid-spring when young foliage, unfurling bronze-red, coincides with single pink flowers, and again early in autumn when the leaves turn brilliant orange and red. Inedible, glossy crimson fruits follow the flowers. Hardy.

Height: 20m (65ft) **Spread:** 15m (50ft)
Site: Sun. Moist but well-drained soil
Use: Specimen tree
Good companions: *Gentiana asclepiadea*, *Hydrangea* 'Preziosa', *Sarcococca hookeriana* var. *digyna*

4 Quercus coccinea 'Splendens'
Scarlet oak

When mature, this fast-growing deciduous tree develops a broad head. The lobed leaves are glossy green throughout summer then turn rich scarlet in autumn. Hardy.

Height: 20m (65ft) **Spread:** 15m (50ft)
Site: Sun, partial shade. Lime-free, well-drained soil
Use: Specimen tree, woodland garden
Good companions: *Amelanchier canadensis*, *Disanthus cercidifolius*, *Pseudolarix amabilis*

5 Rosa 'Fru Dagmar Hastrup'
Rugosa rose

Compact prickly rose with matt leaves. Scented, pink single flowers are borne throughout summer and followed by impressive red hips. Hardy.

General care: In late winter or early spring cut back main stems by about a third and sideshoots by up to two-thirds.

Height: 1m (3ft) **Spread:** 1.2m (4ft)
Site: Sun. Well-drained soil
Use: Hedge, sunny border
Good companions: *Geranium sanguineum* var. *striatum*, *Rosa* 'Blanche Double de Coubert', *Stachys byzantina* 'Silver Carpet'

6 Rosa 'Geranium'
Shrub rose

Blood-red single flowers spangle this deciduous open, thorny bush in summer, but the late summer and autumn display of large, scarlet, curiously shaped hips is longer lasting. Hardy.

General care: Cut out about a quarter of the oldest stems and trim other stems lightly in late winter or early spring.

Height: 2.5m (8ft) **Spread:** 1.5m (5ft)
Site: Sun. Moist but well-drained soil
Use: Sunny or lightly shaded border
Good companions: *Rosa xanthina* 'Canary Bird', *Viburnum opulus* 'Compactum', *Viburnum tinus* 'Gwenllian'

7 Rosa The Times Rose
Floribunda rose

In summer and autumn this deciduous bush rose bears clusters of lightly scented, dark crimson double flowers over purplish green foliage. Hardy.

General care: Prune between late winter and early spring, cutting back main stems to a height of about 25cm (10in) and shortening sideshoots to two or three buds.

Height: 60cm (2ft) **Spread:** 75cm (2ft 6in)
Site: Sun. Fertile and moist but well-drained soil
Use: Formal bedding, sunny border
Good companions: *Nepeta* 'Six Hills Giant', *Paeonia lactiflora* 'White Wings', *Rosa* Elina *Sorbus commixta* 'Embley'

8 Sorbus sargentiana

Slow-growing deciduous tree with large leaves, composed of many leaflets, opening from sticky crimson buds. White flowers in early summer are followed by red fruits that ripen to coincide with the orange and red of the autumn foliage. Hardy.

Height and spread: 10m (33ft)
Site: Sun, partial shade. Well-drained soil, preferably lime-free
Use: Specimen tree, woodland garden
Good companions: *Ilex aquifolium* 'Bacciflava', *Malus* 'Red Sentinel', *Viburnum tinus* 'Gwenllian'

9 Viburnum opulus 'Compactum'
Guelder rose

In late spring and early summer this deciduous shrub bears flat heads of heavily scented white flowers surrounded by showy sterile florets. Inedible translucent red berries ripen before the lobed leaves turn red. Hardy.

Height and spread: 2m (6ft)
Site: Sun, partial shade. Moist, well-drained soil
Use: Sunny or lightly shaded border, woodland garden
Good companions: *Eranthis hyemalis*, *Erythronium dens-canis*, *Galanthus elwesii*

yellow and orange

10 Cotoneaster salicifolius 'Rothschildianus'

Large evergreen shrub with arching stems and narrow tapered leaves. Small white flowers in early summer are followed by long-lasting clusters of inedible, creamy yellow fruits. Hardy.

Height and spread: 5m (15ft)
Site: Sun, partial shade. Well-drained soil
Use: Canopy in border
Good companions: *Colchicum speciosum* 'Album', *Corylus avellana* 'Contorta', *Osmanthus delavayi*

11 Ginkgo biloba
Maidenhair tree

This upright deciduous tree is a survivor of a primitive plant group most closely allied to the conifers. The leaves, which form a notched fan up to 8cm (3in) across, are bright green in summer then turn clear yellow in autumn. Female trees may produce fruits, which have an edible kernel but a rank-smelling outer coating. Hardy.

Height: 25m (80ft) **Spread:** 8m (25ft)
Site: Sun. Fertile, well-drained soil
Use: Specimen tree
Good companions: *Euonymus alatus* 'Compactus', *Prunus laurocerasus* 'Otto Luyken', *Sorbus sargentiana*

12 Malus tschonoskii
Crab apple

Deciduous tree of upright, loosely conical shape with glossy green leaves that colour yellow, orange, red and purple in autumn. The pink-tinged, white single flowers of spring are followed by red-flushed yellow-green crab apples. Hardy.

Height: 12m (40ft) **Spread:** 8m (25ft)
Site: Sun. Moist but well-drained soil
Use: Canopy in border, specimen tree
Good companions: *Geranium macrorrhizum* 'Ingwersen's Variety', *Hosta* 'Halcyon', *Tiarella cordifolia*

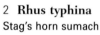

(continued)

1 Nyssa sylvatica
Black gum, Sour gum, Tupelo
A dense head and drooping lower branches give this deciduous tree a broadly columnar shape. The dark green leaves turn brilliant yellow, orange and scarlet in autumn. There are insignificant yellow-green flowers in early summer. Hardy.
Height: 20m (65ft)
Spread: 10m (33ft)
Site: Sun, partial shade. Lime-free, moist but well-drained soil
Use: Specimen tree, woodland garden
Good companions: *Acer japonicum* 'Vitifolium', *Hamamelis* x *intermedia* 'Arnold Promise', *Rhododendron luteum*

2 Rhus typhina
Stag's horn sumach
Deciduous suckering shrub or small tree with few but wide-spreading branches, with red hairs on young shoots. The leaves, which are composed of numerous dissected leaflets, turn brilliant yellow, orange and red in autumn. Female cultivars, such as 'Dissecta', carry inedible, furry, crimson fruits in autumn. Hardy.
General care: To encourage large leaves, cut stems to near base in late winter or early spring.
Height: 3m (10ft) **Spread:** 5m (15ft)
Site: Sun. Moist but well-drained soil
Use: Border, specimen shrub, woodland garden
Good companions: *Cornus alba* 'Sibirica', *Cornus stolonifera* 'Flavirimea', *Cotinus* 'Flame'

3 Sorbus 'Joseph Rock'
Deciduous small tree with a compact head of branches. The green leaves are composed of numerous leaflets and turn rich shades of red, orange and purple in autumn. Heads of creamy white flowers in late spring are followed by clusters of inedible, pale yellow fruits, which ripen to amber and persist after leaf fall. Hardy.
Height: 9m (30ft) **Spread:** 6m (20ft)
Site: Sun, partial shade. Moist but well-drained soil, preferably lime-free

Use: Specimen tree, woodland garden
Good companions: *Cornus kousa* var. *chinensis* 'Satomi', *Malus* 'John Downie', *Prunus sargentii*

4 Arbutus unedo
Strawberry tree
Evergreen small tree, often with multiple stems, with deep brown and shredding bark. The glossy, nearly oval leaves are toothed. Pendent clusters of small white flowers are borne in late autumn and coincide with unpalatable orange-red fruits from the previous season's flowers. Hardy.
Height and spread: 8m (25ft)
Site: Sun. Well-drained soil
Use: Canopy in border, specimen tree
Good companions: *Bergenia* 'Ballawley', *Helleborus foetidus*, *Pachysandra terminalis*

5 Hydrangea macrophylla 'Madame Emile Mouillère'
Mophead hydrangea
Deciduous rounded shrub with coarsely toothed leaves, topped in late summer and early autumn by globular heads of sterile white florets. On alkaline soils the eye of each floret is red, on acid soils it is blue. The florets themselves usually

General care: To maintain as a shrub with colourful juvenile foliage cut back all stems to near base in early spring.
Height: 20m (65ft) **Spread:** 9m (30ft)
Site: Sun. Moist but well-drained soil, preferably lime-free
Use: Border (as shrub), formal bedding (as shrub), specimen tree
Good companions: *Cortaderia selloana* 'Sunningdale Silver', *Eucalyptus pauciflora* subsp. *niphophila*, *Genista aetnensis*

10 Fatsia japonica
Evergreen shrub with handsome, glossy green fingered leaves up to 40cm (16in) long. In mid-autumn stiff sprays made up of rounded clusters of tiny creamy flowers stand out against the foliage. Small, inedible black berries follow. Hardy.
General care: Trim lightly in mid-spring to keep shape balanced.
Height and spread: 3m (10ft)
Site: Sun, partial shade. Moist, well-drained soil
Compost: Soil-based (John Innes No. 3)
Use: Container, sunny or lightly shaded border
Good companions: *Fargesia nitida*, *Hedera colchica* 'Dentata Variegata', *Pleioblastus auricomus*

11 Ilex x altaclarensis 'Camelliifolia'
Highclere holly
Large conical shrub or tree with almost spineless glossy leaves, which are red-purple when young and carried on purplish stems. This female clone produces red berries if near a pollinating male plant. Hardy.
General care: Trim hedges in mid-spring, clip shaped specimens in late summer.
Height: 15m (50ft) **Spread:** 12m (40ft)
Site: Sun, partial shade. Moist, well-drained soil
Use: Hedge, topiary, specimen tree, woodland garden
Good companions: *Corylus avellana* 'Contorta', *Hamamelis mollis*, *Magnolia stellata*

12 Juniperus scopulorum 'Skyrocket'
Rocky mountain juniper
The shoots of this slow-growing evergreen conifer are covered with scale-like leaves that hug the stem to form a grey-green column. Hardy.
Height: 6m (20ft) **Spread:** 35cm (14in)
Site: Sun, partial shade. Well-drained soil
Use: Avenue, gravel garden, heather garden, specimen tree
Good companions: *Calluna vulgaris* 'Peter Sparkes', *Erica carnea* 'Vivellii', *Erica x darleyensis* 'Arthur Johnson'

---

develop a pink tinge as they age. Hardy.
General care: Deadhead and, in early to mid-spring, cut out up to a quarter of old stems.
Height: 2.5m (8ft) **Spread:** 2m (6ft)
Site: Sun, partial shade. Moist but well-drained soil
Compost: Soil-based (John Innes No. 3)
Use: Container, sunny or lightly shaded border, woodland garden
Good companions: *Fuchsia magellanica* 'Versicolor', *Halesia carolina*, *Viburnum plicatum* 'Mariesii'

6 Rosa Elina
Hybrid tea rose
Deciduous bush rose with dark green foliage. During summer and early autumn it bears scented, white double flowers with a pale yellow centre. The buds are cone shaped. Hardy.
General care: Prune between late winter and early spring, cutting back main stems to a height of about 25cm (10in) and shortening sideshoots to two or three buds.
Height: 1m (3ft) **Spread:** 75cm (2ft 6in)
Site: Sun. Fertile and moist but well-drained soil
Use: Formal bedding, sunny border
Good companions: *Alchemilla mollis*, *Campanula persicifolia*, *Viola cornuta* Alba Group

7 Rosa Iceberg
Floribunda rose
Deciduous bush rose well covered with light green leaves. Throughout summer and autumn it

---

bears numerous clusters of creamy white double flowers. Hardy.
General care: Prune between late winter and early spring, cutting back main stems to a height of about 35cm (14in) and shortening sideshoots to two or three buds.
Height: 1m (3ft) **Spread:** 75cm (2ft 6in)
Site: Sun. Fertile and moist but well-drained soil
Use: Formal bedding, sunny border
Good companions: *Geranium* x *magnificum*, *Paeonia lactiflora* 'Bowl of Beauty', *Viola cornuta*

8 Sorbus hupehensis
Hubei rowan
Deciduous tree with a compact head of purplish brown branches clothed with foliage that is conspicuously blue-green throughout summer but colours red in autumn. Heads of white flowers in late spring are followed by clusters of round white berries, sometimes tinged with pink, which last into winter. Hardy.
Height: 8m (25ft) **Spread:** 6m (20ft)
Site: Sun, partial shade. Moist but well drained soil, preferably lime-free
Use: Specimen tree, woodland garden
Good companions: *Acer griseum*, *Hamamelis mollis*, *Malus tschonoskii*

green

9 Eucalyptus gunnii
Cider gum
Evergreen tree with striking greenish white bark that is shed in late summer to reveal new grey-green bark, usually warmed by an orange-pink flush. Juvenile leaves are rounded and silver-blue while mature leaves are sickle shaped and grey-green. In favourable conditions trees bear clusters of small cream flowers during late summer and early autumn. Not fully hardy.

acers

Among the deciduous maples, several shrubs and trees are outstanding for their rich autumn colouring and are suitable for specimen planting or for woodland gardens. Although most tolerate some lime in the soil, the best results are on moist but well-drained acid soil in sun or partial shade. All of the following are hardy.

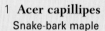

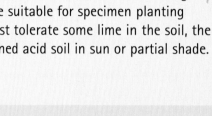

1 Acer capillipes
Snake-bark maple

The young shoots of this small tree are coral-red, but the mature bark is bright green with white vertical stripes. The small greenish flowers develop into more conspicuous tassels of winged fruits, and the three-lobed leaves turn vivid shades of orange and red in autumn.

Height and spread: 10m (33ft)

Good companions: *Acer griseum*, *Enkianthus campanulatus*, *Magnolia* x *kewensis* 'Wada's Memory'

2 Acer tataricum subsp. ginnala
Amur maple

In summer the three-lobed leaves of this large shrub or small tree are bright green, but in autumn they turn vivid crimson. Reasonably tolerant of dry conditions.

Height: 8m (25ft) **Spread:** 6m (20ft)

Good companions: *Cotoneaster lacteus*, *Gaultheria mucronata* 'Bell's Seedling', *Ilex aquifolium* 'Pyramidalis'

3 Acer japonicum 'Vitifolium'
Full-moon maple, Japanese maple

Slow-growing tree or large shrub with multi-lobed fan-shaped leaves that colour magnificently in autumn. In spring, produces drooping clusters of red flowers.

Height and spread: 8m (25ft)

Good companions: *Acer grosseri* var. *hersii*, *Amelanchier canadensis*, *Picea breweriana*

4 Acer rubrum 'October Glory'
Red maple, scarlet maple, swamp maple

Tree with a rounded crown grown mainly for the brilliant red of the glossy five-lobed leaves in autumn.

Height: 20m (65ft) **Spread:** 9m (30ft)

Good companions: *Eucryphia* x *nymansensis* 'Nymansay', *Magnolia denudata*, *Rhododendron* 'Palestrina'

5 Acer palmatum 'Sango-kaku'
Japanese maple

Shrub or round-headed small tree with deeply cut five-lobed leaves. These are warm yellow in spring, green in summer and soft yellow in autumn, when they stand out against the red twigs, which remain a feature over winter.

Height: 6m (20ft) **Spread:** 5m (15ft)

Good companions: *Acer cappadocicum* 'Aureum', *Halesia carolina*, *Magnolia* 'Elizabeth'

6 Acer circinatum
Vine maple

The red-purple-and-white flowers of this large shrub or small tree are a mid-spring feature, but it is the orange to red autumn foliage that makes the plant worth growing. The deeply lobed leaves are almost circular. More tolerant of dry conditions than most maples.

Height: 5m (15ft) **Spread:** 6m (20ft)

Good companions: *Betula pendula*, *Cercis canadensis* 'Forest Pansy', *Lonicera* x *purpusii* 'Winter Beauty'

7 Acer cappadocicum 'Aureum'
Cappadocian maple, Caucasian maple

Rounded tree with fingered leaves up to 10cm (4in) long that are yellow in spring, green in summer and yellow again in autumn.

Height: 15m (50ft) **Spread:** 10m (33ft)

Good companions: *Acer palmatum*, *Davidia involucrata*, *Magnolia denudata*

alpines

These small perennials and shrubs generally thrive in well-drained conditions and do not need a rock garden. Most look well in a raised bed and many are suitable for containers or paving. Plant in mild weather between autumn and early spring.

purple, blue and violet

1 Campanula poscharskyana 'Stella'
Dalmatian bellflower

In the second half of summer and early autumn mats of neat toothed leaves are almost covered by violet-blue starry flowers. This perennial is too vigorous for small rock gardens. Hardy.

Height: 15cm (6in) **Spread:** 60cm (2ft)

Site: Sun, partial shade. Moist, well-drained soil

Use: Dry wall, paving, raised bed, rock garden

Good companions: Hebe cupressoides 'Boughton Dome', Saxifraga 'Peter Pan', Viola biflora

2 Gentiana sino-ornata
Gentian

Semi-evergreen perennial that forms dense mats of prostrate stems clothed with narrow green leaves. The trumpet-shaped flowers are usually brilliant blue with greenish white and blue-purple stripes on the outside and in the throat. Hardy.

Height: 15cm (6in) **Spread:** 35cm (14in)

Site: Sun, partial shade. Lime-free, humus-rich and moist but well-drained soil

Compost: Ericaceous with added sand and leaf-mould

Use: Container, front of border, raised bed, rock garden

Good companions: Erythronium dens-canis, Fritillaria meleagris, Lithodora diffusa 'Heavenly Blue'

3 Gentiana 'Strathmore'
Gentian

Hybrid perennial producing sprawling stems with paired linear leaves. In autumn it bears sky-blue, trumpet-shaped flowers that are silver streaked on the outside and just under 8cm (3in) in length. Hardy.

Height: 15cm (6in) **Spread:** 30cm (12in)

Site: Sun, partial shade. Lime-free, humus-rich and moist but well-drained soil

Compost: Ericaceous with added sand and leaf-mould

Use: Container, front of border, raised bed, rock garden

Good companions: Erythronium californicum 'White Beauty', Narcissus 'Cedric Morris', Viola cornuta

4 Viola 'Belmont Blue'
Cornuta hybrid viola

The horned violet (Viola cornuta) and the violas derived from it are evergreen perennials that usually produce an autumn flush of flowers if plants are trimmed over after the main spring and summer season. The pale flowers of 'Belmont Blue' have clearly separated petals. Hardy.

Height: 15cm (6in)

Spread: 35cm (14in)

Site: Sun, partial shade. Humus-rich and moist but well-drained soil

Compost: Soil-based (John Innes No. 2) or soil-less

Use: Container, front of border, raised bed, rock garden

Good companions: Primula marginata 'Kesselring's Variety', Saxifraga 'Peter Pan', Thuja occidentalis 'Danica'

pink and mauve

5 Astilbe chinensis var. pumila

In late summer and autumn slender spikes of dark mauve-pink flowers top the reddish green, broadly cut leaves of this perennial. Ideal for the edge of a rock garden pool. Hardy.

Height: 30cm (12in) **Spread:** 45cm (18in)

Site: Partial shade. Humus-rich and moist soil

Use: Ground cover, front of border, rock garden, waterside

Good companions: Campanula poscharskyana 'Stella', Tiarella wherryi, Viola 'Belmont Blue'

6 Diascia 'Salmon Supreme'

Throughout summer and autumn this perennial produces slender spires of salmon-pink spurred flowers over mats of heart-shaped leaves. Not fully hardy.

Height: 15cm (6in)

Spread: 45cm (18in)

Site: Sun. Moist but well-drained soil

Compost: Soil-based (John Innes No. 2) or soil-less

Use: Container, front of sunny border, raised bed, rock garden

Good companions: Campanula carpatica, Festuca glauca 'Seeigel', Geranium cinereum 'Ballerina'

pink and mauve (continued)

1 Erodium 'County Park'
Heron's bill, Stork's bill

The common names refer to the pointed beaks of the fruits, but the appeal of this modest perennial lies in the long succession of mauve-pink flowers borne in clusters over the finely cut grey-green leaves throughout summer and autumn. Hardy.

Height and spread: 25cm (10in)
Site: Sun. Gritty well-drained soil
Compost: Soil-based (John Innes No. 1) with added grit
Use: Container, paving, raised bed, rock garden
Good companions: *Crocus chrysanthus* 'Zwanenburg Bronze', *Euphorbia myrsinites*, *Lavandula angustifolia* 'Nana Alba'

2 Origanum amanum
Marjoram, Oregano

In summer and autumn this compact evergreen bush bears numerous long-tubed curved flowers that emerge from among pale green bracts, which take on pink tints as they age. Hardy.

General care: Protect from excessive winter wet.
Height: 15cm (6in) **Spread:** 30cm (12in)
Site: Sun. Well-drained, preferably alkaline soil
Compost: Soil-based (John Innes No. 1) with added grit
Use: Container, raised bed, rock garden
Good companions: *Erodium* 'County Park', *Geranium cinereum* 'Ballerina', *Lavandula angustifolia* 'Hidcote'

3 Persicaria vacciniifolia
This semi-evergreen perennial produces upright spikes packed with small, deep pink flowers in late summer and autumn. The tiny glossy leaves on red-tinted stems turn red in autumn. Hardy.

Height: 20cm (8in) **Spread:** 50cm (20in)
Site: Sun, partial shade. Moist, well-drained soil
Use: Ground cover, front of border, raised bed, rock garden
Good companions: *Astilbe chinensis* var. *pumila*, *Hebe cupressoides* 'Boughton Dome', *Viola* 'Belmont Blue'

4 Scabiosa graminifolia
Pincushion flower, Scabious

Easily grown evergreen perennial that makes a tuft of narrow grey-green leaves. Slender stems carrying soft mauve flowerheads with 'pincushion' centres emerge in summer and early autumn. Good for cutting. Hardy.

Height: 25cm (10in) **Spread:** 35cm (14in)
Site: Sun. Well-drained soil. Good on lime
Use: Front of sunny border, raised bed, rock garden
Good companions: *Aubrieta* 'Greencourt Purple', *Gypsophila repens* 'Rosa Schönheit', *Iberis sempervirens* 'Weisser Zwerg'

red and russet

5 Sedum 'Bertram Anderson'
Stonecrop

From late summer to mid-autumn the arching to prostrate purple stems of this perennial, which are clothed with small purple-blue leaves, bear loose clusters of wine-red starry flowers. Hardy.

Height: 15cm (6in) **Spread:** 30cm (12in)
Site: Sun. Well-drained soil
Use: Front of border, raised bed, rock garden
Good companions: *Artemisia schmidtiana* 'Nana', *Campanula cochleariifolia*, *Festuca glauca* 'Seeigel'

6 Zauschneria californica 'Dublin'
Californian fuchsia

In late summer and early autumn this narrow-leaved woody-based perennial produces sprays of bright orange-red tubular flowers that flare at the mouth. Not fully hardy.

General care: Grow in a sheltered position.
Height: 25cm (10in) **Spread:** 35cm (14in)
Site: Sun. Well-drained soil
Use: Dry wall, front of sunny border, raised bed, rock garden
Good companions: *Aubrieta* 'Doctor Mules', *Aurinia saxatilis* 'Citrina', *Cytisus* x *beanii*

cream and white

7 Rhodanthemum hosmariense

In autumn this shrubby perennial continues to produce yellow-centred, white daisy-like flowers over deeply cut silver leaves. Not fully hardy.
Height: 25cm (10in) **Spread:** 35cm (14in)
Site: Sun. Well-drained soil
Compost: Soil-based (John Innes No. 2) with added grit
Use: Container, front of sunny border, raised bed, rock garden
Good companions: *Lavandula angustifolia* 'Hidcote', *Muscari botryoides* 'Album', *Tulipa saxatilis* Bakeri Group 'Lilac Wonder'

silver and grey

8 Festuca glauca 'Seeigel'
Fescue

Evergreen perennial grass grown for the hair-like, silvery blue-green leaves, which make a spiky clump, rather than its blue-green flowers. Hardy.
Height and spread: 15cm (6in)
Site: Sun. Well-drained soil
Use: Front of sunny border, gravel garden, raised bed, rock garden
Good companions: *Armeria maritima* 'Düsseldorfer Stolz', *Crocus chrysanthus* 'Ladykiller', *Oxalis adenophylla*

green

9 Chamaecyparis lawsoniana 'Gimbornii'
Lawson cypress

Slow-growing, dwarf evergreen conifer valued as a foliage plant. This dense globular bush has blue-green leaves with tips that are tinged purple in cold winters. After many years it may double the dimensions given. Hardy.
Height and spread: 60cm (2ft)

Site: Sun. Moist but well-drained soil
Compost: Soil-based (John Innes No. 3)
Use: Container, heather garden, sunny border, raised bed, rock garden
Good companions: *Campanula poscharskyana* 'Stella', *Persicaria vacciniifolia*, *Viola* 'Belmont Blue'

10 Chamaecyparis lawsoniana 'Green Globe'
Lawson cypress

Dwarf conifer with congested sprays of bright green foliage that make a neat bun when young, but are less regular with age. Hardy.
Height and spread: 25cm (10in)
Site: Sun. Moist but well-drained soil
Compost: Soil-based (John Innes No. 3) with added leaf-mould
Use: Container, raised bed, rock garden
Good companions: *Campanula carpatica*, *Hebe cupressoides* 'Boughton Dome', *Viola biflora*

11 Thuja occidentalis 'Danica'
White cedar

The white cedar is itself a large evergreen conifer, but there are numerous attractive dwarf forms grown as foliage plants. This slow-growing example, which may eventually exceed the dimensions given, makes a rounded bush composed of erect stems carrying sprays of bright green leaves. Hardy.
Height and spread: 45cm (18in)
Site: Sun. Moist but well-drained soil
Compost: Soil-based (John Innes No. 3)
Use: Container, heather garden, sunny border, raised bed, rock garden
Good companions: *Daphne cneorum* 'Eximia', *Gentiana verna*, *Hebe cupressoides* 'Boughton Dome'

black

12 Viola 'Molly Sanderson'
Viola

Although it may be short-lived, this compact evergreen perennial flowers freely throughout summer and into autumn. A yellow eye brightens the medium-sized velvet-black flowers. Hardy.
General care: Deadhead to prolong flowering.
Height: 10cm (4in) **Spread:** 25cm (10in)
Site: Sun, partial shade. Humus-rich, moist but well-drained soil
Compost: Soil-less or soil-based (John Innes No. 2)
Use: Container, front of border, raised bed, rock garden
Good companions: *Astilbe chinensis* var. *pumila*, *Erythronium dens-canis*, *Viola biflora*

waterside & water plants

As the days shorten, a few perennials that thrive in reliably moist soil put on a late show. Plant in the dormant season.

purple, blue and violet

1 Lobelia syphilitica
Blue cardinal flower

Short-lived perennial with leafy upright stems and light green foliage. In late summer and early autumn it produces spikes of clear blue flowers that are tubular but open at the lips. Hardy.

General care: Divide plants every few years and move to fresh soil.

Height: 1m (3ft) **Spread:** 30cm (12in)

Site: Sun, partial shade. Fertile and moist soil

Use: Moist border, waterside

Good companions: *Lobelia* 'Queen Victoria', *Lythrum salicaria* 'Feuerkerze', *Primula pulverulenta* Bartley hybrids

pink and mauve

2 Eupatorium purpureum
Joe-pye weed

Large impressive perennial with stiff upright stems that are conspicuously purple among the toothed mid-green leaves, which sometimes also have a purple tinge. In late summer and autumn, domed heads of pink flowers top the foliage. Hardy.

Height: 2.5m (8ft) **Spread:** 1.2m (4ft)

Site: Sun, partial shade. Moist soil

Use: Moist border, waterside, wild garden

Good companions: *Cortaderia selloana* 'Sunningdale Silver', *Lythrum salicaria* 'Feuerkerze', *Miscanthus sinensis* 'Silberfeder'

bronze and maroon

3 Azolla filiculoides
Fairy moss, Mosquito plant

This aquatic fern forms patches of scale-like fronds that float freely on the water's surface and trail fine roots. The foliage is light green in summer but turns red-bronze in autumn. Half hardy.

General care: In frost-prone areas overwinter several fronds on damp soil under cover. When

there is no longer risk of frost scatter them on the water's surface.

Spread: Indefinite

Site: Sun, partial shade

Use: Pond

Good companions: *Aponogeton distachyos*, *Caltha palustris* 'Flore Pleno', *Myosotis scorpioides* 'Mermaid'

4 Rodgersia podophylla
This rhizomatous perennial produces a modest display of rounded sprays of tiny, greenish cream flowers in late summer but bears magnificent foliage. The leaves are up to 40cm (16in) long and consist of five jaggedly lobed leaflets. Newly unfolded, these are crinkled and dark brown. They then turn green and in autumn become bronze-red. Hardy.

Height and spread: 1.5m (5ft)

Site: Sun, partial shade. Humus-rich and moist soil

Use: Moist border, waterside

Good companions: *Miscanthus sinensis*

'Silberfeder', *Rheum palmatum* 'Atrosanguineum', *Rodgersia aesculifolia*

red and russet

5 Osmunda regalis
Flowering fern, Royal fern

Large deciduous fern that forms a substantial mound of broadly triangular fronds, which are copper tinted when they unroll in spring. In summer upright, rust-coloured partially fertile fronds contrast with bright green infertile fronds, which in autumn turn yellow, tan and buff. Hardy.

Height and spread: 1.5m (5ft)

Site: Sun, partial shade. Humus-rich and reliably

moist soil, preferably lime-free

Use: Damp border, waterside

Good companions: *Cornus alba* 'Sibirica', *Matteuccia struthiopteris*, *Salix irrorata*

yellow and orange

6 Ligularia dentata 'Desdemona'
Golden groundsel

This perennial makes an impressive clump of large, bronze-purple heart-shaped leaves with magenta-purple undersides. In late summer and early autumn sturdy stems carry clusters of orange-yellow daisy-like flowers. Hardy.

Height: 1.2m (4ft) **Spread:** 1m (3ft)

Site: Sun, partial shade. Reliably moist soil

Use: Moist border, waterside

Good companions: *Ligularia* 'The Rocket', *Miscanthus sinensis* 'Zebrinus', *Rodgersia aesculifolia*

7 Luzula sylvatica 'Aurea'
Greater woodrush

In summer the tussock of glossy leaves, topped early in the season by warm brown flowers, is yellow-green. In late autumn and winter the leaves turn bright yellow. Hardy.

Height: 75cm (2ft 6in) **Spread:** 45cm (18in)

Site: Partial shade, sun. Humus-rich and reliably moist but well-drained soil

Use: Ground cover, moist border, waterside, woodland garden

Good companions: *Carex pendula*, *Filipendula ulmaria* 'Aurea', *Trollius europaeus*

cream and white

8 Aponogeton distachyos
Cape pondweed, Water hawthorn

This perennial aquatic may be evergreen in mild winters. The floating light green leaves are frequently mottled maroon. The heavily scented, forked flower clusters are white at first then fade to green, their season extending from early summer until mid-autumn. Not fully hardy.

Spread: 1.2m (4ft)

Site: Sun. Still water 30cm–1m (1–3ft) deep

Compost: Soil-based (aquatic)

Use: Pond

Good companions: *Myosotis scorpioides* 'Mermaid', *Nymphaea* 'James Brydon', *Zantedeschia aethiopica* 'Crowborough'

silver and grey

9 Miscanthus sacchariflorus
Silver banner grass

Non-invasive perennial grass that makes a magnificent summer and autumn feature for large gardens. Leaves, up to 1m (3ft) long and blue-green in summer, flutter from bamboo-like canes. Their rustling movement remains appealing when they turn beige-brown in autumn. Silky, silvery brown flowers are produced only after a hot summer. Hardy.

General care: Leave foliage for winter effect but cut to the ground by early spring.

Height: 2.5m (8ft) **Spread:** 1.2m (4ft)

Site: Sun. Moist but well-drained soil

Use: Moist border, waterside, wild garden

Good companions: *Eupatorium purpureum*, *Ligularia* 'Gregynog Gold', *Rodgersia pinnata* 'Superba'

10 Miscanthus sinensis 'Silberfeder'

The value of most cultivars of this clump-forming grass lies in their foliage. The blue-green ribbon-like leaves of 'Silberfeder' arch elegantly from tall stems that in autumn are topped by feathery, pink-tinted silver-beige plumes. These remain attractive throughout winter. Hardy.

Height: 2.5m (8ft) **Spread:** 1.2m (4ft)

Site: Sun. Moist but well-drained soil

Use: Sunny border, waterside

Good companions: *Aconitum carmichaelii* 'Arendsii', *Cimicifuga simplex* Atropurpurea Group, *Molinia caerulea* subsp. *arundinacea* 'Windspiel'

11 Molinia caerulea subsp. caerulea 'Heidebraut'
Purple moor grass

This perennial grass makes a tussock of narrow tapered blades. In autumn, even after these have died down, stiff columns of straw-coloured stems topped with glittering seedheads remain eye-catching. Hardy.

Height: 1.5m (5ft)

Spread: 40cm (16in)

Site: Sun, partial shade. Moist soil, preferably lime-free

Use: Moist border, waterside

Good companions: *Astilbe* 'Professor van der Wielen', *Carex pendula*, *Hosta* 'Royal Standard'

herbs, vegetables & fruit

Autumn is the traditional season for harvesting fruit and vegetables, but it is also when gardeners need to plan for early crops the following year.

herbs

1 Aniseed
Pimpinella anisum
With a froth of feathery leaves this annual makes a dainty edging and container plant. The strongly flavoured fresh foliage and dried seeds are used in Indian and Middle Eastern cooking. Tender.
General care: Sow seed in late spring in pots or *in situ,* then thin to 20cm (8in) apart. Harvest seeds in early autumn when seedpods turn grey and hang up to dry in a cool dark place.
Height: 45cm (18in) **Spread:** 30cm (12in)
Site: Sun, sheltered. Light, well-drained soil
Compost: Soil-based (John Innes No. 3)
Use: Container, edging, front of border

2 Bay
Laurus nobilis
Large shrub or small tree with evergreen foliage that can be trimmed into simple topiary shapes and kept to required size. In very hot summers, creamy white flowers are produced. The leaves are used to flavour soups, stews and stocks. Use fresh or harvest to dry in early summer. Fairly hardy when established, but frost-sensitive while young and in exposed gardens.
General care: Plant in spring or autumn and

protect from frosts for two years. Insulate containers against frost. Water regularly in dry summers. Trim to shape in late spring.
Height: 12m (40ft) **Spread:** 3m (10ft)
Site: Sun, sheltered. Well-drained soil
Compost: Soil-based (John Innes No. 3) with good drainage
Use: Large container, specimen tree in border, topiary

3 Caraway
Carum carvi
Easily grown biennial herb. Although young leaves are used in salads, the seeds, used for flavouring bread and biscuits, are the main crop. Harvest these in autumn just before they ripen, as the capsules change colour. Hardy.

4 Winter savory
Satureja montana
This semi-evergreen perennial is an attractive plant for indoor and patio containers. It is more strongly flavoured than summer savory. Hardy.
General care: Sow seed indoors in small pots in early spring and plant out 15cm (6in) apart, or divide established clumps. Pick or trim regularly to maintain good shape and condition.
Height and spread: 45cm (18in)
Site: Sun. Fairly poor, well-drained soil
Compost: Soil-based (John Innes No. 3) with added grit
Use: Container, edging, front of border

General care: Sow seed outdoors in rows in autumn or indoors in a plug tray in early spring. Thin or plant out 20cm (8in) apart each way. Mark the position of the plants as they die down completely over winter. Check for carrot root fly.
Height: 1m (3ft) **Spread:** 30cm (12in)
Site: Sun. Well-drained soil
Use: Herb or vegetable garden

5 Brussels sprout
Brassica oleracea Gemmifera Group

Sprouts are normally picked after the first frost, which improves their flavour. Firm ground or staking is essential for taller varieties. The leafy tops make tasty 'greens', especially if cut off when the lowest sprouts are nearly ready. 'Oliver' and 'Peer Gynt' are the first to crop. Hardy.
Site: Sun, light shade. Deep, rich very firm soil, limed to pH7 or higher

How to grow: Sow seed outdoors in mid-spring. Thin seedlings to 8cm (3in) apart and transplant 60cm (2ft) apart each way when five or six weeks old. Water freely in dry weather. Feed with high-nitrogen fertiliser in midsummer. Remove yellowing leaves and net against birds. Snap off sprouts cleanly, starting at the bottom.

6 Cabbage, autumn
Brassica oleracea Capitata Group

Hardier and slower growing than summer cabbage, this produces large heads that remain in good condition for weeks. Varieties include pointed 'Winnigstadt', round 'Stonehead', white 'Polinius', savoy 'Celtic' and red 'Hardoro'. Hardy.
Site: Sun. Rich firm soil, with added lime if acid
How to grow: Sow outdoors in mid-spring. Thin seedlings to 8cm (3in) apart and transplant 50cm (20in) apart, less for compact varieties, when six to eight weeks old; plant firmly. Water in dry

weather and protect from birds. Cut heads off when large enough. If hard frost threatens, dig up mature heads and hang in a cool frost-free place.

7 Carrot, maincrop
Daucus carota

Large autumn and winter carrots are maincrop varieties, sown later than summer kinds and allowed to grow for at least 12 weeks. Whole crops can be dug up for storing when mature, but in mild gardens with light soils, roots remain sound over winter if mulched. Varieties include 'Autumn King' and 'Major'. Hardy.
Site: Sun. Light, well-drained soil with plenty of added compost
How to grow: Sow seed outdoors in late spring, in rows 15cm (6in) apart. Thin seedlings to 5–8cm (2–3in) apart and mulch. Water every two to three weeks in dry weather. Start forking up roots when large enough. Clear crops in mid-autumn; twist off tops and store in boxes in just damp sand, or mulch rows with straw or leaves 15cm (6in) deep, held down with netting or soil.

8 Celery, self-blanching
Apium graveolens var. dulce

Self-blanching and green (American) celery is Fast-growing and harvested from late summer until the first frosts, or later if grown under cover. The tasty green leaves can be picked at any time for use as flavouring. Good varieties include 'Celebrity', 'Lathom Self Blanching', 'Green Utah' and 'Greensleeves'. Tender.
Site: Sun, sheltered or in a coldframe. Moist soil with plenty of added compost
How to grow: Sow seed indoors in early spring and prick out into trays or small pots. Harden off and plant out in late spring, at least 23cm (9in) apart each way in blocks. Water weekly during dry weather and feed with high-nitrogen fertiliser in midsummer. Start harvesting when large enough and clear before the first frosts.

9 Jerusalem artichoke
Helianthus tuberosus

This produces nutritious tubers and tall leafy stems, which make an effective 3m (10ft) high windbreak if grown in rows. Stems can be shortened in midsummer to 2m (6ft). 'Fuseau' has the smoothest tubers; 'Dwarf Sunray' is short. Hardy.
Site: Sun, light shade. Fertile soil with plenty of added compost
How to grow: Plant small tubers in early spring, 10–15cm (4–6in) deep and 30cm (12in) apart. Water freely in dry weather. Earth and mulch stems for extra support. For larger tubers remove flowers. Lift as required from very early autumn.

10 Kohl rabi
Brassica oleracea Gongylodes Group

This cabbage relative has smooth swollen stems that are crisp and mildly flavoured. Ready just seven to eight weeks after sowing, even on soils that are too dry for other brassicas. The 'bulbs' are best when the size of tennis balls, although modern varieties grown on moist soils remain crisp when much larger. Not fully hardy.
Site: Light shade. Fertile sandy soil
How to grow: Sow small batches of seed *in situ* about every three to four weeks, in rows 30cm (12in) apart, from mid-spring until midsummer. Thin seedlings to 15–20cm (6–8in) apart. Water regularly in dry weather and mulch. Pull plants when large enough. Late crops can be cleared and stored in boxes of sand, or left outdoors in mild weather.

11 Leek, early
Allium porrum

Mild-flavoured member of the onion family with non-bulbing white stems. Early varieties, such as 'Albinstar' and 'King Richard', are juicy but cannot withstand frost. Mini-leeks, grown by thinning leek seedlings to 2.5cm (1in) apart, are ready when the size of spring onions. Tender.
Site: Sun, light shade. Deep rich soil with plenty of added compost
How to grow: Sow seed under glass in late winter then prick out into trays, or outdoors in mid-spring, thinning seedlings to 4cm (1½in) apart. Plant out from late spring onwards, when 20cm (8in) high, dropping a single seedling into a 15cm (6in) deep hole, spaced 15cm (6in) in rows 30cm (12in) apart. Water occasionally in dry weather. Start lifting with a fork when large enough.

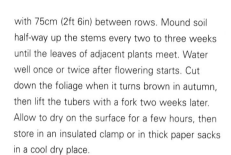

1 Marrow
Cucurbita pepo

Marrows can be cut eight weeks after planting and will continue cropping until the first frosts. The last can be 'cured' (see below), then stored in a dry airy place at about 10ºC (50ºF) for several weeks. Trailing varieties can be planted on a compost heap. Varieties include 'Long Green Trailing' and 'All Green Bush'. Tender.

Site: Sun, sheltered. Rich, deeply dug soil with plenty of added compost

How to grow: Sow seed indoors in small pots two to three weeks before the last frosts and plant out when all risk of frost is past. Space bush varieties 1–1.2m (3–4ft) apart and trailing kinds 2m (6ft) apart. Water and mulch liberally. Pinch out trailing kinds when five leaves have opened and spread out resulting sideshoots across the ground or tie to trellis. Harvest regularly. To cure fruits for storing, dry them in the sun (in a greenhouse or on a windowsill) for two weeks.

2 Onion, maincrop
Allium cepa

Can be raised from seed or, more easily, from sets (immature bulbs). A combination of spring and autumn sowing or planting (see 5, Onion in Summer, page 115) can ensure a year-round supply. Check varieties for flavour, which can range from mildly sweet to ferociously hot. Not fully hardy.

Site: Sun. Fertile, well-drained soil with plenty of added compost

How to grow: Sow seed *in situ* in early spring in rows 30cm (12in) apart and thin seedlings to 5cm (2in) apart for small bulbs and 10–15cm (4–6in) for large ones. Plant sets at the same distances, with their tips just covered. Water frequently until midsummer. In late summer to early autumn fork up bulbs carefully and spread out on trays or under glass to dry. When skins are papery, store in nets or boxes; they will keep until spring.

3 Potato, maincrop
Solanum tuberosum

Maincrop potatoes yield heavily on most soils. Although they occupy space for most of the growing season, they can be stored until spring. Good varieties are 'Marfona', 'Cara', 'Romano', 'Sante' and 'Picasso'. Not fully hardy.

Site: Sun. Fertile, deeply dug and well-drained soil

How to grow: Set seed potatoes to sprout, or 'chit', in late winter and plant out in mid-spring 10–15cm (4–6in) deep, spaced 40cm (16in) apart

with 75cm (2ft 6in) between rows. Mound soil half-way up the stems every two to three weeks until the leaves of adjacent plants meet. Water well once or twice after flowering starts. Cut down the foliage when it turns brown in autumn, then lift the tubers with a fork two weeks later. Allow to dry on the surface for a few hours, then store in an insulated clamp or in thick paper sacks in a cool dry place.

4 Squash, winter
Cucurbita maxima and C. moschata

With thick skins protecting their well-flavoured flesh, pumpkins and other winter squashes can be stored for months over winter. These vigorous trailing plants need plenty of space, but tolerate light shade so make good ground cover under sweetcorn, runner beans and fruit trees. Tender.

Site: Sun, light shade. Rich, deeply dug soil with plenty of added compost or rotted manure

How to grow: Sow and plant as for marrows (see 1, Marrow), or sow *in situ* after the last frosts. Water well in dry weather and feed every two to three weeks while fruits are swelling. To grow large squashes, thin fruitlets to three to four on each plant. Move or remove leaves to expose ripening fruits to the sun. Cut when large enough or, for storing, leave until fully coloured in early autumn. Cure and store as for marrows.

fruit

5 Apple
Malus domestica

Apart from the earliest varieties, most apples ripen at various times during the autumn and need regular inspection to judge the best moment to start harvesting. Some kinds, such as 'Sunset', can be eaten straight after picking, while others, especially late keepers such as 'Ribston Pippin' and 'Orleans Reinette', need storing for a few weeks after harvest before they are ready to eat. These will keep well into winter or early spring. Hardy.

Site: Sun, sheltered. Deep, fertile, well-drained soil

How to grow: Plant during the dormant season. Support if necessary, especially dwarf trees in exposed gardens. Water regularly during the first season, and feed and mulch in spring. Prune trained trees in mid or late summer, other kinds

during winter. Gather fruits as soon as the stalks part easily from the tree (some varieties need several partial harvests). Store in a cool airy place.

6 Blackberry
Rubus fruticosus

Cultivated blackberries have larger fruit than wild plants, but are still vigorous and need firm training on wires or a fence. A range of varieties offers fruit from late summer until the frosts. 'Ashton Cross' and 'Fantasia' have good flavour; parsley-leaved 'Oregon Thornless' is thornless. Hardy.

Site: Sun, sheltered. Fertile, well-drained soil

How to grow: Plant while dormant, spacing the plants 4m (12ft) apart. Water in dry weather, and feed and mulch in spring. Train in new canes and prune out fruited ones after harvest. Pick fruit when fully coloured and soft.

7 Damson
Prunus insititia

Grow as specimen trees for spring blossom and heavy crops of blue-black, richly flavoured fruits. 'Farleigh Damson' and 'Prune Damson' are among the best varieties. Hardier but less vigorous than other plums.

Site: Sun, sheltered. Rich, deep soil with plenty of added compost

How to grow: Plant in late autumn, 5m (15ft) apart. Mulch in spring with rotted manure. Prune while in leaf. Harvest fruit when fully coloured and starting to fall.

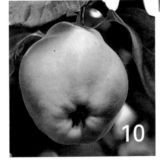

9 Melon
Cucumis melo

For the best crops, grow in a greenhouse or coldframe, but cantaloupe varieties can be grown in the open, especially if trained over a hard surface such as paving, which absorbs heat. Tender.

Site: Sun, sheltered. Fertile, well-drained soil.

How to grow: Sow seed indoors in mid-spring in small pots. Plant out 1m (3ft) apart, after danger of frosts is past. Pinch out the growing tip after five leaves and spread out resulting sideshoots on the ground or on vertical wires. Select the best fruit on each shoot, remove any others and pinch out the growing tips. Flowers on indoor plants may need hand pollinating. Harvest when melons are strongly fragrant, with cracking around the stalk base.

10 Quince
Cydonia oblonga

Small, decorative deciduous tree bearing large pinkish white blooms in spring and perfumed golden pear or apple-shaped fruits. Bush, standard trees and fans for training on a wall are available.

Look for 'Vranja' and 'Meech's Prolific'. Hardy.

Site: Sun, sheltered. Deep, light, fertile soil

How to grow: Plant while dormant, 4.5–6m (15–20ft) apart. Feed or mulch with rotted manure annually in early spring. Prune in winter, removing misplaced, crossing and congested shoots. Leave fruits until fully coloured but harvest before frosts. Store in boxes in a cool airy place for a month to allow the powerful flavour to develop; keep away from other fruit to avoid cross-flavouring.

11 Raspberry, autumn
Rubus idaeus

Autumn-fruiting raspberries yield heavy crops of firm red, sometimes golden fruits until the frosts. They need plenty of space and produce a dense screen of tall canes, which can be useful for shading leafy vegetables in a hot summer. Try 'Autumn Bliss', 'Heritage' or yellow 'Fallgold'. Hardy.

Site: Sun. Deep, light soil with added compost

How to grow: Plant while dormant, 45–60cm (18–24in) apart in rows 1.2m (4ft) apart, and cut down to 23cm (9in) high. In early spring feed and mulch with compost. Train in the canes as they grow, fanning them evenly about 10cm (4in) apart on parallel wires. Harvest fruit when fully coloured. Leave canes over winter, cutting to ground level in late winter to allow for the new season's canes.

8 Grape
Vitis vinifera and Vitis cultivars

With firm training these elegant vines may be grown as an intensive fruit crop, or they can be used as decorative climbers for screens and pergolas. Outdoor dessert grapes are best trained on a warm wall; wine grapes are hardier and can crop heavily after a hot summer. Good varieties include 'Siegerrebe' (white) and 'Brant' (black, good autumn colour). Hardy.

Site: Sun, sheltered. Fertile, well-drained soil

How to grow: Plant while dormant, 1.2–1.5m (4–5ft) apart. Mulch in spring with rotted manure and water regularly during dry weather. Train climbers on wires, with a maximum of three to four stems. Prune after fruiting, cutting all sideshoots back to the main branches.

the greenhouse

Tender plants that are ornamental in autumn and winter are a great source of colour for those who have a greenhouse. Make sure those plants you moved outdoors for summer are brought into a greenhouse or conservatory before the frost approaches.

purple, blue and violet

1 Achimenes 'Ambroise Verschaffelt'
Cupid's bower, Hot-water plant

Trailing perennial suitable for growing in a hanging basket. It has a tuber-like rootstock and dies down in winter. The flowers, borne prolifically in summer and autumn, consist of a long, curved white tube that opens out to five rounded lobes with strong purple veining. Tender.

General care: Water sparingly to start into growth in spring. Dry off in late autumn and store roots in frost-free conditions.

Height: 25cm (10in) **Spread:** 40cm (16in)

Under glass: Bright light. Soil-based (John Innes No. 2) or soil-less compost

Use: Container, conservatory or greenhouse minimum 10°C (50°F), houseplant

2 Agave americana

Succulent that forms a large rosette of heavy, grey-blue, spiny sword-shaped leaves. There are variegated forms, such as yellow-edged 'Variegata'. All are impressive as container plants in a sunny outdoor position in summer. Fragrant cream flowers, on a 6m (20ft) stem, appear on 30-year-old specimens, after which the rosette dies, leaving offsets. Tender.

Height: 2m (6ft) **Spread:** 3m (10ft)

Under glass: Full light. Soil-based compost (John Innes No. 2) with added grit

Use: Container, conservatory or greenhouse minimum 5°C (41°F), sunny patio

3 Campanula isophylla
Falling stars, Italian bellflower,
Star-of-Bethlehem

Low-growing perennial with trailing stems. Blue star-shaped flowers, about 2–3cm (1in) across, almost hide the toothed heart-shaped leaves in late summer and early autumn. Good for hanging baskets, as is white-flowering 'Alba'. Half hardy.

Height: 15cm (6in) **Spread:** 30cm (12in)

Under glass: Bright light. Soil-based compost (John Innes No. 2)

Outdoor site: Sun. Well-drained soil

Use: Container, conservatory or greenhouse minimum 0°C (32°F), front of sunny border

4 Exacum affine
Persian violet

Compact, bushy, short-lived evergreen perennial usually grown as an annual. In summer and early autumn the shiny, deep green leaves are covered with scented, mauve-blue saucer-shaped flowers with conspicuous yellow stamens. Tender.

General care: Sow seed under glass at 18°C (64°F).

Height and spread: 25cm (10in)

Under glass: Full light. Soil-based compost (John Innes No. 2)

Use: Container, conservatory or greenhouse minimum 10°C (50°F), houseplant

5 Plumbago auriculata
Cape leadwort

This scrambling evergreen shrub is best trained up and tied into supports. Clusters of sky-blue flowers are borne during summer and autumn, but maintaining a temperature above 13°C (55°F) will extend flowering into winter. Half hardy.

General care: Prune after flowering, reducing all growths by about a third. Tie in weak stems as they make growth.

Height: 5m (15ft) **Spread:** 2.5m (8ft)

Under glass: Full light. Soil-based compost (John Innes No. 3)

Use: Conservatory or greenhouse minimum 0°C (32°F)

6 Rhodochiton atrosanguineus

Slender perennial climber usually grown as an annual outdoors or under glass. The heart-shaped leaves have twining leaf stalks, which twist around supports. Intriguing purple-red pendent flowers are borne throughout summer and into autumn. Tender.

General care: Sow seed under glass at 15–18°C (59–64°F).

Height: 3m (10ft) **Spread:** 60cm (2ft)

Under glass: Full light. Soil-based compost (John Innes No. 2)

Outdoor site: Sun. Humus-rich, moist but well-drained soil

Use: Container, conservatory or greenhouse minimum 3°C (37°F), tripod, wall shrub

pink and mauve

7 Justicia carnea
Brazilian plume, Flamingo plant

Evergreen shrub with prominently veined, glossy tapered leaves. In late summer and early autumn it bears dense, flesh-pink flower spikes. Tender.

General care: Prune hard in late winter or early spring to prevent plants from becoming leggy.

Height: 2m (6ft) **Spread:** 1m (3ft)

Under glass: Bright light. Soil-based compost (John Innes No. 3)

Use: Container, conservatory or greenhouse minimum 7°C (45°F)

8 Lapageria rosea
Chilean bellflower

Twining evergreen climber that sometimes succeeds outdoors in a lightly shaded but warm and sheltered corner. The waxy, red-pink, elongated bell-shaped flowers are borne in late summer and autumn. Not fully hardy.

General care: Limit pruning to the removal of weak growths immediately after flowering.

Height: 5m (15ft) **Spread:** 1.2m (4ft)

Under glass: Bright indirect light. Ericaceous compost

Outdoor site: Partial shade. Lime-free, humus-rich and moist but well-drained soil

Use: Container, conservatory or greenhouse minimum 7°C (45°F), wall climber

red and russet

9 Abutilon 'Souvenir de Bonn'
Flowering maple, Indian mallow

A number of abutilon hybrids of mixed parentage are evergreen shrubs that flower freely from spring to autumn. 'Souvenir de Bonn', which can make a large shrub or small tree, has cream-variegated lobed leaves and orange nodding bell-shaped flowers. Other hybrids to extend the colour range include white 'Boule de Neige', yellow 'Canary Bird' and deep crimson 'Nabob'. Half hardy.

General care: In early spring cut back main stems by half and shorten laterals to 10cm (4in).

Height and spread: 2.5m (8ft)

Under glass: Full light. Soil-based compost (John Innes No. 2)

Use: Container, conservatory or greenhouse minimum 0°C (32°F)

10 Passiflora racemosa
Red passion flower

Glossy-leaved evergreen climber that attaches itself to supports by tendrils. Bright red starry flowers hang in drooping sprays from summer to autumn. At the centre of each flower is a ring of purple-and-white filaments. Tender.

General care: Thin out tangled growths and shorten laterals to about 15cm (6in) between late winter and early spring.

Height: 5m (15ft) **Spread:** 2m (6ft)

Under glass: Full light. Soil-based compost (John Innes No. 3)

Use: Container, conservatory or greenhouse minimum 16°C (61°F)

yellow and orange

11 Chrysanthemum 'Bronze Mayford Perfection'

A large group of late flowering florists' chrysanthemums are grown in pots outdoors in summer and moved under glass in early autumn. The double flowers vary in form and come in a wide range of colours, measuring 20cm (8in) or more across. This apricot example bears intermediate blooms with partially incurved and partially reflexed ray-florets in late autumn and early winter. Tender.

General care: To achieve flowers of good quality, grow from newly rooted cuttings, pot on in three stages and control growth. Pinch out the growing tip of young plants between mid-spring and early summer to encourage sideshoots, then from late summer remove buds and sideshoots except the central bud on a stem. Stake plants.

Height: 1.2m (4ft) **Spread:** 45cm (18in)

Under glass: Bright light. Soil-based compost (John Innes No. 2, potting on finally to No. 3)

Use: Container, conservatory or greenhouse minimum 10°C (50°F)

yellow and orange (continued)

1 Chrysanthemum Charm hybrids

These dwarf chrysanthemum hybrids are widely grown as pot plants. They require no training to form a topiary-like dome that is densely covered with scented, long-lasting single flowers in autumn. Cultivars are often sold unnamed, but the colour range includes yellow, white and shades of red and bronze. Tender.

Height and spread: 1m (3ft)

Under glass: Bright light. Soil-based (John Innes No. 2, potting on finally to No. 3)

Use: Container, conservatory or greenhouse minimum 10°C (50°F)

2 Fuchsia 'Thalia'
Triphylla Group fuchsia

This erect shrub has dark, strongly veined leaves that are purplish on the underside. In summer and autumn it bears small scarlet-orange flowers. These have long tubes, as do those of other Triphylla hybrids, and hang in clusters from the stem tips. Plants can be moved outdoors in summer. Tender.

General care: To keep plants in flower all year maintain a temperature of 15°C (59°F).

Height: 75cm (2ft 6in) **Spread:** 50cm (20in)

Under glass: Bright light. Soil-based compost (John Innes No. 3) or soil-less

Use: Container, conservatory or greenhouse minimum 5°C (41°F), sunny or lightly shaded patio

3 Ipomoea lobata
Spanish flag

This short-lived perennial is usually grown as an annual. It has climbing stems and toothed leaves with three finger-like lobes. In summer and autumn it bears spikes of up to 12 tubular flowers. These have protruding stamens and are scarlet at first but gradually age to orange and yellow. Tender.

General care: Soak seed before sowing under glass at 18°C (64°F).

Height: 3m (10ft) **Spread:** 2m (6ft)

Under glass: Full light. Soil-based compost (John Innes No. 2)

Outdoor site: Sun. Well-drained soil

Use: Conservatory or greenhouse minimum 10°C (50°F), wall climber

4 Lantana camara cultivars

The parent of the various forms in cultivation is a hairy, often prickly, evergreen shrub that is a naturalised weed in many parts of the tropics. The cultivars have crinkly leaves. Over a long season that extends well into autumn, they bear domed compact heads of small flowers. The blooms deepen in colour as they age, with two or more shades being present in a flowerhead at any one time. The colour range encompasses white, yellow, orange, pink, red and purple. Some cultivars are bicoloured, their flowerheads showing a contrast of, for example, pink and yellow. Tender.

General care: Prune plants in late winter to control size and shape.

Height: 1.2m (4ft) **Spread:** 1m (3ft)

Under glass: Full light. Soil-based compost (John Innes No. 3)

Use: Container, conservatory or greenhouse minimum 10°C (50°F)

5   Nerine sarniensis
Guernsey lily

This bulb starts into growth in early autumn, a few strap-shaped leaves emerging with the flower stems. These carry compact rounded heads of 10 or more flowers, which are usually orange-red although the colour range includes pink and crimson. Conspicuous stamens jut out from the swept-back segments, which have wavy edges. Half hardy.

General care: Plant in autumn or spring with the tip of the bulb above the surface of the compost.

Height: 45cm (18in) **Spread:** 8cm (3in)

Under glass: Full light. Soil-based compost (John Innes No. 2)

Use: Container, conservatory or greenhouse minimum 0°C (32°F)

6   Nertera granadensis
Bead plant

This perennial forms a close mat of tiny leaves and is usually grown as an annual. Large numbers of small round berries follow inconspicuous greenish yellow flowers. The berries are glossy yellow-orange to orange-red and scattered liberally over the foliage. Half hardy.

General care: Sow seed under glass at 13–16°C (55–61°F)

Height: 2cm (¾in) **Spread:** 20cm (8in)

Under glass: Indirect light. Soil-less compost

Outdoor site: Partial shade. Humus-rich, moist but well-drained soil

Use: Container, greenhouse or conservatory minimum 0°C (32°F), rock garden

7   Tecoma capensis
Cape honeysuckle

Although it can be kept as a bush, in the greenhouse or conservatory this scrambling evergreen shrub is best trained up as a climber. The glossy dark green leaves are composed of diamond-shaped leaflets. Sprays of orange-scarlet tubular flowers are produced in late summer and autumn. Tender.

General care: Thin out tangled growths and shorten laterals to about 15cm (6in) between late winter and early spring.

Height: 6m (20ft) **Spread:** 2.5m (8ft)

Under glass: Full light. Soil-based compost (John Innes No. 3)

Use: Conservatory or greenhouse minimum 5°C (41°F)

cream and white

8   Camellia sasanqua 'Narumigata'

Most *C. sasanqua* cultivars begin flowering in mid-autumn. The best results are achieved if plants are exposed to full sun outdoors in summer, while the roots are kept shaded, then brought under glass for the winter. All cultivars bear small fragrant, white single flowers but those of 'Narumigata' have a pink tinge. Hardy, though flowers may be browned by frost.

Height: 3m (10ft) **Spread:** 2.5m (8ft)

Under glass: Bright light. Soil-based ericaceous compost

Outdoor site: Sun, partial shade. Lime-free, moist but well-drained soil

Use: Container, conservatory or greenhouse, sunny or lightly shaded border

9   Pteris cretica var. albolineata
Brake

Evergreen fern with arching fronds that have strap-shaped segments. These are light green and each is marked with a bold white central band. Needs a humid atmosphere. Not fully hardy.

Height: 75cm (2ft 6in) **Spread:** 60cm (2ft)

Under glass: Bright light. Soil-based compost (John Innes No. 1) with added leaf-mould

Use: Container, conservatory or greenhouse minimum 5°C (41°F), houseplant

green

10   Grevillea robusta
Silky oak

In the wild this evergreen makes a tall tree that bears sprays of rich yellow or orange flowers in summer. Under glass it is usually grown as a foliage shrub and maintained at a manageable height. The ferny leaves, which are covered with silky hairs, are bronze when young, darkening on the upper surface to deep green as they mature. Tender.

General care: Prune to restrict size in early spring.

Height and spread: 1.2–2m (4–6ft)

Under glass: Full light. Soil-based ericaceous compost

Use: Container, conservatory or greenhouse minimum 5°C (41°F), houseplant

11   Peperomia caperata

This evergreen perennial makes a mound of deeply corrugated heart-shaped leaves. These are deep velvety green with a purple tinge, variably lightened by a silver-grey sheen. Spikes of tiny white flowers stand on brown stems above the foliage from spring to early winter. Tender.

General care: Maintain a humid atmosphere in summer.

Height and spread: 20cm (8in)

Under glass: Bright indirect light. Soil-based (John Innes No. 1) or soil-less compost

Use: Container, conservatory or greenhouse minimum 15°C (59°F), houseplant

choosing the best plants

The following plant lists draw on all the plants described in the preceding pages of the Plant Selector, but they are grouped together here to help you choose plants for particular conditions, situations and uses.

plants for coastal sites

Where windbreaks and hedges give protection from salt-laden winds, a wide range of plants can be grown in coastal gardens, including many that benefit from the sea's moderating influence on temperatures.

- *Amaryllis belladonna*
- *Arbutus unedo*
- *Arctotis* x *hybrida* 'Flame'
- *Aster* (short-growing kinds)
- *Calluna vulgaris* (all)
- *Campanula poscharskyana* 'Stella'
- *Caryopteris* x *clandonensis* 'Kew Blue'
- *Ceanothus* 'Autumnal Blue'
- *Cotoneaster conspicuus* 'Decorus'
- *Cyclamen hederifolium*
- *Erodium* 'County Park'
- *Euphorbia seguieriana* subsp. *niciciana*
- *Festuca glauca* 'Seeigel'
- *Fuchsia* (most)
- *Geranium sanguineum*
- *Hebe* 'Autumn Glory'
- *Hydrangea* (all)
- *Ilex* x *altaclarensis* 'Camelliifolia'
- *Isotoma axillaris*
- *Juniperus communis* 'Green Carpet'
- *Kniphofia* (all)
- *Lagurus ovatus*
- *Lavatera trimestris* 'Silver Cup'
- *Limonium sinuatum* Forever Series
  - *Nerine bowdenii*
  - *Penstemon* (all)
  - *Rhodanthemum hosmariense*
  - *Rosa* 'Fru Dagmar Hastrup'
  - *Scabiosa* (all)
  - *Schizostylis coccinea* 'Sunrise'
    - *Sedum* (all)
    - *Sternbergia lutea*

Penstemon 'Raven'

plants for moist shade

The following plants tolerate or more commonly thrive in moist shade, although many will also grow in full sun provided the soil is reliably moist. Plants marked with an asterisk* will grow in boggy conditions.

- *Acer* (all)
- *Amelanchier canadensis*
- *Anemone* x *hybrida* (all)
- *Aster divaricatus*
- *Aster lateriflorus* 'Horizontalis'
- *Astilbe chinensis* var. *pumila*
- *Cercidiphylum japonicum*
- *Cimicifuga simplex* Atropurpurea Group
- *Disanthus cercidifolius*
- *Euphorbia schillingii*
- *Fatsia japonica*
- *Fuchsia* (all)
- *Galax urceolata*
- *Gaultheria mucronata* 'Mulberry Wine'
- *Hydrangea macrophylla* 'Madame Emile Mouillère'
- *Hydrangea* 'Preziosa'
- *Impatiens* New Guinea Group
- *Iris foetidissima*
- *Lobelia syphilitica**
- *Molinia* (all)
- *Nicotiana langsdorffii*
- *Nicotiana sylvestris*
- *Ophiopogon planiscapus* 'Nigrescens'
- *Osmunda regalis**
- *Rodgersia podophylla**
- *Saxifraga fortunei*
- *Tricyrtis formosana*
- *Viburnum opulus* 'Compactum'
- *Viola* 'Belmont Blue'
- *Viola* 'Molly Sanderson'

Acer palmatum

plants for acid soil

Plants in the following list that are marked with an asterisk* will only grow satisfactorily on soils that are free of lime. Other plants in the list thrive on acid soils, although they may also grow satisfactorily on soils that are neutral or to some degree alkaline.

- *Acer* (all)
- *Amelanchier canadensis*
- *Calluna vulgaris* (all)*
- *Camellia sasanqua* 'Narumigata'*
- *Disanthus cercidifolius**
- *Eucalyptus gunnii*
- *Galax urceolata**
- *Gaultheria mucronata* 'Mulberry Wine'
- *Gentiana sino-ornata**
- *Gentiana* 'Strathmore'*
- *Lapageria rosea**
- *Liquidambar styraciflua* 'Worplesdon'
- *Molinia* (all)
- *Osmunda regalis*
- *Quercus coccinea* 'Splendens'*
- *Sorbus* (most)

plants for dry chalky soil

A large number of plants are automatically excluded from this list because they will not tolerate alkaline (limy) soil. The improvement of shallow chalky soil by the addition of moisture-retaining organic matter allows lime-tolerant but moisture-loving plants, notably clematis, to be grown successfully.

- *Arbutus unedo*
- *Aster amellus*
- *Caryopteris* x *clandonensis* 'Kew Blue'
- *Cotoneaster conspicuus* 'Decorus'
- *Crocus kotschyanus*
- *Crocus speciosus*
- *Cyclamen hederifolium*
- *Euonymus europaeus* 'Red Cascade'
- *Euphorbia seguieriana* subsp. *niciana*
- *Iris foetidissima*
- *Lavatera trimestris* 'Silver Cup'
- *Liriope muscari*
- *Origanum amanum*
- *Scabiosa* (all)
- *Sedum* (all)
- *Sternbergia lutea*

plants for clay soil

Although the following plants generally succeed on close-textured clay soils, they do better when the ground has been improved by the addition of grit and organic matter such as well-rotted garden compost.

- *Acer* (most)
- *Amelanchier canadensis*
- *Anemone* x *hybrida* (all)
- *Chamaecyparis lawsoniana* 'Gimbornii'
- *Clematis* (some)
- *Cotinus* 'Flame'
- *Cotoneaster* (all)
- *Crataegus persimilis* 'Prunifolia'
- *Eucalyptus gunnii*
- *Hibiscus syriacus* 'Woodbridge'
- *Ilex* x *altaclarensis* 'Camelliifolia'
- *Juniperus communis* 'Green Carpet'
- *Kniphofia* (all)
- *Malus* 'John Downie'
- *Miscanthus* (all)
- *Molinia* (all)
- *Panicum virgatum* 'Rubrum'
- *Parthenocissus quinquefolia*
- *Parthenocissus tricuspidata* 'Veitchii'
- *Prunus sargentii*
- *Rodgersia podophylla*
- *Rosa* (all)
- *Sorbus* 'Joseph Rock'
- *Sorbus sargentiana*
- *Thuja occidentalis* 'Danica'
- *Viburnum opulus* 'Compactum'
- *Vitis coignetiae*

Acer circinatum

plants for sandy or gravelly soil

The following plants require free drainage and are generally drought tolerant. The range of plants that can be grown in dry sunny gardens can be enlarged if the soil is improved by the addition of organic matter.

- *Bassia scoparia* f. *tricophylla*
- *Bidens ferulifolia*
- *Calluna vulgaris* (all)
- *Caryopteris* x *clandonensis* 'Kew Blue'
- *Convolvulus tricolor* 'Royal Ensign'
- *Cotoneaster conspicuus* 'Decorus'
- *Cotoneaster salicifolia* 'Rothschildianus'
- *Crocus kotschyanus*
- *Crocus speciosus*
- *Erodium* 'County Park'
- *Euphorbia seguieriana* subsp. *niciciana*
- *Festuca glauca* 'Seeigel'
- *Gaura lindheimeri* 'Siskiyou Pink'
- *Isotoma axillaris*
- *Juniperus communis* 'Green Carpet'
- *Juniperus scopulorum* 'Skyrocket'
- *Lagurus ovatus*
- *Lavatera trimestris* 'Silver Cup'
- *Limonium sinuatum* Forever Series
- *Nerine bowdenii*
- *Origanum amanum*
- *Pennisetum villosum*
- *Rhodanthemum hosmariense*
- *Sedum* (all)
- *Sternbergia lutea*
- *Tagetes* (all)
- *Tithonia rotundifolia* 'Goldfinger'
- *Vitis* 'Brant'
- *Xeranthemum annuum*
- *Zauschneria californica*

Erodium 'County Park'

flowering plants for containers

As well as the plants listed here as suitable for general container gardening, a number of alpine, or rock garden, plants are suitable for troughs and all the greenhouse plants described on pages 112–115 can be grown in containers.

- *Amaranthus caudatus* 'Viridis'
- *Anagallis monellii*
- *Arctotis* x *hybrida* 'Flame'
- *Begonia semperflorens* Organdy Series
- *Calluna vulgaris* (all)
- *Convolvulus tricolor* 'Royal Ensign'
- *Dahlia* 'Figaro Red'
- *Diascia* 'Salmon Supreme'
- *Fuchsia* (most)
- *Heliotropium arborescens* 'Marine'
- *Hydrangea macrophylla* 'Madame Emile Mouillère'
- *Hydrangea* 'Preziosa'
- *Impatiens* New Guinea Group
- *Isotoma axillaris*
- *Petunia* 'Purple Wave'
- *Rudbeckia hirta* 'Rustic Dwarf'
- *Salvia farinacea* 'Victoria'
- *Tagetes* (all)
- *Viola* 'Belmont Blue'
- *Viola* 'Molly Sanderson'

plants for ground cover

Close planting of shrubs and perennials will help to create an attractive weed-excluding cover. However, effective cover can only be achieved by planting into soil from which perennial weeds have been eliminated. The following plants are particularly useful because of their dense foliage.

- *Astilbe chinensis* var. *pumila*
- *Calluna vulgaris* (all)
- *Cotoneaster conspicuus* 'Decorus'
- *Galax urceolata*
- *Liriope muscari*
- *Persicaria vaccinifolia*

choosing the best plants/2

flowers for cutting

In addition to the following, many other plants provide material for small, sometimes short-lived, displays. The flowers of plants marked with an asterisk* are suitable for drying.

- *Aconitum carmichaelii* 'Arendisii'
- *Amaranthus caudatus* 'Viridis'
- *Amaryllis belladonna*
- *Aster* (most)
- *Callistephus chinensis* Princess Series
- *Calluna vulgaris* (all)*
- *Chrysanthemum* 'Clara Curtis'
- *Chrysanthemum* 'Mary Stoker'
- *Cimicifuga simplex* Atropurpurea Group
- *Cosmos bipinnatus* 'Sea Shells'
- *Cosmos sulphureus* 'Sunset'
- *Crinum* x *powellii*
- *Dahlia* (all)
- *Echinacea purpurea* 'White Lustre'
- *Fuchsia* (most)
- *Helenium* 'Sonnenwunder'
- *Helianthus annuus* 'Velvet Queen'
- *Helianthus* 'Lemon Queen'
- *Kniphofia* (most)
- *Lavatera trimestris* 'Silver Cup'
- *Layia platyglossa*
- *Limonium sinuatum* Forever Series*
- *Liriope muscari*
- *Nerine bowdenii* (all)
- *Physostegia virginiana*
- *Rosa* (most)
- *Sanguisorba obtusa*
- *Saxifraga fortunei*
- *Scabiosa caucasica* 'Miss Willmott'
- *Schizostylis coccinea* 'Sunrise'
- *Sedum* 'Herbstfreude'
- *Tricyrtis formosana*
- *Xeranthemum annuum**

Rosa Iceberg

annuals, perennials and grasses with ornamental seed heads or berries

Some grasses are grown mainly for their foliage, but those marked with an asterisk* are grown principally for the long-lasting display of their flowers and seed heads.

- *Cortaderia selloana* 'Aureolineata'*
- *Helianthus annuus* 'Velvet Queen'
- *Iris foetidissima*
- *Lagurus ovatus**
- *Miscanthus sinensis* 'Silberfeder'*
- *Molinia caerulea* subsp. *arundinacea* 'Windspiel'*
- *Molinia caerulea* subsp. *caerulea* 'Heidebraut'*
- *Ophiopogon planiscapus* 'Nigrescens'
- *Panicum virgatum* 'Rubrum'*
- *Physalis alkekengi* var. *franchetii*
- *Scabiosa stellata* 'Paper Moon'
- *Sedum* 'Herbstfreude'

trees for small gardens

None of the following is suitable for very small gardens, where climbers on structures such as arches are a better way of creating height and shade. Some are more commonly grown as large shrubs rather than as trees.

- *Acer japonicum* 'Vitifolium'
- *Acer palmatum* 'Sango-kaku'
- *Amelanchier canadensis*
- *Arbutus unedo*
- *Clerodendrum trichotomum* var. *fargesii*
- *Cotinus* 'Flame'
- *Crataegus persimilis* 'Prunifolia'
- *Euonymus europaeus* 'Red Cascade'
- *Juniperus scopulorum* 'Skyrocket'
- *Malus* 'John Downie'
- *Sorbus hupehensis*
- *Sorbus* 'Joseph Rock'
- *Sorbus sargentiana*
- *Rhus typhina* 'Dissecta'

shrubs, trees and climbers for autumn colour

In most years the foliage of the following plants colours well in autumn, but the display is more reliable in a continental climate.

- *Acer cappodocicum* 'Aureum'
- *Acer japonicum* 'Vitifolium'
- *Acer palmatum* 'Sango-kaku'
- *Acer rubrum* 'October Glory'
- *Amelanchier canadensis*
- *Calluna vulgaris* 'Robert Chapman'
- *Cercidiphyllum japonicum*
- *Chamaecyparis lawsoniana* 'Gimbornii'
- *Cotinus* 'Flame'
- *Crataegus persimilis* 'Prunifolia'
- *Disanthus cercidifolius*
- *Euonymus alatus* 'Compactus'
- *Euonymus europaeus* 'Red Cascade'
- *Ginkgo biloba*
- *Hydrangea* 'Preziosa'
- *Liquidambar styraciflua* 'Worplesdon'
- *Metasequoia glyptostroboides*
- *Nyssa sylvatica*
- *Parthenocissus quinquefolia*
- *Parthenocissus tricuspidata* 'Veitchii'
- *Prunus sargentii*
- *Quercus coccinea* 'Splendens'
- *Rhus typhina*
- *Sorbus* 'Joseph Rock'
- *Sorbus sargentiana*
- *Viburnum opulus* 'Compactum'
- *Vitis* 'Brant'
- *Vitis coignetiae*

Sorbus 'Joseph Rock'

plants with large and boldly cut leaves

The following plants have impressively large leaves and shapes that make a strong impact in the garden.

- *Acer cappadocicum* 'Aureum'
- *Acer japonicum* 'Vitifolium'
- *Acer palmatum* 'Sango-kaku'
- *Acer rubrum* 'October Glory'
- *Agave americana*
- *Cotinus* 'Flame'
- *Fatsia japonica*
- *Ginkgo biloba*
- *Ligularia dentata* 'Desdemona'
- *Liquidambar styraciflua* 'Worplesdon'
- *Miscanthus sacchariflorus*
- *Osmunda regalis*
- *Quercus coccinea* 'Splendens'
- *Rhus typhina* 'Dissecta'
- *Rodgersia podophylla*
- *Sorbus* 'Joseph Rock'
- *Sorbus sargentiana*
- *Vitis* 'Brant'
- *Vitis coignetiae*

plants with fragrant flowers

Age of flower, time of day, temperature and other factors affect the strength of floral scents and their appreciation is highly personal. Some of the following are worth siting to give the best chance of their perfumes being enjoyed, but the fragrance of others can only be fully appreciated close to.

- *Aponogeton distachyos*
- *Camellia sasanqua* 'Narumigata'
- *Chrysanthemum* 'Clara Curtis'
- *Cimicifuga simplex* Atropurpurea Group
- *Clematis rehderiana*
- *Clerodendrum trichotmum* var. *fargesii*
- *Crinum* x *powellii*
- *Disanthus cercidifolius*
- *Heliotropium arborescens* 'Marine'
- *Isotoma axillaris*
- *Nicotiana sylvestris*
- *Rosa* Elina
- *Rosa* 'English Miss'
- *Rosa* 'Felicia'
- *Rosa* 'Fru Dagmar Hastrup'
- *Rosa* The Times Rose
- *Verbena rigida*

plants with aromatic foliage

In the case of many aromatic plants the scent of the leaves is only detectable when they are bruised.

- Bay (*Laurus nobilis*)
- *Caryopteris* x *clandonensis* 'Kew Blue'
- *Chrysanthemum* (all)
- *Eucalyptus gunnii*
- *Iris foetidissima* (rank)
- *Tagetes* (all, pungent)
- *Thuja occidentalis* 'Danica'

plants with colourful foliage

The red, purple, copper, yellow, blue or cream foliage colour of plants in the following list is generally strongest in spring and early summer. For other colourful foliage see Shrubs and Trees for Autumn Colour and Perennials for Autumn Colour.

- *Acer cappadocicum* 'Aureum'
- *Calluna vulgaris* 'Robert Chapman'
- *Cimicifuga simplex* 'Atropurpurea Group'
- *Dahlia* 'Yellow Hammer'
- *Eucalyptus gunnii*
- *Impatiens* New Guinea Group
- *Ligularia dentata* 'Desdemona'
- *Ophiopogon planiscapus* 'Nigrescens'
- *Pteris cretica* var. *albolineata*
- *Sedum* 'Bertram Anderson'
- *Sedum* 'Vera Jameson'

evergreen shrubs and trees

The following shrubs and trees create a year-round structure for the garden.

- *Arbutus unedo*
- *Calluna vulgaris*
- *Cotoneaster salicifolius* 'Rothschildianus'
- *Ceanothus* 'Autumnal Blue'
- *Chamaecyparis lawsoniana* 'Gimbornii'
- *Eucalyptus gunnii*
- *Fatsia japonica*
- *Gaultheria mucronata* 'Mulberry Wine'
- *Hebe* 'Autumn Glory'
- *Ilex* x *altaclarensis* 'Camelliifolia'
- *Juniperus communis* 'Green Carpet'
- *Juniperus scopulorum* 'Skyrocket'
- *Thuja occidentalis* 'Danica'

perennials for autumn colour

In most years the foliage of the following plants, which include grasses and ferns, colours well in autumn.

- *Miscanthus sacchariflorus*
- *Molinia caerula* subsp. *arundinacea* 'Windspiel'
- *Molinia caerulea* subsp. *caerulea* 'Heidebraut'
- *Osmunda regalis*
- *Panicum virgatum* 'Rubrum'
- *Persicaria vaccinifolia*
- *Rodgersia podophylla*

shrubs, trees and climbers with ornamental fruits, berries or seed heads

The plants in the following list are of value because they have more than one ornamental attribute.

- *Ampelopsis glandula* var. *brevipedunculata*
- *Arbutus unedo*
- *Callicarpa bodinieri* var. *giraldii* 'Profusion'
- *Celastrus orbiculatus*
- *Clematis* 'Bill MacKenzie'
- *Clerodendrum trichotomum* var. *fargesii*
- *Cotoneaster conspicuus* 'Decorus'
- *Cotoneaster salicifolius* 'Rothschildianus'
- *Crataegus persimilis* 'Prunifolia'
- *Euonymus alatus* 'Compactus'
- *Euonymus europaeus* 'Red Cascade'
- *Gaultheria mucronata* 'Mulberry Wine'
- *Malus* 'John Downie'
- *Prunus sargentii*
- *Rhus typhina* 'Dissecta'
- *Rosa* 'Fru Dagmar Hastrup'
- *Rosa* 'Geranium'
- *Sorbus* 'Joseph Rock'
- *Sorbus sargentiana*
- *Viburnum opulus* 'Compactum'
- *Vitis* 'Brant'

Euonymus europaeus 'Red Cascade'

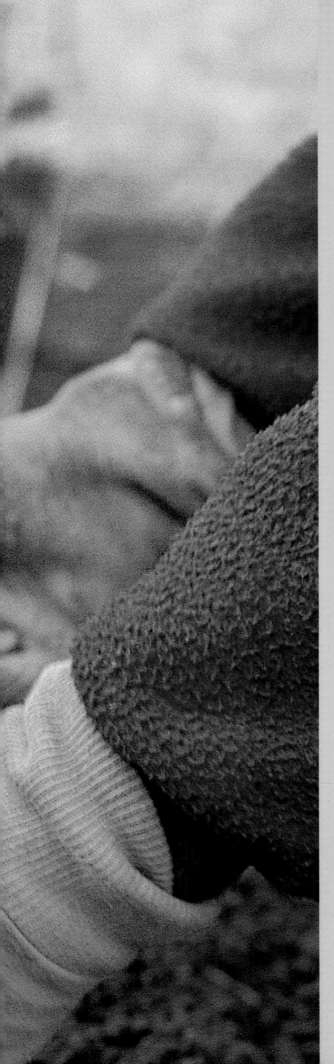

Autumn presents an ideal opportunity to breathe life into ideas and plans for improving your garden. Adding new fences and walls can transform a plot, lending much-needed winter structure, valuable vertical surfaces for climbing plants and backdrops for beds and borders. Choose materials carefully and perhaps learn some new skills in the process. Now might be a good time to put up some compost bins ready for the falling leaves. Or you could build on what is already in the garden, perhaps by improving an area where the soil is poor and uncultivated. Even a simple project like adding a fruit tree can enhance a garden for years to come.

garden projects

garden boundaries

Choosing the structure for a garden boundary is an important decision that involves a number of practical issues, such as privacy, security and longevity, as well as visual considerations, which will affect the style and type of boundary as well as its height.

the role of a boundary

As well as defining and enclosing your property, you may want a boundary to keep prying eyes or unwanted visitors out, to keep children and pets in, or to reduce traffic noise and pollution. In an exposed site a boundary can provide a useful windbreak, creating shelter in which you can enjoy the garden and where plants are able to thrive. Since it is an intrinsic part of a garden's structure, a boundary should ideally be in keeping with the house and surrounding area, so use local materials – the right colour of bricks or type of stone – where possible.

The construction of a wall or solid fence introduces an architectural element into the garden. Check local building or planning regulations as height limits are often set for boundary walls.

brick and stone walls

High boundary walls are a great asset, creating a warm, sheltered microclimate within the garden, though in a small plot they may cast too much shade. A tall wall must be built by a professional bricklayer and is costly, so creating one from scratch may not be an option. You can, however, tackle a low wall as a DIY job (see page 124).

fences and screens

If you want an instant effect, wooden fences are unbeatable. They come in different styles, both open and closed, and the choice of design and size will depend on how much privacy you want and the sturdiness required. Basic panel fencing (see page 126) comes in different heights and styles, or you can have fencing designed to your own requirements. Other options include picket fences, palings and post and rail.

Metal screens or railings are an alternative to traditional wooden fences; they come in period or contemporary designs. You can also buy less durable but attractive screens made of bamboo, willow, reed and heather. These make excellent temporary windbreaks for establishing shrubs, particularly evergreens.

Metal railings are best suited to city plots. Their starkness can be alleviated by plants, such as the yucca and *Pyracantha rodgersiana* seen in this front garden (left).

For a continuous boundary, a gate of the same design and the same height has been let into this sturdy wooden custom-made fence (below).

hedges

A hedge makes a superb living screen that becomes more beautiful with the passage of time, unlike a wooden fence or screen that will inevitably deteriorate. Many hedging plants also help to mitigate traffic noise and pollution. Bear in mind, however, that a hedge occupies considerably more room than a fence, an important factor where space is limited. And remember that even the fastest-growing plants take several years of growth before they provide a decent degree of privacy and shelter (see page 131). Hedges also need a considerable amount of maintenance each year.

'living' boundaries

An open material such as trellis or wire makes an economical boundary that is quick to erect. While such material does not provide much privacy or noise protection initially, planting it with

The high brick walls surrounding a traditional kitchen garden are useful for training fruit trees, as the heat stored by the bricks helps the fruit to ripen (below).

climbers will transform it into a colourful, near-solid boundary within a few years. Planting will similarly soften the hard texture of a wall or expanse of panel fencing (see page 136).

Another variation on a living boundary is willow 'trellis', made using 1.8m (6ft) long willow rods planted in the ground

deterring burglars

If security is a priority, the following tips will help you to create a burglar-proof garden boundary.

- **an intruder** will find it much harder to climb a flimsy barrier such as a trellis, bamboo or reed screen than a strong, solid fence. Consider fixing trellis panels along the top of walls and fences.
- **erect** an open picket fence around the front garden.
- **fit** movement-detector lights.
- **fit and use** locks to gates that give access to the back garden.
- **plant** a dense, thorny hedge (see pages 132–133).

while dormant and woven together to form a diamond pattern. Willow takes root incredibly easily and the rods soon sprout and eventually fuse together where they overlap. However, this type of screen takes a long time to make and needs trimming several times a year.

combination boundaries

A mixed boundary can provide the best of both worlds in a number of situations. Top a low to medium-height wall or fence with trellis panels, which will create extra screening and privacy without appearing claustrophobic or dominant. You can then grow climbing plants in swathes along the trellis.

If you are presented with an unattractive fence or wall that belongs to a neighbour and is outside your control, you may be able to cover it with rolls of reed, bamboo or willow screening, or fix trellis panels to it.

Beech hedges remain attractive in autumn and winter, as the leaves die but remain on the plant. The gap cut into this hedge (below) brings a 'borrowed landscape' into the garden.

garden walls

Garden walls built of brick or stone can fulfil a number of different purposes – they may form a boundary, screen a patio, or retain earth in terraces on a sloping site. You can build a low wall yourself, but the construction of a high boundary or retaining wall is best left to a professional.

boundary walls

Building a wall of solid masonry round your property, or at least along the road frontage, is without doubt the most imposing and permanent type of boundary you can erect. However, it is a major structural project – and an expensive one. For example, a wall 1.8m (6ft) high and one-and-a-half bricks (32cm/13in) thick, requires an astonishing 360 bricks per linear metre.

The recommended safe height for a brick wall depends on its thickness and exposure to strong winds. The chart suggests maximum safe heights for sheltered and exposed areas. Higher walls may be acceptable if reinforcing piers are incorporated into the structure.

Natural and man-made (reconstituted) stone walling blocks can be used as alternatives to brick for boundary walls. Natural stone is expensive and difficult for an amateur to work with, but man-made blocks are easy to lay and they often come in multiple units. Made in standard sizes, with flat top and bottom surfaces, they can be laid and bonded in courses like bricks. Roughly twice the price of bricks, they are relatively cheap compared to natural stone.

retaining walls

Retaining walls are used to hold back soil on a sloping site to create terraces. They can be built using stone, man-made walling blocks or frost-proof bricks, but need to be strong enough to hold back the weight of the retained earth plus the moisture it contains after rain. The recommended minimum thickness is 21cm (8½in), but if the wall is higher than about 1m (3ft),

maximum safe heights for brick (and stone) walls

thickness	SHELTERED AREAS height	EXPOSED AREAS height
10cm (4in)	52cm (21in) or 7 courses of standard bricks	38cm (15in) or 5 courses
21cm (8½in)	1.5m (5ft) or 20 courses	1.1m (44in) or 15 courses
32cm (13in)	2.5m (8ft) or 32 courses	1.8m (6ft) or 24 courses

building a stone-block retaining wall

YOU WILL NEED
• pegs and string • wheelbarrow • spade • cement • soft sand • bricklaying trowel • walling blocks • long spirit level • pointing trowel or piece of garden hose • large paintbrush • liquid waterproofer • gravel

1 Set up pegs and string to mark out the position of the outer face of the wall. Mix up some mortar, trowel a 1cm (½in) layer on the foundation strip (see above right) and lay a row of blocks end to end along the wall line (multiple units have been used here). Fill the gaps between blocks with mortar, but leave every other one open as a weep hole. Trim off excess mortar from joints as you go.

2 Spread mortar on top of the first course. Stagger the blocks in the second course to avoid two vertical joints aligning, which would be a weak point in the wall. Check the blocks are level and in line by laying a long spirit level along the top and sides.

or 12 courses, it should be reinforced by steel rods set into the concrete foundation. All retaining walls should incorporate weep holes at ground level to let moisture drain away. For a wall higher than about 1.2m (4ft), it is best to hire a professional bricklayer.

foundations

All walls need a solid foundation – a strip of concrete cast in a trench to form the base of the wall. For a wall up to about 75cm (2ft 6in), or 10 courses high, the strip should be twice the width of the wall it will support, and a minimum of 15cm (6in) deep. For anything higher, the foundation width needs to be three times the thickness of the wall and 23cm (9in) deep, or 30cm (12in) on clay soils.

A long foundation strip needs to be laid in sections or it will crack. Use wooden shuttering to contain the concrete until it sets hard.

If the subsoil is not well compacted, fill the base of the trench with a layer of hardcore (broken bricks and gravel) and ram it hard with something like a fence post before pouring in the concrete.

If you want to hide the concrete and plant right up to the face of the wall, dig the trench deep enough so that the top of the concrete will be 15–23cm (6–9in), or two to three brick courses, below

ground level. Allow for these courses in estimating how many bricks to buy.

For concrete that is suitable for foundations, you need to mix one part cement to two and a half parts sharp sand and three and a half parts aggregate (size 2cm/¾in). Or you can buy all-in ballast, which is sand and aggregate already combined. If you give a builders' merchant the length and depth of the foundations you intend to lay, they will work out the quantities required, all of which are measured by volume. For small foundations, you could simply buy a dry ready-made concrete mix.

Leave the foundation to harden for at least 48 hours, but preferably for seven days, before building on it.

3 **Complete the second course** and fill all the joints with mortar. After completing the two courses or within two hours, point the joints by smoothing them into a concave shape with a pointing trowel or a piece of garden hose (inset). Continue adding courses to the required height.

4 **Brush two coats** of liquid waterproofer onto the inner face of the wall. This will help to prevent the formation of white stains (efflorescence) on the wall's outer face.

5 **Fill the area** immediately behind the wall with gravel to a depth of about 30cm (12in). This will assist drainage and prevent the weep holes from becoming blocked with soil. Once the mortar has set, back-fill behind the wall with soil.

A retaining wall built of natural stone looks very attractive (right), but man-made walling blocks make a good alternative and are easier to lay.

fences

There are so many different types and styles of fencing available that it can be difficult to decide which would be best for a particular garden or specific purpose. Start by narrowing down the choice to fences that will not look out of place within the setting of your garden and, where possible, are decorative as well as functional.

Woven willow hurdles have a pleasantly natural appearance. They come in panels that have to be wired to sturdy wooden fence posts (above).

A rustic, open fence can be made by nailing split chestnut palings vertically to horizontal arris rails of the same material (below).

considerations

Your reason for wanting a fence may well influence the type you choose and the material you use. For instance, if the fence is to provide a visual rather than a physical barrier, opt for an open fence, which is ideal for training plants along and through. Interwoven materials, such as wood, willow or hazel hurdles, all provide good wind protection, filtering the wind rather than blocking it completely, which can cause damaging turbulence. A solid, enclosed pattern, such as larch-lap, is an excellent choice if you need more privacy.

fence types

● **panel** Possibly the most commonly used type of garden fencing, these prefabricated panels are made up of standard units 2m (6ft) wide, although they do vary in height, from 60cm (2ft) up to 2m (6ft) high, in 30cm (12in) gradations. The panels are made up of strips of softwood such as larch, which either overlap horizontally or are interwoven vertically and horizontally, and are held inside a frame of battens around the edge of the panel.

● **close-board** A close-board fence is made up of overlapping 10–15cm (4–6in) wide featherboards, nailed vertically onto two or three horizontal rails. A capping rail may then be fastened onto the top. A range of different woods can be used for this type of fence and although softwoods, such as larch, are the most common, unseasoned oak is also popular.

● **hurdles** This type of traditional fencing is made from willow or hazel woven together to form panels up to 2m (6ft) wide and 2m (6ft) high. The flexible stems are woven horizontally through upright rods or 'staves' to form a basket-weave pattern. They are usually bought as ready-made panels for fixing between upright posts and last up to five years.

● **palings** These fences are made from split sections of chestnut, spaced 5–8cm (2–3in) apart and held together by strands of strong wire fastened close to the top and bottom of the vertical posts, or pales. The pales are usually 1.2m (4ft) high and come in rolls up to 10m (33ft) in length.

● **picket** This type of low fence, usually up to 1m (3ft) in height, is very popular for traditional gardens, and particularly cottage-style gardens where a high fence or barrier is not required. The narrow vertical pieces of wood, or pales, are fastened onto two or more horizontal arris rails, usually with the pales set

about 5–8cm (2–3in) apart. Often the tops of the pales are shaped to give a more decorative effect. You can assemble these fences on site or buy them as a kit in ready-made sections 2–3m (6–10ft) long.

● **wire** These fences are usually made from galvanised or plastic-coated wire mesh suspended from heavy gauge wire, tensioned between supporting posts. The type of wire used can vary from relatively cheap 'chicken wire' through to strong, woven 'chain link' fences, as well as more decorative welded wire mesh. The thinner gauge wires and those not protected with a plastic coating will last only about five to seven years.

choice of materials

In addition to the more usual choices of wood, there is an ever-increasing range of fencing materials. Some of these, such as willow and hazel, are traditional and have come back into fashion, while others, like bamboo, are more recent introductions. It is worth bearing in mind that few of these alternative materials will last as long as well-maintained wood.

● **bamboo** Available as thick poles up to 10cm (4in) in diameter for posts and as thinner 2–3cm (1in) diameter poles held together with wire for open fencing or a screen, bamboo can also be used to make a trellis-like fence. Particularly appropriate in oriental-style gardens, bamboo is very good for boundary fences, windbreaks and screening, and lasts for 10–15 years.

● **heather** Long branches of heather interwoven with thin strands of wire to hold the branches in place can be bought in rolls up to 2m (6ft) high and up to 10m (33ft) in length. This can be mounted on a wooden framework to give it rigidity. Heather is very good for

windbreaks and screening, with a lifespan of three to five years.

● **wattle** Stronger than willow and very similar to hazel in the way it is woven to form panels or an open trellis, wattle is particularly good for barriers, boundary fences, windbreaks and screening. It can last for over five years.

● **willow and hazel** These flexible stems are made into hurdles (see opposite).

An immaculate bamboo fence makes a fitting backdrop for grasses and bamboos (top).

For a Japanese-inspired garden a bamboo fence is given an authentic treatment, the canes carefully interwoven and tied in a traditional manner (above left).

An ivy-covered heather screen (above) is held together with horizontal wires and mounted on a wooden frame, on which a basket of busy lizzies is suspended.

fences/2

putting up a panel fence

This type of fencing, which is 'hung' between a series of posts, is the most common boundary screen. Panel fences are less expensive than walls, and although regarded by many as unsightly when new, they do gradually blend into the surroundings, especially if used to support climbers and wall shrubs. They can also be painted or stained.

Before you dig any holes, it is important to mark out the intended line of the fence with a garden line or string. This will help to ensure that you put up the fence exactly where you want it and that it runs in a straight line. Whether all the posts are put in place first, or one at a time along with the other fencing components, will depend on the type of fence.

Wooden fence posts, even when treated with preservative, are likely to rot where they come in contact with the soil. For this reason the bases should be sunk in concrete or set in a spiked metal post holder.

If you concrete posts in place, a quarter of their length should be below ground. Measure accurately between posts to ensure the panel fits before concreting or banging in the spikes.

If you are building a fence using close-boards and arris rails, nail metal arris-rail brackets to the posts and fix the rails to them before nailing on the vertical boards.

erecting a close-board fence using metal post holders

YOU WILL NEED • sledgehammer • canes or wooden pegs • garden line or string • post driver (or offcut of wood slightly smaller than the socket) • fence posts (use 2.5m/8ft posts for 2m/6ft panels) • metal post holder (use a 60cm/2ft post holder for fences up to 1.2m/4ft high, and a 75cm/2ft 6in post holder for fences 2m/6ft high) • spirit level • fence panels • fence brackets • claw hammer or screwdriver • nails or screws • circular or panel saw • wooden post tops

1 Start by knocking a peg into the ground at each end of the intended line of the fence and stretch a string line between the two points.

2 Position the first post holder by driving the spike about 7–10cm (3–4in) into the ground. To do this, place the post driver or an offcut of wooden post into the socket at the top (to protect the metal socket), and hold a spirit level against the sides of the socket to check that the spike is upright. Adjust if necessary using the handles on the post driver. Using a sledgehammer, hit the post driver or wooden offcut until the flat plate on the spike is resting on the ground.

3 Position the post inside the socket, knocking it into place with the sledgehammer. Use a spirit level held against adjacent faces to check that the post is vertical in both planes. Fix the post to the holder by driving several nails through the slots.

4 Fix two metal brackets to the side of the fence post (inset), and slide the first panel into the brackets.

setting posts in concrete

1 Using a spade, dig a hole at least a spade's width and to a depth of a quarter of the post's length. Taper the sides of the hole outwards slightly towards the top so that you can pack hardcore and concrete around the post. Place a layer of hardcore in the bottom of the hole to support the base of the post and provide drainage. Insert the post in the hole.

2 Ram loose hardcore around the post, leaving a hole about 30cm (12in) deep for filling with ready-mixed concrete. Check the post is vertical before you use a trowel or shovel to drop concrete into the hole all round the post.

3 Tamp the concrete in place with the end of a piece of wood. Build it up to just above the level of the soil and smooth it to slope away from the post. This will help to shed water and prevent wooden posts from rotting too quickly. Check finally that the post is upright and leave the concrete to harden for about a week.

5 Rest the panel on bricks or slabs to hold it in place while you check for height and level before nailing it permanently to the brackets. (The panels can, alternatively, be fixed to the posts by hammering nails through the outer frame into the fence post.)

6 Place the second post holder at the other end of the panel, mark its position, then slide out the panel before fixing the metal post holder in place and driving the post into it. Attach brackets to each side. Replace the panel and fix it to the brackets using screws or nails. Repeat these steps until the whole fence is in place.

7 Use a string line and spirit level all along the fence to mark where to cut the posts, leaving about 5cm (2in) above the top of the fence.

8 Saw each post to length and nail a wooden cap onto each cut post.

Close-board fence panels come in several designs, including a style topped with trellis panels (below). Treated wooden post caps finish a fence off and help to shed water, preventing the wood from rotting.

boundary hedges

Although it will take several years for a hedge to become an effective screen, your patience will be well rewarded. You will eventually be the proud owner of an attractive living boundary offering great ornamental value in terms of colour, texture and structure.

formal or informal?

First of all you need to decide whether to have a formal or an informal style of hedge. A formal hedge is close-clipped on the top and sides, creating a neat shape that is maintained by trimming two or three times a year. An informal hedge is looser and more open in design, as plants are allowed to grow naturally and are pruned just once a year. Consequently, an informal hedge takes up more space than a formal one. The other main difference between the

Looking its best in autumn, when it produces masses of red berries, *Cotoneaster lacteus* (right) forms a dense evergreen hedge midway between formal and informal in style.

Privet lends itself to tight clipping and makes a superb formal hedge. This immaculate divider (below) incorporates an archway through to another part of the garden.

two types of hedge is that a formal hedge is grown solely for foliage effect, while an informal one is also grown for other ornamental attributes such as flowers and fruit.

mixed hedges

Mixed hedges of native plants look very attractive in a rural setting, and are superb for wildlife. They provide flowers for bees, plenty of fruits and berries for birds, as well as shelter for nests. Choose deciduous plants, such as hawthorn, blackthorn, field maple and hazel, for about three-quarters of the hedge, and evergreens, such as holly and yew, for the remainder. It is best to plant this type of hedge in a double staggered row (see page 133).

growth rates

Different plants grow at dramatically different rates, which is usually a prime consideration when deciding what to plant as a hedge. The table below outlines the approximate rates of growth of good hedging plants, but it must be stressed that this is only a general guide. Many other factors influence speed of growth, including the quality of soil preparation prior to planting, attention to watering and feeding after planting, and local climate and weather conditions, such as exposure to wind.

growth rates for hedges

FORMAL HEDGES	GROWTH RATE	SPACING BETWEEN PLANTS
BEECH (*Fagus sylvatica*)	Slow	30cm (12in)
HAWTHORN (*Crataegus monogyna*)	Medium	30cm (12in)
HOLLY (*Ilex aquifolium*)	Slow	45cm (18in)
HORNBEAM (*Carpinus betulus*)	Slow	45cm (18in)
LAUREL (*Prunus laurocerasus*)	Fast	60cm (2ft)
LAWSON'S CYPRESS (*Chamaecyparis lawsoniana*)	Medium	60cm (2ft)
LEYLAND CYPRESS* (x *Cupressocyparis leylandii*)	Fast	75cm (2ft 6in)
LONICERA NITIDA	Medium	45cm (18in)
PRIVET (*Ligustrum ovalifolium*)	Fast	30cm (12in)
WESTERN RED CEDAR (*Thuja plicata* 'Atrovirens')	Medium	60cm (2ft)
YEW (*Taxus baccata*)	Slow	60cm (2ft)

INFORMAL HEDGES	GROWTH RATE	SPACING BETWEEN PLANTS
BERBERIS (many, such as *B. darwinii*, *B.* x *stenophylla*)	Medium	45cm (18in)
ELAEAGNUS x EBBINGEI	Medium	60cm (2ft)
ESCALLONIA	Medium	45cm (18in)
FLOWERING CURRANT (*Ribes sanguineum*)	Fast	45cm (18in)
GRISELINIA LITTORALIS	Medium	45cm (18in)
LAURUSTINUS (*Viburnum tinus*)	Medium	60cm (2ft)
PYRACANTHA COCCINEA	Medium	60cm (2ft)
ROSA RUGOSA	Fast	45cm (18in)
SNOWBERRY (*Symphoricarpos*)	Medium	30cm (12in)

Slow = up to 23cm (9in) of growth per year
Medium = 23–45cm (9–18in) of growth per year
Fast = over 45cm (18in) of growth per year

* not for small gardens; plant only if you are prepared to clip regularly and limit its height.

hedges as windbreaks

In exposed sites, and especially near the coast where the wind is laden with salt, hedges are essential for shelter. They make excellent windbreaks because the wind is filtered through them, unlike solid barriers that create turbulence. If space permits, choose an informal belt of tough, mixed plants rather than a close-clipped hedge. Exceptionally windy sites will benefit from more than one line of protection, such as an informal shelter belt of trees outside a tall hedge.

Coastal windbreaks must be made of salt-tolerant plants. *Elaeagnus* x *ebbingei* and tamarisk (*Tamarix ramosissima*) make lovely informal hedges, as does *Escallonia*, which is widely grown for its colourful flowers. You can also trim *Escallonia* to make a more formal hedge, albeit one that will flower less freely. *Griselinia littoralis* can also be trimmed into a formal shape. In mild areas, *Fuchsia magellanica* and tall hebes such as *Hebe salicifolia* make excellent flowering hedges.

thorns and prickles

Plants packed with vicious thorns or prickly leaves are excellent deterrents to would-be intruders, particularly if you trim them to encourage the growth to form a dense barrier. The following are among the best for hedges.

- *Berberis darwinii* • *Berberis gagnepainii* • *Berberis* x *stenophylla*
- holly (*Ilex aquifolium*) • pyracantha
- *Rosa rubiginosa* • *Rosa rugosa*

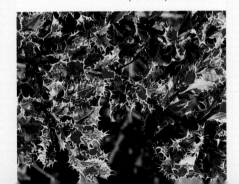

Holly (*Ilex aquifolium*)

planting a new hedge

A hedge is a long-lasting feature of the garden, so the attention you give to soil preparation, planting and aftercare is particularly important.

the best time to plant

Autumn is the ideal time to plant a hedge because this is when plants establish themselves best. You can also make considerable savings during the dormant season: until late winter, you can buy bare-rooted (field-grown) deciduous plants, which are much cheaper than pot-grown ones. You can also buy evergreens, such as holly and laurel, as large, root-wrapped plants for a similar price to smaller container-grown ones. Garden centres usually supply a limited range of bare-rooted hedging plants, sold in packs of five or ten. Alternatively, you can buy these by mail order, which is less expensive if you need larger quantities.

preparing the ground

Rather than prepare individual planting sites, tackle the area as one long strip. Its width will range from 60cm (2ft) for a single-row hedge to 1m (3ft) for a double. Most hedges are planted in a single row (see below), but a mixed native hedge or a dense, wide hedge is planted in two rows, with the plants staggered to offset one another. Within each row of a double hedge, position the plants at one-and-a-half times the spacings given on page 131.

Ideally, carry out the preparation of the soil in summer to early autumn. Clear the weeds first, using weedkiller if necessary to get rid of any perennial weeds. Mark out the site using canes and string, to ensure you prepare the strip in a straight line, then double-dig the soil (see page 151) in early autumn, to allow a few weeks for it to settle before planting. Water container-grown plants well and soak bare-rooted plants before planting the hedge.

aftercare

The way you care for a new hedge during its first year can make all the difference. Mulch the soil with a 5cm (2in) layer of chipped bark or cocoa shells straight after planting. This will help to keep the roots moist, even out the soil temperature and prevent weed growth that would compete with the hedge plants. Top-dress with a general fertiliser in early spring and water well during dry spells in the first spring and summer, giving plants a soaking two or three times a week.

planting a single-row holly hedge

1 Set up a string guideline to ensure that you position the plants in a straight line. Cut a bamboo cane to the length of the spacing between plants and use this as a spacer when planting. If the space between plants is uneven, this will be very obvious later, when the plants have grown.

2 Take the plants out of their pots and unwind any roots that are spiralling around the bottom of the rootball. Make individual planting holes and put the plants in the ground at the same depth as they were growing previously.

3 With your toe, firm the soil all around the roots and water well.

A thick layer of bark chippings around new hedge plants acts as a mulch to keep the roots moist and suppress weeds.

If your garden is visited by deer or rabbits you will need to protect young hedge plants with plastic tree guards for at least the first six to twelve months after planting.

low hedges

In open areas where tall planting is inappropriate or not permitted, low hedges can make useful boundaries. Within the garden itself, you can use low hedges in a number of different ways: along paths, fronting borders, and as dividers between different parts of the garden. While box (*Buxus sempervirens*) has long been a favourite for low hedges, the spread of the fungal disease *Cylindrocladium*, to which box is susceptible, may make alternatives more appealing. These include:
- *Berberis thunbergii* 'Atropurpurea Nana' • hyssop (*Hyssopus officinalis*)
- ivy (*Hedera helix* varieties), growing on a low wire fence • japanese holly (*Ilex crenata*) • lavender (most varieties except *Lavandula stoechas*) • santolina

temporary windbreaks

If the site for planting is at all exposed, put up a temporary windbreak of plastic netting, available from garden centres, to help your plants establish well. Evergreen plants, in particular, need protection because they lose moisture through their leaves all year round. Make sure the netting is at least as high as the plants and secure it to temporary stakes pushed in the ground.

If you want instant privacy as well as a hedge, put up an ornamental screen of reed, bamboo or willow with a view to leaving it in place until the hedge is well established – provided it does not block light to the plants. The hedge will also grow faster in a sheltered environment.

planting a double-row beech hedge

1 Set up two strings 45cm (18in) apart as marker lines. Cut a cane to the required plant spacing (one-and-a-half times the spacing given on page 131). Measure out the plant positions, staggering the plants in the second row.

2 Soak bare-rooted plants in a bucket for a couple of hours before planting. Then use secateurs to shorten any long roots and to trim off any damaged ones.

3 Put the plants in their holes at the same depth as they were growing previously (the part of the stem originally below ground is usually a darker colour). Firm the roots thoroughly. Immediately after planting, cut back all deciduous plants by a third, which includes shortening any long sideshoots. Water well to settle the soil around the roots.

gates & gateways

Gates complete a boundary, allowing you to close it to the world. Ready-made gates are available in a wide range of sizes and designs, so all you have to do is choose a suitable style and hang it.

types of gate

Gates are made of wood or metal and can be of open or solid construction. An open style is appropriate where the gate is needed as a barrier but not a screen, for example at the front of a property or

A tall, attractively weathered wooden gate in a brick wall is fitted with a traditional Suffolk latch (above).

Metal gates are a good solution where an open style is suitable (left). They are usually made of wrought iron, which is traditionally painted black but can be any other colour.

between areas of the garden with a view beyond. A solid, fully boarded style is suitable where privacy is required, for instance at the side of the house. The height of a gate should match that of the boundary in which it is placed.

The choice of material depends on the style of gateway. Timber gates generally have a pleasant rustic or modest feel to them. They can be left to weather naturally or can be stained or painted whether constructed from hardwood or preservative-treated softwood such as larch.

Metal gates are more formal in appearance but are less visually obtrusive. They often work best as entrance gates, especially if hung from masonry piers.

gate sizes

Off-the-peg gates are available at timber merchants in a range of standard sizes.

- **single timber gates** come in several widths, from 1m–1.5m (3–5ft). Heights range from 1m (3ft) for a simple boundary gate in solid or palisade style, to 1.8m (6ft) for gates styled to match fence panels and 2m (6ft 6in) for a solid ledged-and-braced gate.
- **traditional 'five-barred' farm gates** are made in several widths from 2.7–3.6m (9–11ft) and are usually 1.2m (4ft) high. Suppliers offer a range of styles and many will make gates to your own design if required.
- **wrought iron gates** are about 1m (3ft) or 1.8m (6ft) high; they come in three common widths for single gates and 1.2m (4ft) for driveway gates, which are hung in pairs. They can also be ordered in non-standard sizes.

gate supports

How you hang a gate depends on its position – whether part of a boundary or simply closing an existing gap. A gate in a wooden fence can be hinged to one of the posts framing the opening, so these must be spaced to match the gate size. A gate set in a boundary wall is hung from masonry piers constructed at each side of the opening, either on pivots built into the brickwork or on timber battens fixed to it. The latter method is usually used for gates within existing openings, such as a side gate between a house and the boundary.

Fence or gate posts must be strong enough to carry the weight of the gate without flexing and must be well set in the ground. Use 10cm (4in) square posts for gates up to 1m (3ft) high, and 12cm (5in) or 15cm (6in) posts for high side gates or wide driveway gates. Set the posts 45cm (18in) deep for a 1m (3ft) high gate, and 60cm (2ft) deep for a gate up to 1.8m (6ft) high. For wide driveway gates, increase the buried section to 75cm (2ft 6in).

Masonry piers should be at least one brick square for 1m (3ft) high gates and a brick-and-a-half square for taller or wide driveway gates.

Unless you have a non-standard opening, buy a ready-made gate and the necessary hardware – two strap hinges for a low gate, three for a tall one, plus a latch and keeper and a handle if you are fitting a Suffolk latch. Your gate supplier will make sure you have the right hardware for the gate's size and style. If there is no suitable fence or post for the gate to hang on, set one in place (see opposite above) and allow a week for the concrete to harden.

foundations for gate posts and piers

Gate posts must have a solid foundation to remain stable. For a single narrow gate they are best set in individual concrete collars.

• **for each post,** dig a hole 30cm (12in) across and deep enough to take the buried section (see opposite). Prop each post upright in position, ram hardcore around its base and top this with a collar of concrete about 20cm (8in) deep (left above). A ready-made fast-setting concrete mix is ideal.

• **improve the stability of tall gates** by linking the collars with a continuous strip of concrete about 20cm (8in) wide and deep (left below). This prevents the hinge post from being pulled inwards by the weight of the gate when opening.

• **brick piers** need to be built on a concrete foundation. For low gates the foundation needs to be twice the width and depth of the pier and 15cm (6in) deep, and for tall gates three times the pier's dimensions and 23cm (9in) deep. Use the concrete mix given for wall foundations on page 125; allow it to harden for a week before constructing the piers.

hanging a new gate

YOU WILL NEED • gate • tape measure • softwood batten (optional) • exterior paint or varnish • gate hinges • bradawl • power drill plus twist and masonry drill bits • screwdrivers • latch • panel or circular saw • spirit level • pencil • hammer

3 **Screw the latch** faceplate to the outer face of the gate and fit the lifter bar and its keeper to the inner face of the latch stile.

6 Hold the latch bar horizontal and screw the latch hook to the gate post.

7 **Remove the wedges** and check that the gate swings freely and the latch works smoothly.

1 **Prop the gate** between the posts and check that there is 1cm (½in) clearance at each side. If the gate is to be attached to a house wall at one side, leave 5–8cm (2–3in) clearance for a timber batten.

2 **Paint or varnish** the gate and posts, if wished, before hanging. When dry, lay the gate flat on the ground and position the hinges across the horizontal boards on the back of the gate – the hanging stiles – so the hinge knuckle projects just beyond the edge of the wood. Using a bradawl, mark screw holes through all the holes in each hinge, then drill the holes and attach the hinges.

4 **Wedge the gate in place** between the posts, raising it off the ground with a wood offcut to ensure adequate ground clearance.

5 **Check** that the clearances are equal at each side, then screw the hinges to the post.

softening boundaries

Although boundary walls and fences primarily have a practical role,
they can also look gorgeous when planted with climbers and wall shrubs.
The range of suitable plants to choose from is impressive and,
with a little planning, you can have something that looks good
for every season of the year.

plants for walls and fences

Before choosing your plants, check the aspect or the direction in which the boundary faces, since most climbers and wall shrubs are particular about the amount of sun or shade they get. Remember that sunny walls soak up heat to create a storage-heater effect, making it possible to grow plants that might not otherwise survive in your garden.

It is vital to choose plants with flower and foliage colours that will be shown off well by their background. Dark backgrounds, such as red brick walls and dark-coloured fences, are flattered by golden or variegated foliage and pale flowers, while lighter backgrounds, such as pale stone and wood and whitewashed brick, make a superb foil for rich, vibrant flower colours and purple foliage.

climbers in hedges

Although probably already attractive in their own right, boundary hedges appear much more colourful when threaded through with climbers, to create a bonanza of summer flowers. Be sure to match the vigour and growth habit of the climber to that of its support. Partner hedges (see Late Summer) with climbers that can tolerate hard pruning. Alternatively, choose annual or herbaceous climbers such as the bright red *Tropaeolum speciosum*, which looks wonderful growing through a sombre yew hedge.

choosing suitable climbers

Identifying the different ways in which plants grow is immensely useful when it comes to matching them to the most suitable supports.

● **self-clinging climbers**, such as ivy and virginia creeper, attach themselves by means of aerial roots. Grow them on walls, trellis and wire fences, but not on old walls where the mortar is crumbling, nor on wooden fences as the stems will force the boards apart.

In a warm, sunny position, *Campsis* x *tagliabuana* with its scarlet trumpet flowers thrives on a white-painted wall (right).

positioning climbers and wall shrubs

To perform at their best, most climbers and wall shrubs have a preference for sun or shade but, inevitably, there is some crossover. For example, many climbers for full sun will thrive in a site that receives warm afternoon and evening sun, while large-flowered hybrid clematis will grow in full sun if their roots are cool and shaded.

SHADE • *Chaenomeles* • *Clematis alpina* • *Clematis macropetala* • *Garrya elliptica* • ivy (*Hedera colchica* and *H. helix* varieties) • *Hydrangea anomala* subsp. *petiolaris* • *Jasminum nudiflorum* • *Lonicera* x *tellmanniana*

SUN/PART SHADE • all climbers suitable for shade • clematis (large-flowered hybrids) and clematis species (all except those for full sun) • *Humulus lupulus* 'Aureus' • *Jasminum officinale* • *Lonicera japonica* • *Lonicera periclymenum* • *Parthenocissus* • *Schisandra* • *Schizophragma*

FULL SUN • *Campsis* • *Ceanothus* • *Chimonanthus praecox* • *Clematis armandii* • *Clematis cirrhosa* • *Clematis texensis* • climbing roses • *Fremontodendron* • *Passiflora caerulea* • *Solanum laxum* syn. *S. jasminoides* • *Trachelospermum* • *Vitis vinifera* 'Purpurea' • wisteria

Solanum laxum

- **twining climbers,** like jasmine (*Jasminum officinale*) and honeysuckle, have stems that wind upwards. Grow these plants on any surface, provided that you place the trellis or wires in a vertical or fan-shaped design.
- **plants that climb by means of tendrils** or curling leaf stems include clematis and passionflower. They are suitable for any surface, as long as there is closely spaced trellis or wire mesh over which

they can scramble. Many of these climbers are also good for growing through other, well-established plants such as large shrubs, conifers or trees to give an extra season of colour.
- **wall shrubs** have an upright habit and can be trained closely to any surface furnished with trellis or wires. Tie them in regularly to their supports and prune occasionally to keep their growth flat against the wall.

With its large, heart-shaped leaves and red and russet autumn tones, *Vitis coignetiae* clothes a boundary fence to perfection (top).

Virginia creeper, seen at its finest in autumn, clings to the framework of a trellis support (above left).

Raspberry canes encouraged to grow through the slats of this traditional picket fence will quickly enliven the boundary (above right), but will need to be kept in check by pruning regularly after fruiting.

plants for trellis and wire fences

Climbers and wall shrubs designated for trellis screens and wire fences must not be too vigorous, or the plant will eventually swamp the support. The following plants will all do well: • annual climbers such as morning glory (*Ipomoea*), sweet pea (*Lathyrus odoratus*) and nasturtium (*Tropaeolum majus*) • *Chaenomeles* • clematis (all except *C. armandii, C. cirrhosa, C. texensis*) • climbing roses • ivy (*Hedera helix* varieties) • *Humulus lupulus* 'Aureus' • *Jasminum officinale* • *Lathyrus latifolius* • honeysuckle (*Lonicera*) • passionflower (*Passiflora caerulea*) • pyracantha • *Tropaeolum speciosum*

Tropaeolum speciosum

making an entrance

The front of your house merits special attention, for this is the public face of the garden that also welcomes you home every day. Along the front path and around the door, it is well worth including shapely evergreens for year-round effect as well as scented spring bulbs and summer-flowering plants for seasonal interest.

assessing what you have

Too often the main entrance to a house is neglected, so take a good look at this all-important part of the garden. First, walk around your neighbourhood and look at all the house fronts. Notice how the well-planted ones look friendly and welcoming, with climbers around the door or trained across the front of the house, tubs of plants framing the doorway and, most beguiling of all, perfume wafting across as you pass by. Then, stand outside the front of your own house and consider the impression it gives. If it looks bare, or neglected and unwelcoming, it is time to make some changes.

planting around doorways

Plants to go around the entrance need to be chosen with care. Long-lasting good looks are essential, for it is pointless having a two-week wonder that looks dull for the rest of the year. Try to include a good proportion of plants with attractive foliage, both deciduous and evergreen, to form the foundation of a year-round planting scheme.

Growth must be either naturally neat or made so with ease. This is particularly relevant to climbing plants because nobody wants to do battle through a curtain of growth or rain-soaked foliage in order to reach the front door. Keep climbers round the door secured to their supports and perhaps plant a neat, low hedge either side of the front path to contain plants in the borders. For obvious reasons, position thorny plants only where they can be trained well out of the way.

using containers

You can use containers in many different ways to bring interest to the front of the house. Frame the doorway with large containers of bold-featured plants chosen for their year-round good looks, coloured foliage, attractive shape or striking outline. Make the most of the front of the building by using flat-sided wall pots, troughs or mangers, which you can fix to the wall, as well as window boxes, which can sit on sills or be supported on stout brackets attached to the wall beneath (see Early Spring).

planting suggestions

• **long-lasting foliage and soft flowers for shade** On the walls, a small-leaved ivy (*Hedera helix* varieties) will give attractive year-round foliage, or try a climbing hydrangea (*Hydrangea anomala* subsp. *petiolaris*), which is deciduous but has white flowerheads in summer. Frame the door with large tubs of the glossy-leaved *Fatsia japonica*, underplanted with masses of busy lizzies (*Impatiens*) for summer-long flowers.

• **formal foliage for sun or shade** Train ivy and pyracantha on the walls and trim regularly to a neat, formal shape. Continue this theme with

Trained box spirals on either side of a front door produce a formal effect and look good all year (above); they need clipping annually.

Climbing roses and clematis are trained up trellis panels on either side of a portico (right). The roses bring scent to the entranceway, while pots of petunias, helichrysum and annuals provide plenty of colour in high summer.

plants for seasonal fragrance

Unseen yet powerful, the perfume of flowers and the scent of aromatic foliage add a welcoming touch to the front of your house. The following plants are among the most enchanting.

SPRING • bulbs, especially hyacinths and narcissi • *Clematis armandii* • lily of the valley (*Convallaria majalis*) • *Daphne odora* • sweet william (*Dianthus barbatus*) • *Erysimum* • *Osmanthus* x *burkwoodii* • *Osmanthus decorus*

SUMMER TO AUTUMN • climbing roses (many) • *Dianthus* • *Jasminum officinale* • lavender (*Lavandula*) • lilies (many, especially *Lilium regale*) • tobacco plant, white varieties (*Nicotiana alata*) • night-scented stock (*Matthiola bicornis*) • *Trachelospermum* • *Viburnum* (most)

WINTER • *Chimonanthus praecox* • *Sarcococca*

Trachelospermum jasminoides

topiary plants, such as bay clipped into various designs like pyramids or lollipops, or ivies trained on wire 'topiary' frames. Add a touch of sophisticated seasonal colour with plants such as richly coloured regal pelargoniums or white marguerites (*Argyranthemum*).

• **foliage, flowers and fruit for partial shade**
Pyracantha makes excellent coverage for walls because it is amenable to close pruning and training. It looks attractive over several seasons, with flowers, berries and evergreen leaves. Partner it with large-flowered hybrid clematis for the bonus of summer blooms. Neat evergreens like variegated

A climbing hydrangea in flower has a skirt of *Alchemilla mollis* at its foot (above). In winter the hydrangea's bare branches create a handsome outline against the wall.

Tubs of mophead hydrangeas mark the approach to the door in this informal front garden in a rural setting (left).

Aucuba or *Euonymus japonicus* 'Ovatus Aureus' are handsome all year and make a fine backdrop to seasonal flowers, such as blue violas or trailing *Scaevola aemula*.

• **flowers and foliage for full sun**
One of the best climbers for a sunny, sheltered wall is star jasmine (*Trachelospermum*), which is evergreen, self-clinging, long-flowering and scented. For fast growth, opt for passionflower (*Passiflora caerulea*) with attractive foliage, flowers all summer long and bright orange fruits in autumn. Climbing roses give a lovely summer display, but it is best not to choose varieties that are too vigorous. *Rosa* 'Zéphirine Drouhin' is popular for its thornless stems, although it can suffer from mildew.

• **good evergreen feature plants**
For borders or containers, include new zealand flax (*Phormium*) with colourful, sword-shaped leaves, and mexican orange blossom (*Choisya*) with glossy lobed leaves and summer flowers.

planning a fruit garden

Fruit can be grown in a smaller space than you might imagine possible, but to ensure regular and high-quality crops, you need to select a site that satisfies the requirements of the chosen plant.

assessing the site

Local climate is probably the strongest influence on the type of fruit you can grow. Although you can relieve the effects of high rainfall with efficient drainage, and compensate for too little rain by improving the soil and watering, other factors are critical to productivity.

● **temperature** Fruits such as peaches, apricots and figs do well in long, hot summers, while apples, pears, plums, gooseberries and currants need cooler conditions, especially in winter. Late spring frosts can damage buds, flowers and young shoots.

In very mild districts, the only option is to choose fruits that revel in heat. In cold gardens, note where frost lingers longest and plant elsewhere; never plant at the bottom of a slope, where cold air tends to collect. If you have no choice, plant taller fruit trees and late flowering bush fruit varieties in the cold spots, reserving the warmer sites for smaller and earlier flowering plants.

● **wind** Strong winds discourage pollinating insects, injure flowers and cause fruits to drop prematurely. The best protection is a windbreak of netting or open-board fencing, a hedge of beech, or a row of trees such as willow. Avoid building a wall or solid fence that will block the wind and cause turbulence.

● **sun and shade** Warm-climate crops, like peaches and greengages, and late

A standard red currant bush takes up little room in the centre of a vegetable bed (above), but provides decorative value as well as fruit.

'Stepover' apples make ideal dividers in small spaces, as in this potager (left).

fruit for walls

NORTH WALL (shaded, cool) ● acid cherries ● blackberries ● cooking apples ● damsons ● gooseberries ● red and white currants

EAST WALL (cold, dry, afternoon shade) ● blackberries ● cherries ● early apples and pears ● gooseberries ● plums ● raspberries ● red and white currants

SOUTH WALL (sunny, warm, dry) ● apples ● apricots ● cherries ● figs ● grapes ● peaches ● pears ● plums and gages ● red and white currants

WEST WALL (moist, windy, afternoon sun) ● all currants and berries ● apples ● apricots ● cherries ● grapes ● peaches ● pears ● plums and gages

Pear 'Doyenné du Comice' trained against a south-facing wall.

ripening top, or tree, fruit need the most sunshine, whereas most soft fruits will tolerate some shade for up to half the day. You can train certain fruits on a fence or wall, saving space and allowing the fruits to benefit from the reflected warmth of the sun. Avoid areas of deep shade, especially under overhanging trees.

● **soil** Most soils are suitable for growing fruit, provided they are well drained. You should dig heavy clay deeply to prevent waterlogging and work plenty of compost or well-rotted manure into light soils to improve water retention (see page152).

when to start

Ideally, carry out preparation in summer to early autumn, clearing the weeds first and using weedkiller, if necessary, to get rid of any perennial weeds. In early autumn dig the ground, to allow it several weeks to settle before planting.

fruit in small spaces

By using compact varieties and restricted forms, you can assemble a large amount of fruit in a small area. A garden about 6 x 4m (20 x 12ft) could include a row each of gooseberries, red currants and blackcurrants; two rows of raspberries; loganberries, blackberries, cordon apples and pears, and fan-trained peaches around the perimeter on posts and wires or a 2m (6ft) fence.

In a tiny garden, you could plant cordon apples on very dwarfing rootstocks, 75cm (2ft 6in) apart against a fence; train three or four raspberry plants in a cluster round a pillar; and plant a thornless cut-leaved blackberry to make an attractive arch.

Strawberries are good edging plants, standard gooseberries and red currants are decorative highlights in flower borders, and many tree fruits will grow well in generous-sized pots.

rootstocks and fruit tree sizes

Most fruit trees are grafted onto a standardised rootstock, which controls the vigour of the tree and reduces its natural size. Some fruits, such as apples and, to a lesser degree, pears, are supplied on a range of rootstocks, from vigorous to very dwarfing, whereas only one or two kinds are available for plums, peaches and cherries. To get the most from a limited space, you need to combine a restrictive form of training with an appropriate rootstock. Good fruit catalogues list the rootstocks available, the trained forms they suit, and their ultimate sizes and recommended spacing.

pruning and training

Top fruits, such as apples, pears and 'stone fruits' like plums, cherries and peaches, grow naturally into large trees, but you can prune and train most of them to create a more attractive and productive shape that occupies much less space (see also Rootstocks, above). Soft fruits that can be pruned and trained into restricted shapes include bushes such as gooseberries and red and white currants.

● **standards, bushes and pyramids** In most open ground, you can train tree fruits like apples, pears, plums and cherries as standards with 1.5–2.2m (5–7ft) trunks, half-standards with 1–1.5m (3–5ft) trunks, bushes with stems up to 1m (3ft) high and cone-shaped dwarf pyramids, 2.2–2.5m (7–8ft) high. Gooseberries and red currants are grown as bushes, with a 15cm (6in) stem, or a standard with a 1–1.2m (3–4ft) stem.

● **cordons, espaliers and fans** You can train all tree and bush fruits (except blackcurrants) flat against walls and fences, or on wires stretched between posts. The commonest forms are cordons, which are upright or angled straight stems with short fruiting sideshoots (see page 142); these are used for apples, pears, gooseberries and red or white currants. The same fruits are also suitable for growing as espaliers, which have a central trunk with pairs of opposite, horizontal branches. Fans,

which have branches radiating from a short central trunk, are best for plums, cherries, figs, apricots and peaches; they also suit apples, pears and gooseberries.

Blackberries and hybrid berries can be grown flat on wires, informally or as neat fans, and thornless varieties on pillars and arches, like a climber.

To save space in small gardens, plant four or five strong raspberry canes round a central 8cm (3in) post buried 45—60cm (18–24in) in the ground. Tie the canes in a group with loops of string or, in windy gardens, attach them individually to vertical wires stapled to each face of the post. Grow and prune in the usual way.

creating a fruit garden

Unless your soil is already well cultivated, you will need to prepare the site thoroughly at least a month before planting.

1 Dig a bed 1m (3ft) wide and at least one spade blade deep, and add plenty of garden compost or rotted manure (see page 144). Drive in an 8cm (3in) diameter post every 3m (10ft) along the strip, and staple taut horizontal wires to the posts about 60–75cm (2–2ft 6in) apart. Space the cordons 60cm (2ft) apart, marking the position of each with a cane inserted at 45° and tied to the wires.

preparing the ground

The best way of preparing the ground is to do it in simple stages.

● **mark out the fruit garden area** with canes and string or a garden line, marking approximate planting positions (these depend on fruit type and form).

● **spray weeds** with a systemic weedkiller such as glyphosate, and leave for three weeks for it to take full effect. Alternatively, fork out perennial weeds.

● **dig the whole area** – single digging is sufficient for good soil, but double digging is advisable for soil that is impoverished or overgrown with weeds, or where drainage is poor (see page 152).

● **feed the soil** and improve drainage by digging in garden compost or well-rotted manure, spreading an 8cm (3in) layer in each trench as you dig.

● **leave to settle** for at least a month before lightly forking and levelling the surface prior to planting.

If making a bed in an old lawn, skim off the top 5–8cm (2–3in) of turf with a spade and bury this upside down while you are digging. This will improve the soil's texture as well as its water-holding qualities.

planting the fruit

Store trees and bushes safely if you can't plant them immediately. If they look dry, plunge the roots in a bucket of water for two to three hours before planting. Trim back any damaged roots, and shorten excessively long ones to 30cm (12in).

planting a bare-rooted tree

● **mark the planting position** of the tree with a cane, spacing it an adequate distance from any neighbours. Dig a hole large enough to take the roots comfortably when spread out, and at a depth that leaves the old soil mark on the stem at ground level.

● **drive in a vertical stake** 8–10cm (3–4in) off-centre and on the lee side of the tree (the side away from the prevailing wind). The top of the stake should reach a third of the way up the trunk, or up to the first branches in exposed positions.

● **in a bucket, mix** 5 litres (1 gallon) of planting mix, using equal parts of well-rotted manure and garden compost or leaf-mould, plus 140g (5oz) each of seaweed meal and bone meal. Fork this into the excavated topsoil.

● **hold the tree upright** in its hole, spread a few trowelfuls of the planting mix over the roots, and gently shake the tree up and down so that the mix settles. Repeat and firm the mix lightly with your foot.

● **half-fill the hole** with planting mix, and gently tread firm. Check that the tree is still at the right depth, then fill the hole up, firm again and level the surface. Attach the tree to its support with an adjustable tie fixed near the top of the stake. Water in well.

planting a container-grown tree

● **mark out the planting position** of the tree, and dig out a hole large enough to

allow for 10cm (4in) of planting mix below and all round the rootball.

● **water the plant thoroughly** and stand it in the hole on the layer of planting mix. Cut down the side of the container and remove it carefully.

● **fill in around the rootball** with planting mix (see left), firming it as you go with your fists or a trowel handle; level the surface. Water in.

● **position the stake** on the side away from the prevailing wind. Drive it in at a 45° angle to avoid damaging the roots, and secure the tree with an adjustable tie.

soft fruit

Plant bush fruits in the same way as tree fruits, following the appropriate bare-rooted or container-grown method. Bury blackcurrants 5–8cm (2–3in) lower than their original growing depth to encourage branching from below ground. Staking is unnecessary, except for standard red currants and gooseberries, which will need supporting with stakes treated with preservative and adjustable ties near the

2 Plant a cordon beside each cane, at the same angle, and attach the main stem to the cane with two or three adjustable tree ties. Either prune now, shortening sideshoots by half, or wait until spring, when the trees are also fed and mulched. A low sideshoot has been retained on the first tree to train vertically on an upright cane to fill the empty triangular space.

top of the plant's stem. Blackberries, raspberries and fan or cordon-trained gooseberries and currants need tying in to a system of horizontal wires attached to vertical posts, or to vine eyes screwed into a wall or fence.

RASPBERRY TIP Raspberries dislike wet soils. Where drainage is poor, spread builders' rubble or gravel into the hole as you dig, or add extra topsoil to create planting ridges 8–10cm (3–4in) high.

after planting

Some fruits need pruning at planting time to stimulate plenty of new growth where it is needed. You do not have to prune fruit trees at planting time, unless you are training a restricted form such as a fan or espalier from a one-year-old tree (maiden). Cut down all stems of

blackcurrant to 2–3cm (1in) high after planting. Prune the main stems on gooseberry and red or white currant bushes by half, making the cuts just above outward-facing buds. Cut raspberries down to a bud about 23cm (9in) above the ground.

the formative years

For best results, keep an area about 1m (3ft) around the fruits weed-free for at least the first two to three seasons. Do this by hoeing, spraying with weedkiller, or by mulching with manure or compost. Water regularly in dry periods, especially if the soil is light; continue this until the beginning of winter for bush fruits, and for one to two years for tree fruits. Feed plants every spring (see Late Spring), and prune at the appropriate season for shapely, productive plants (see Winter).

planting raspberries

1 Dig a strip 1m (3ft) wide and about one spade blade deep, more if the ground is heavy or poorly drained, then spread a bucketful of garden compost or rotted manure per plant on the surface. Fork this into the top 10–15cm (4–6in) of soil. Space the canes on the surface 38–45cm (15–18in) apart to mark the planting positions.

2 Make sure the roots of the raspberries have been soaked for two to three hours beforehand. Dig a hole for each cane so that it sits comfortably at the same depth as it was growing previously, or about 5cm (2in) deeper on light sandy soils. Thin or poorly rooted canes can be doubled up by planting in pairs.

3 Firm gently with your foot, continue with the rest of the plants, then level the surface.

4 Prune each cane to about 23cm (9in) high to stimulate strong buried buds to start growing in the coming season – they will produce fruit the following year. Once this new growth appears next spring, tie it to the wires and cut the pruned stumps to ground level.

compost & leaf-mould

Gather up your garden and kitchen waste and recycle it to provide a free supply of nutrients for the garden. Composting is not difficult or smelly – it is a means of speeding up the natural process of decomposition.

how composting works

Left to itself, a heap of garden waste will warm up in the centre as the softer, greener ingredients start to ferment and rot. This warmth encourages worms and other organisms to feed on the waste and, in time, turn it into a crumbly, sweet-smelling substance rich in plant foods that holds water like a sponge.

making compost

The secret of making good compost is to mix quick-rotting green waste and tougher fibrous materials in roughly

A box on wheels is used to gather up fallen leaves from the garden to turn into leaf-mould.

equal amounts, and keep them warm and moist in a container, preferably insulated, as the beneficial aerobic bacteria need warmth, moisture and air in order to break down waste. A lid ensures that the compost does not become too wet or dry out, and helps to retain much of the heat, which accelerates decay.

- **add a mixture of materials** (see page 147) in 15cm (6in) layers, or fork them into the heap. If you have a lot of one type of material stack it to one side and cover with black plastic sheeting until there is sufficient variation to mix together. Large quantities of grass cuttings will not go slimy if mixed with torn crumpled paper or egg boxes, while fibrous waste will rot faster mixed with grass cuttings, nettle tops or comfrey leaves.
- **continue to add waste** until the container is full, although the level will sink as the contents rot.
- **check that the heap is moist;** water it occasionally in hot weather.
- **cover the top** with an old blanket, piece of carpet or a layer of straw if there is no lid, and leave to rot for at least six months in summer – rotting will tend to slow down over winter.
- **turn the heap** once or twice to speed up the rotting process, mixing the outer materials into the centre. The easiest way to do this is to fork the materials into a second bin.

recycling perennial weeds

The roots of perennial weeds can survive and even multiply in a compost heap, while seeds and spores on mature or diseased weeds will only be killed if the temperature is sufficiently high. You

In six to twelve months, raw kitchen and garden waste (top) will have rotted down into a dark, crumbly mass at the bottom of the heap (above) – a valuable source of organic matter.

can compost these weeds separately in a black plastic bag, mixed with a bucketful of mowings to help build up heat. Tie the bag tightly and leave for at least six months in summer, longer over winter, after which the contents can safely be added to the compost heap.

making leaf-mould

1 **Rake up autumn leaves,** preferably after rain. Stack them outdoors in a simple low enclosure. (You can make one easily by driving four stakes into the ground and wrapping them round with chicken netting.) Tread down the leaves to make room for more. Leave the heap open, or cover with old carpet or sacking.

2 **The level of leaf-mould** will fall dramatically as the leaves decay, and you can sometimes combine two heaps into one after a year. By this time, the partially decomposed leaf-mould makes an excellent soil conditioner and mulching material.

3 **If you allow leaf-mould to** rot for two years, you can sieve out the finer material and add it to potting composts and top-dressings for lawns.

shredding woody waste

Thick stems and tough prunings take years to decompose unless you chop them into fragments in a shredder. Petrol or electric models are available, usually capable of dealing with bundles of plant stems and branches up to 2–3cm (1in) in diameter. Make sure that the blades are kept sharp and don't overload the machine. Add the fibrous shreddings to the compost heap to aerate the mixture and break it down much more quickly.

resolving problems

● **unpleasant smells** Turn or fork the heap, working in fibrous materials such as torn newspapers and straw.
● **a dry heap that does not rot** Water it well or, if the contents are mostly fibrous, mix in plenty of soft green waste such as grass cuttings.
● **a cold wet heap** Turn or remix the contents, adding plenty of fibrous material. In cold weather, cover with old blankets, a piece of carpet, sacking or bubble plastic.

● **flies** They are harmless and part of the decomposition process, but if you find flies unpleasant cover the bin with a close-fitting lid.

composting autumn leaves

You can mix small amounts of leaves into the compost heap, but large quantities are better stacked separately (see above). Leaf-mould is slower to make than compost but should need no attention after you have packed the leaves into netting cages or plastic bags.

making leaf-mould in bags

Rake up fallen leaves after rain and pack them into black plastic bags; tie the tops and punch a few holes in the sides with a garden fork. Stack the bags in a hidden corner of the garden for a year while the leaves decay.

COMPOST TIP For faster leaf-mould, spread the leaves on the lawn and use a rotary mower to chop them into fragments before bagging them up. The grass cuttings help the leaves to decay faster.

An electric shredder makes quick work of chopping up thick plant stems. For safety, wear gloves as well as face and ear protectors when using a shredder.

compost & leaf-mould/2

compost containers

Although garden waste can be left in a heap, it is tidier and more efficient to contain it in a bin. Various models are available, or you can easily make your own wooden compost containers.

Timber is one of the best materials for a compost bin as it is an efficient insulator and you can recycle old pallets or wooden boards in its construction (see below). The minimum sized container to make sure you get sufficient heat at the centre measures 1 x 1 x 1m (3 x 3 x 3ft) and the loose front panels allow you easy access. Attach a second bin alongside the first if you have enough space, so that the contents of the first mature while you fill up the other.

Timber is one of the best materials for a compost bin and blends well into the garden.

alternative compost containers

- **wire-mesh cage** with four corner posts and lined with cardboard or straw.
- **large plastic barrel** with 2–3cm (1in) holes drilled 30cm (12in) apart around the base and halfway up the sides.
- **proprietary square or conical** plastic bin with a close-fitting lid.
- **compost tumbler,** a barrel that is turned daily for fast results, mounted on a frame.
- **old beehives** with removable wooden slats.
- **whole builders' pallets** make excellent 'instant' compost bins set on end and lashed together. For extra insulation, fill the gaps with straw or newspaper.

building a compost bin

YOU WILL NEED
- 4 x 1m (3ft) lengths of 5 x 5cm (2 x 2in) wood for posts • 10 x 1m (3ft) lengths of 9 x 2cm (3½ x ¾in) timber for the side and back boards • hammer and galvanised nails • 2 x 1m (3ft) lengths of scrap wood for support • 4 x 1m (3ft) lengths of 2.5 x 2.5cm (1 x 1in) timber for front panel battens • 10 x 1m (3ft) lengths of 15 x 2.5cm (6 x 1in) timber for the front boards • timber preservative and paintbrush

1 **Make the first side** by laying two posts on the ground, parallel to each other. Nail on the side boards, butting them up against each other. Make a second side in the same way.

2 **Stand the two sides upright** and hold them in place by nailing one of the lengths of scrap wood across the tops of the back posts. Nail on the lowest back board. Then nail another piece of scrap wood across the tops of the front posts. This will keep the structure firm and square.

worm compost

Small amounts of kitchen waste can be recycled in a worm bin or 'wormery' to produce a very rich compost that you can use as a fertiliser for potting mixtures, lawn top-dressings, fruit or large container plants. Kits are available supplying everything you need, including the worms. The container usually has a facility for draining off a concentrated solution that you can dilute and use as a liquid feed.

A wormery can run for a year or more before it is full, depending on how much it is 'fed', and you can remove the finished compost from the bottom of most proprietary bins.

compost ingredients

QUICK-ROTTING MATERIALS These are the active ingredients of a compost heap.
• soft, sappy, green waste such as weeds, young plants, soft prunings, fruit and vegetable peelings.
• lawn cuttings and nettles – these heat up very fast, and are used as accelerators to stimulate a dry compost heap into life.
• horse and poultry manure, tea and coffee grounds, and litter from small pets (rabbits, guinea pigs and pigeons).

SLOW-ROTTING MATERIALS These add bulk and prevent the softer materials from turning into a wet and evil-smelling mass.
• fibrous materials such as shredded paper and card products, straw, vegetable stems, leaves, eggshells and soft hedge prunings.
• thick stems and woody material: these need to be chopped or crushed with a spade, or shredded (see page 145).

DO NOT USE: meat and fish scraps; cat and dog faeces; plastic and synthetic fibres; coal ashes; wood, metal or glass; diseased plant material; perennial and seeding weeds.

3 Nail on the rest of the back boards, butting them up against each other.

4 For the front, nail two battens vertically to one side of each front post to form a channel for the boards. Slide in the first board and nail it at an angle to the battens to stabilise the base. Add more boards as the compost level builds up, then slide them out as required to take out rotted compost.

5 Paint the finished bin with one or two coats of timber preservative, wearing heavy-duty gloves. Pay particular attention to the bottom of the posts. Leave the preservative to dry thoroughly before starting to use the bin.

understanding your soil

We cannot all achieve the perfect loam treasured by gardeners, but we can go a long way towards improving our soil, provided we understand it and know how to treat it.

soil type and texture

Soil is the raw material of a garden, made up of four basic components: sand, silt, clay and organic material. The varying proportions of these will determine soil texture and how well plants grow.

You need to know what type of soil you are dealing with and its pH value (acidity/alkalinity), as this will influence how you cultivate the soil and the time of year you do it. Heavy clay soils are best cultivated in autumn before they become too wet, and sandy soils in late winter and spring. The pH will to an extent dictate the plants you can grow – you should avoid trying to grow acid-loving plants on chalk soil, for example. You can test the pH using a kit; it is a good idea to take samples from different areas of the garden.

- **sandy soils** are at least 70 per cent sand and gravel and no more than 15 per cent clay. The colour varies, depending on their organic matter content. They are very free-draining and often lack fertility, but do have the advantage of warming up quickly in spring. They feel gritty when rubbed between finger and thumb.
- **clay soils** contain at least 45 per cent clay, and less than 40 per cent sand. Their high water-holding capacity means they drain slowly; some are prone to waterlogging. Most are quite fertile and good at holding plant nutrients, but they can be difficult to cultivate and are slow to warm up in spring. They have a smooth, soapy texture when moistened and rubbed between finger and thumb.
- **chalky soils** have a high concentration of chalk or limestone (it may be visible as pieces of rock) and are often shallow, with soil depth less than 30cm (12in) over the rock below. They can be very

soil testing

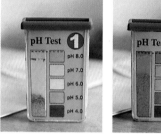

1 Following the instructions with the kit, use an old spoon or a trowel to dig up a sample of moist soil from the top 15cm (6in) and place it on a sheet of absorbent paper. With the back of the trowel or spoon, crush the sample lightly to break down lumps, and remove and discard any stones or roots. Put a measured amount of soil into the test tube with a measured amount of test chemical, and add distilled water to the level indicated on the tube. Seal the top and shake the contents vigorously for about a minute, then allow the solution in the tube to settle and clear.

2 The liquid will gradually change colour as it settles. Check its final colour against the pH indicator card to get a reasonably accurate reading of the lime content in the soil. The three samples tested above show a range of soils from the acid end of neutral to the alkaline.

pH scale

0	1	2	3	4	5	6	7	8	9	10	11	12	13	14
acid							neutral							alkaline

fertile and are usually biologically active, with high populations of worms and beneficial bacteria. They tend to be free-draining, but high pH limits the range of plants they can support.

- **peaty soils** are correctly termed 'organic' as a relatively high level of organic matter (minimum 15 per cent) influences their characteristics. They are good at retaining water and can be very fertile (unless they are pure peat). Although this type of soil is usually associated with plants that love acid

conditions, there are many alkaline organic soils. They are crumbly and fibrous when handled.

- **silty soils,** often referred to as loams, contain at least 70 per cent silt with a clay content below 12 per cent. Many gardeners view these as ideal soils. They are usually good at holding water and are also free-draining, fertile, productive and easier to work than other types. They are smooth but slightly gritty when moistened and rubbed between finger and thumb.

understanding pH values

Whether soil is acid, alkaline or neutral will determine the range of plants that can be grown in it. Acidity and alkalinity are measured using the pH scale, which ranges from 0–14; pH 7 is neutral, neither acid nor alkaline (see opposite).

Most natural soils range from pH 4 to pH 9; few plants grow in soil with pH above 9 or below 4. Gardeners usually aim at a soil of pH 6.5–7 to ensure they can grow the maximum range of plants. TESTING TIP Avoid handling soil samples with your bare hands as the pH of your skin may affect the final reading.

adding lime

Lime raises the pH and neutralises soil acidity. This often benefits plant growth because many plant nutrients are more readily available when there is lime present in the soil, and many soil organisms can only function well in a soil where there is lime. Ideally, lime should be added to the soil after digging but before it is cultivated down to a finer tilth – this ensures that the lime is evenly distributed. Apply lime in small quantities rather than run the risk of overliming.

single digging

The most commonly practised form of digging cultivates the soil to the depth of a spade blade (called a spit), usually about 25–30cm (10–12in) deep. Cultivation is concentrated in the area where most plant roots naturally grow, in the top 10–20cm (4–8in) of soil.

If the plot is large, mark out the extent to be dug using canes and a garden line, then dig a trench at one end (see right). A new trench is created each time a section of the plot is dug. Repeat this process until the entire plot has been dug. Keep your back as straight as possible when lifting spadefuls of soil.

single digging

YOU WILL NEED
• garden line and canes to mark out plot (optional) • spade • fork to loosen soil • wheelbarrow

3 Dig a second trench, adjacent to the first, and throw the soil from the second trench into the first. (You can put manure or garden compost in the bottom of the trench first, if you wish to improve the soil's texture.) Turn each block of soil upside down as it is moved, so that the surface soil goes into the bottom of the trench to cover weeds and prevent new weed seeds from germinating.

1 Dig the first trench to one spade width and one spade depth.

2 Place the soil from this trench in a wheelbarrow and take it to the far end of the plot – or place it in a corner of the plot. It will be used to fill in the final trench.

4 Continue to dig trenches across the whole plot. Use the soil from the wheelbarrow to fill the last trench.

understanding your soil/2

improving soil structure

Structure is the term given to the way the individual particles of soil bond together in clusters. If soil particles are fine, they are packed together so that water drains through slowly and the soil stays wet. By adding organic materials the structure can be improved by 'opening' the soil, allowing air and water to penetrate. Conversely, if a soil is too open (drains too quickly), adding organic matter will help the soil particles to stick together more closely, allowing the soil to hold more water.

why add organic matter?

Animal manures and fresh green plant waste provide small amounts of nutrients quite quickly, mainly nitrogen (N), phosphate (P) and potash (K). However, fibrous and woody materials are much better for improving soil structure and 'opening' heavy soils, while on lighter, free-draining soils, they improve moisture retention. The ideal garden compost is a mixture of the two (see page 144).

All bulky organic materials have low levels of nutrients when compared with inorganic concentrated fertilisers, but as the organic matter rots, it produces organic acids that dissolve nutrients already in the soil, making them available to plants.

● **for green manure,** grow borage, comfrey, mustard, red clover or ryegrass and dig into the top soil when the plants are six to eight weeks old. This will improve organic matter and nutrient levels, particularly nitrogen content, and smother germinating weeds.

ORGANIC MATTER TIP For maximum nutrient benefit from bulky organic materials such as manures, incorporate them into the soil when they have only partly rotted. The longer they are stored, the lower their nutritional value, because nutrients can leech away.

improving soil fertility

A healthy, fertile soil must have a biologically active community of different organisms, capable of releasing and recycling nutrients so that plants can feed. For this activity to take place, there must be a balance between the amount of air in the soil (so that the beneficial organisms can live) and water (so that chemical changes can take place).

Time the application of manures, organic mulches or fertilisers so plants gain maximum benefit, applying them either just as growth starts as a base dressing, or part-way through the growing cycle as a top dressing. Apply dry fertilisers to moist soil, as plants absorb nutrients in soluble form.

Bear in mind that over-feeding with high concentrations of fertilisers and manures can severely damage or kill plants by chemically burning their roots.

adding mulches

ORGANIC MULCHES ARE USED TO:

● **suppress weeds;** the mulch needs to be at least 8cm (3in) deep to block out the light.

● **reduce moisture loss;** the mulch needs to be at least 5cm (2in) deep.

● **improve soil fertility** by encouraging high levels of biological activity while the organic material is broken down and incorporated into the soil's upper layers.

FOR BEST RESULTS:

● **in order to work well,** mulches should be spread evenly over the soil, and left to work their way into it. This is particularly important on heavy soil. If they are dug in, decomposition stops due to lack of oxygen. The soil structure may also be damaged when digging takes place.

the benefits of digging

Digging over vacant ground within flower borders and vegetable plots at least once each year is a good way of incorporating organic matter into the soil, improving drainage and root penetration. It is the most effective way of preparing the soil for the next growing season and also keeps the garden tidy by burying unwanted plant waste and weeds. However, especially when soil is being brought back into cultivation from a neglected state, disturbing the soil in this way will lead to the emergence of weeds, as most of their dormant seeds will start to germinate once exposed to daylight.

For shallow-rooted plants, it may not be necessary to dig to a greater depth than about 30cm (12in) unless the soil is compacted or badly drained. For single digging, see page 149.

double digging

This technique is often used where a hard sub-surface layer of soil has formed, or on land that is being cultivated for the first time. It involves digging to the equivalent depth of two spade blades (see opposite). The aim is to improve the crumbliness of the subsoil without bringing it up to the surface, while keeping the most biologically active layer of soil (the topsoil) close to the young roots of the plants. This makes it a useful technique for an area where long-term, deeper-rooted plants, such as roses, shrubs, trees or fruit bushes, are to be grown. The benefits of double digging a plot can last for up to 15 years.

DOUBLE DIGGING TIP Avoid mixing the subsoil with the topsoil. If the two are mixed together, the fertility of the topsoil is diluted, rather than the fertility of the subsoil improved.

double digging

YOU WILL NEED
• garden line and about 10 bamboo
canes to mark out plot • spade
• wheelbarrow • fork to loosen soil
• pickaxe (optional) • organic matter

1 **Mark out the plot** with canes and line, and remove the turf. Dig a trench 60cm (2ft) wide and one spade deep, then place the soil from this trench in the wheelbarrow and take it to the far end of the plot, to be used to fill the final trench.

3 **Mix organic matter** into the lower layer of soil to improve its structure and its drainage.

5 **Repeat the process** until the entire plot has been dug to a depth of about 50cm (20in). Use the soil from the wheelbarrow to fill the last trench and finish the plot.

2 **Fork over the subsoil** in the base of the trench to the full depth of the fork's tines. You may need to use a pickaxe to break through very compacted soil.

4 **Using a spade,** dig the topsoil from an adjacent second trench and throw it into the first, making sure that it gets turned over. (On new ground, or if the soil is not very fertile, you can incorporate a further dressing of compost or manure into the top layer of soil.) Fork over the bottom of the second trench in the same way as the first.

CLEANING TIP Clean the spade blade regularly, using a scraping tool such as a trowel. A clean spade slices through the soil more easily.

improving drainage

A soil that is both moisture-retentive and well-draining is achievable, but it is helpful to know how soil holds water – especially if you need to improve the drainage of a waterlogged area or lawn.

how soil holds water

A soil's ability to hold on to water as it flows through varies from soil to soil. Some water is held in pores, the spaces between soil particles, but the main source of water for growing plants is capillary water, which clings to the surface of each soil particle.

● **dry soils,** predominantly of sand and gravel, have large pores that allow them to drain quickly. Because they are made up of fewer, larger particles, they hold less capillary water and dry out rapidly.

● **wet soils,** usually with a high clay content, are made up of lots of very small particles, giving them the potential to hold plenty of water. The pores in between are much smaller so water is held for longer, and the soil stays wet for prolonged periods.

reasons for poor drainage

Poor drainage, where surplus water cannot drain away, can be caused by:

● **surface compaction,** or 'capping', which occurs most commonly on silty soils where little organic matter is present, or where not much vegetation covers the soil. If soil worked to a fine tilth becomes wet (through rain or irrigation), and then dries quickly, a crust or cap perhaps 1cm (½in) thick may form.

● **deep compaction,** which is most commonly seen in the gardens of new houses where subsoil and topsoil have become mixed, and the soil mass has been pressed by heavy machinery. Deep cultivation through double digging (see page 150) is the only effective solution.

● **hard pans,** which are compacted layers of soil, usually within 30cm (12in) of the surface. These prevent water from draining well, producing waterlogged soil above. The cause can be cultivating wet soil or repeated walking over an area.

● **heavy clay,** which with its minute soil particles may hold onto large volumes of water even where drains are present.

TESTING DRAINAGE TIP Dig a hole to about 50cm (20in) deep and 30–45cm (12–18in) in diameter. This will part-fill with water after two to three hours of rain but should empty within 48 hours as the water drains away. If it does not, you will have to take steps to correct your drainage.

solutions to poor drainage

Techniques for improving drainage will depend on the lie of the land, soil depth and soil type (heavy clay soils have the worst drainage), and how much moisture the intended plants will tolerate. Always avoid walking on soil that is waterlogged

and never attempt to cultivate it, as this makes the problem worse.

Installing a drainage system under lawns or cultivated areas may be the only effective solution to severe water-logging. Although initially disruptive, it should work well for up to 50 years. Even digging a shallow trench, filling it a third deep with a layer of aggregate then replacing the soil, will provide a solution for about 10 years.

● **adding aggregate:** mixing in fine grit, horticultural sand or boiler ash helps to open up heavy soil. On very wet soils, cut narrow slits, about 8cm (3in) wide and 10cm (4in) deep, and fill them with aggregate.

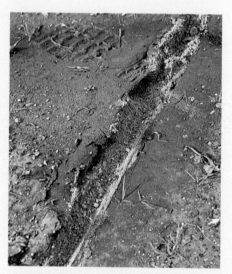

On a wet soil, make narrow slits and fill them with fine-particled aggregate.

● **varying the depth of cultivation** over different areas avoids creating a hard pan. Dig heavy soils in the autumn before they become too wet, and leave as rough lumps over winter so that the wind and frost can dry them out and help break the soil down to a finer tilth.

● **spiking lawns** using a hollow-tined aerator removes cores of soil about 1cm (½in) in diameter and up to 15cm (6in) long. This breaks through the compacted layer, allowing air in and

---

conserving **water in the soil**

● **adding organic matter** to a light sandy soil can improve its water-holding capacity by 25 per cent in the first year and 60 per cent in the second year. It will also open up a clay soil, which tends to dry out and bake hard in summer, improving its water-holding capacity. Annual applications are essential to maintain these improvements.

● **an organic mulch** of up to 5cm (2in) deep will reduce surface evaporation and considerably improve the conservation of water in the soil.

moisture to evaporate. The holes can be filled by brushing in an open, sandy compost, which acts like a wick, drawing moisture up towards the surface.

● **growing plants on mounds** or ridges keeps most of the roots above the saturated soil. Raising the soil level in one part will also help it dry out more quickly. Plants that prefer free-draining soil (like strawberries, lavenders and most herbs) will benefit from being

grown 'high' even if the soil is not particularly wet.

● **raised beds** are ideal for heavy clay soils: water drains from the raised bed, allowing it to dry out ready for sowing or planting, and collects in the trenches where it evaporates. For raised beds, dig a series of trenches 20–30cm (8–12in) deep, placing the soil in between them to create beds approximately 1.2m (4ft) wide.

● **installing a land drain** means that the upper soil layers, at least, will be drier. A sloping narrow trench is dug from the top of the garden, across the land towards the lowest point (see below). Porous clay or perforated plastic pipes are placed within a porous layer (ash or gravel) before the trench is refilled with soil. (Clay pipes are about 40cm/16in long and plastic drains are bought in flexible coils up to 30m/100ft long.)

laying a simple land drain

YOU WILL NEED
• garden line • 10 wooden pegs or bamboo canes • spade and shovel
• wheelbarrow • spirit level • 2 long, broad wooden planks (to place either side of the trench if soil is wet) • gravel and ash or sand • rake
• clay or plastic drainage pipes

1 Mark where the drainage pipes are to be laid using the line and canes. The floor of the trench should slope gently towards the lowest point.

2 Dig a trench 60–75cm (2–2ft 6in) deep, and about 30cm (12in) wide, keeping topsoil and subsoil separate. Use the spirit level to check that there is a slight 'fall' of about 1cm (½in) in 1m (3ft).

3 Place gravel in a 5cm (2in) layer along the bottom of the trench and rake level.

4 Lay or 'bed' the pipes on top, so that they touch one another end-to-end.

5 Cover them with a layer of gravel or ash (see Step 3), refilling the trench to within 25–30cm (10–12in) of the surface. Replace the topsoil, leaving a slight mound along the length of the trench (this will settle within four to five weeks). Never compress soil into the trench, especially if it is wet. As the water moves through the soil, it is intercepted by the gravel and percolates down towards the pipes which carry the water to a ditch or soakaway (below).

autumn index

acknowledgments

Photographs were supplied by the following people and organisations. Where relevant, the number of a picture as it appears on the page is given. Abbreviations are used as follows: t top, c centre, b bottom, l left, r right. CB Chris Burrows, JB Jonathan Buckley, MB Mark Bolton, MBr Martin Brigdale, EC Eric Crichton, HSC Harry Smith Collection, SC Sarah Cuttle, JD Jacqui Dracup, GPL Garden Picture Library, JG John Glover, GGS Georgia Glynn-Smith, JH Jerry Harpur, MH Marcus Harpur, SH Sunniva Harte, NH Neil Holmes, AL Andrew Lawson, MM Marianne Majerus, S&OM S & O Mathews, DM David Murphy, MN Mike Newton, CN Clive Nichols, OBG Oxford Botanical Garden, PH Photos Horticultural, RD Reader's Digest, HR Howard Rice, MLS Mayer le Scanff, SSP Sea Spring Photos, JS J Sira, MT Maddie Thornhill, JW Jo Whitworth, MW Mark Winwood

Front cover HSC **Back cover** tl MW, cl GPL/JS, tcr JW, tr MW, bl MT, br RD **1** MW **2-3** JH **4-5** OBG **8-9** CN **10** tl AL, tr MN, b JW **11** t GPL/JG, cr GPL/JS, bl GPL/MLS, br MH **12** tl JW, bl R Whitworth, r CN (RHS Wisley) **13** tl JW, tr MB (Lady Farm, Somerset), c GPL/François de Heel, b GPL/M Heuff **14** tl GPL/MB, bl GPL/HR, br JH (Design: Beth Chatto) **15** t MB, bl MB (Design: Sheila White), br MT **16** l MT, r JH, **17** tl CN (Trelean, Cornwall), tr GPL/HR, cl RD, cr CN (Design: Piet Oudolf), b JB (Design: Sue & Wol Staines) **18** tl JW, bl AL (Design: Lesley Rosser), r GPL/A l Lord **19** tl GPL/MLS, tc CN, tr GPL/F Strauss, bl CN (Clive Nichols' garden), cr GPL/F Strauss, br MM (RHS Wisley) **20** tl MM (Woodpeckers, Warwickshire), bl MT, JB (Great Dixter) **21** t GPL/J Ferros Sims, c AL (RHS Rosemoor, Devon), bl & br MM (Woodpeckers, Warwickshire) **22** tl GPL/SH, tr S&OM, b AL **23** tl JH (Great Dixter), tr CN (Hadspen House, Somerset), c JH, bl RD, br GPL/JG **24** tl GPL/SH, tr GPL/MB, bl AL, br MB, **25** tl RD, tr JB, bl GPL/B Thomas, br AL **26-28** MW **29** t MB (Design: Sheila White), b MW **30** l OBG, **30-31** MW except bl SC **32** GPL/MB **33** t SC, b MW **34** S&OM **35** tl & tcl SC, tcr, tr & b MW **36-37** t S&OM, bl MW **38** t HSC, b MW, **39** l SC, r S&OM **40** l MB (Design: Sheila White), c & r MW **41** MW **42** t MW bl JH, bc & br MW **43** MW **44** l GPL/MB r SC **45** t MW, bl & br SC **46** MW **47** t SC, b MW **48** t SC, b S&OM **49** MW **50** t MW, b RD **51-52** MW **53** tl & bc SC, br MN **54** CN (Lakemount, Cork, Eire) **55-57** MW **58** t S&OM, c & b MW, **59** t GPL/MLS (Domaine de St Jean de Beauregard, France), b MW **60** tl, bl, br MW, tr SC **61** GPL/GGS **62** MW **63** t GPL/C Perry, c MN, bl & br MW **64** tl & tr MW, b GPL/C Carter, **65** t MN, b MW, **66** b SC **66-67** t RD **67** b MW **68** MW **69** t MW, b RD **70** l HSC, r MW **71** GPL/M Howes **72** MW **73** tl MW, tc & tr DM, b SC **74-75** RD **76-77** (1, 9) GPL/JG, (2) GPL/SH, (3) GPL/CB, (4, 8, 11, 12) RD, (5) GPL/JS, (6) GPL/D Askham, (7, 10) AL **78-79** (1, 4, 5, 7) RD, (2) GPL/SH, (3) PH, (6) GPL/EC, (8) MH, (9) GPL/MB, (10) GPL/E Peios, (11, 12) GPL/HR

80-81 (1, 4, 5) RD, (2, 6, 8, 11, 12) HSC, (3) S&OM, (7) J Willsmore, (9) GPL/JG, (10) SC **82** (1, 2) HSC, (3, 6) RD, (4) GPL/JS, (5) GPL/HR **83** (1, 2, 4) RD, (3) GPL/SH, (5, 6) HSC, (7) GPL/HR **84-85** (1, 4, 8, 9) HSC, (2, 11) GPL/B Carter, (3) GPL/EC, (5) GPL/M Heuff, (6) GPL/JS, (7, 12) RD, (10) AL **86-87** (1, 3, 6, 8, 9, 11, 12) HSC, (2, 4, 5, 10) RD, (7) GPL/JS **88** (1, 2, 4, 6) RD, (3) GPL/HR, (5) GPL/JS **89** (1) GPL/CB, (2, 4) MB, (3) GPL/P Bonduell, (5, 6) RD **90** (1) RD, (2, 3, 4, 5) MB, (6) JH **91** (1, 3, 4, 5, 6, 7) RD, (2) GPL/CB, (8) GPL/NH **92** (1, 4) MB, (2) JD, (3) GPL/J Sorrell, (5) GPL/JS, (6) S&OM **93** (1) RD, (2, 7) HSC, (3, 5) MB, (4) RD **94-95** (1, 9) JW, (2, 5, 8, 12) RD, (3) HSC, (4) MM, (6, 10) GPL/NH, (7) MT, (11) JD **96-97** (1, 2, 3, 5, 6, 7, 9, 10) RD, (4, 12) JW (8) HSC, (11) S&OM **98-99** (1, 10, 11) RD, (2, 8, 12) GPL/HR, (3) JW, (4) GPL/Ron Evans, (5, 7) HSC, (6) JH, (9) MW **100-101** (1, 9, 11) RD, (2) S&OM, (3, 4, 5, 10) JW, (6, 8, 12) HSC, (7) SC **102** (1, 7) GPL/HR, (2, 3, 5) RD, (4) HSC, (6) GPL/JS **103** (1) SC, (2) GPL/Lamontagne, (3) GPL/JS, (4, 5) RD, (6) GPL/JG **104-105** (1) SC, (2) AL, (3) GPL/B Carter, (4, 6, 9, 11) RD, (5) GPL/C Fairweather, (7) GPL/HR, (8) GPL/J Pavia, (10) GPL/NH, (12) GPL/SH **106-107** (1, 5, 10) RD, (2) GPL/JS, (3, 4, 6) HSC, (7) GPL/HR, (8, 11) SC, (9) JH **108-109** (1, 4) PH, (2, 3, 5, 6, 7, 11) MT, (8) GPL/MLS, (9) GPL/JG, (10) GPL/C Carter **110-111** (1, 3 ,4, 5, 6, 7, 8, 10, 11) MT, (2) SSP, (9) S&OM **112-113** (1, 11) HSC, (2) SC, (3) GPL/R Hyam, (4, 5, 8) RD, (6) MW, (7) J Willsmore, (9) GPL/NH, (10) GPL/HR **114-115** (1, 11) HSC, (2, 4, 6, 9) RD, (3) GPL/C Fairweather, (5) GPL/EC, (7) GPL/NH, (8) AL, (10) GPL/S Wooster **116** l S&OM, r MH **117** l GPL/JS, r SC **118** l SC, r JW, **119** MT **120-121** MW **122** l GPL/EC, r GPL/RS **123** l GPL/EC, r GPL/P Hart, **124** MW **125** all MW, except br GPL/J Pavia **126** t MB, b GPL/RS **127** t JB (Design: Maureen & Sid Allen), bl MW, br GPL/RS **128** bl & bc MW, br & tr SC **129** SC except br MW **130** t GPL/HR, b CN **131** RD **132** MW **133** MW **134** t MB (Lady Farm, Somerset), b JH (Charney Well Design: Christopher Holiday) **135** all MW except lct DM **136** b RD **136-7** AL **137** t S&OM, cl MM, cr AL, b RD **138** t GPL/JG, b GPL/JS **139** tl GPL/NH, tr RD, b GPL/S Wooster **140** t JH (Eck & Winterrowd, Vermont, USA), c JH (Old Rectory, Sudborough, Hants), b S&OM **141** SC **142** SC except b MW **143** SC **144** t & br MW, bl SC **145** t SC, b MN **146-153** MW.

Front cover: *Rudbeckia hirta* 'Rustic Colours'. **Back cover,** clockwise from top left: potted chrysanthemums on a patio; *Vitis coignetiae*; *Sorbus* 'Joseph Rock'; preparing a planting site for a tree; *Dahlia* 'Zorro'; apple 'Fiesta'

Amazon Publishing would like to thank Adrian Hall Garden Centres, and Magnet Joinery for supplying the gate on page 135. Thanks also to the following individuals who allowed us to use their gardens for photography: Bridget Heal, Martin Brigdale and Helen Trent, Alison Shackleton, Ian Sidaway. We are grateful to David Murphy for help with the projects.

Autumn is part of a series of gardening books called the **All-Season Guide to Gardening**. It was created for Reader's Digest by Amazon Publishing Limited.

Series Editor Carole McGlynn
Art Director Ruth Prentice

Editors Barbara Haynes, Jackie Matthews, Alison Freegard; also Norma MacMillan
Design Jo Grey, Mary Staples
Photographic art direction Ruth Prentice
Special photography Sarah Cuttle, Mark Winwood
Writers Steve Bradley, Andi Clevely, Sue Fisher, David Joyce, Mike Lawrence, Anne Swithinbank
Picture research Clare Limpus, Mel Watson, Sarah Wilson
Consultants Jonathan Edwards, Mike Lawrence
DTP Felix Gannon
Editorial Assistant Elizabeth Woodland

FOR READER'S DIGEST
Project Editor Christine Noble
Pre-press Accounts Manager Penny Grose

READER'S DIGEST GENERAL BOOKS
Editorial Director Cortina Butler
Art Director Nick Clark

First Edition Copyright © 2002
The Reader's Digest Association Limited,
11 Westferry Circus, Canary Wharf,
London E14 4HE
www.readersdigest.co.uk
Reprinted with amendments 2003

Copyright © 2002 Reader's Digest Association Far East Limited
Philippines copyright © 2002 Reader's Digest Association Far East Limited

We are committed to both the quality of our products and the service we provide to our customers. We value your comments, so please feel free to contact us on 08705 113366, or via our website at www.readersdigest.co.uk If you have any comments about the content of our books, you can email us at gbeditorial@readersdigest.co.uk

Origination Colour Systems Limited, London
Printed and bound in the EEC by Arvato Iberia

ISBN 0 276 42711 4
BOOK CODE 621-004-2
CONCEPT CODE UK0087